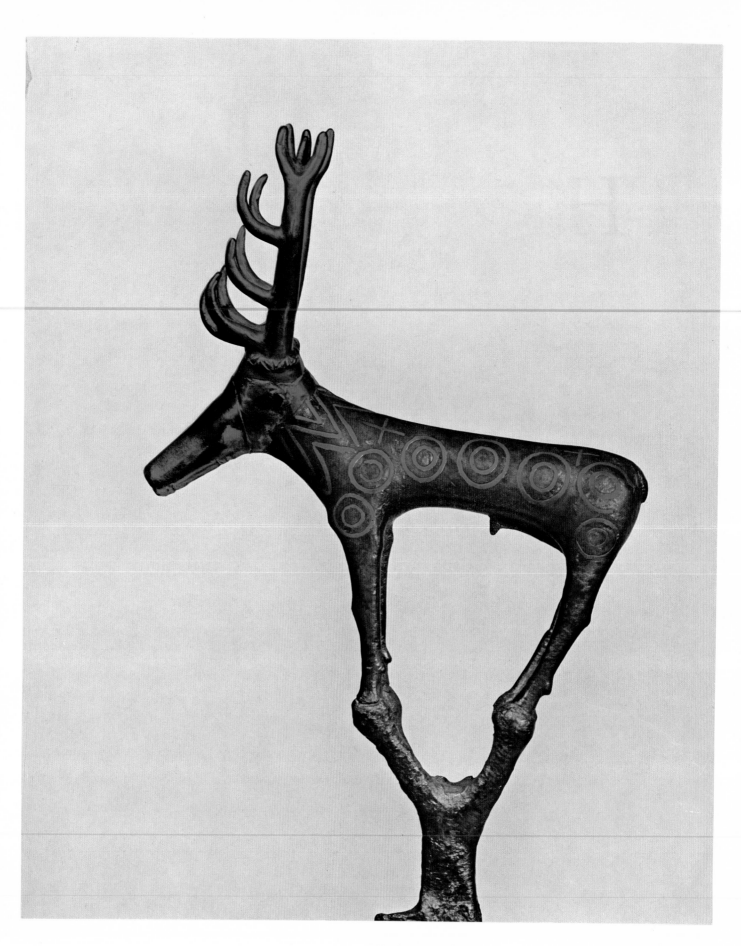

I Ritual standard of a stag. Bronze inlaid with silver. Height 52 cm. (20½ in.). From Alaca Hüyük—Ankara

THE ART OF
THE HITTITES

BY EKREM AKURGAL

PHOTOGRAPHS BY MAX HIRMER

———

HARRY N. ABRAMS, INC. *Publishers*

NEW YORK

TRANSLATED BY CONSTANCE McNAB

LIBRARY OF CONGRESS CATALOGUE NO. 62–11624

HARRY N. ABRAMS INC., NEW YORK

COLOUR AND MONOCHROME PLATES PRINTED IN WEST GERMANY

TEXT PRINTED IN ENGLAND

BOUND IN HOLLAND

CONTENTS

FOREWORD

Hittite art first entered the field of public consciousness at the beginning of the present century. In those days (1906–07) the first German excavations at Boghazköy brought to light splendid buildings and numerous clay tablets inscribed in an unknown script. The deciphering of this newly discovered script by F. Hrozny between 1916 and 1917 awakened considerable interest in Hittite civilization. Towards the end of the twenties American excavations began at Alishar and disclosed further centres of Anatolian culture. An important step in the discovery of Hittite civilization was made by Atatürk with the foundation of the Turkish Historical Society, which has organized several successful excavations since 1939.

The astonishing fruits of these excavations, carried out over half a century by American, German, British, French and Turkish archaeologists, are the marvellous treasures of Hittite culture, now largely housed in Turkish museums. The recent Italian excavations at Malatya promise to yield further decisive results.

Since the thirties Hittite works of art have been the subject of systematic investigations. The valuable research of K. Bittel, H. Th. Bossert, H. G. Güterbock, A. Moortgat and R. Naumann have made important contributions to the understanding of Hittite art. But all these scholars have dealt with special aspects so that until now a really comprehensive presentation of Hittite art has been lacking. It is true that in my essay on 'Late Hittite Sculpture' (Ankara 1949) I have dealt not only with the art of the late period, but have touched as far as possible upon the artistic products of the Great Empire, though my occasional remarks could hardly give a complete picture of Hittite art. Recently published literature has dealt with Hittite civilization in general, presenting us with a complete study but without special emphasis on the history of art or archaeology.

Albrecht Goetze, to whom we owe a synthesis of Hittite culture but not art, was the first to re-create a living world from the chaos of Hittite texts on clay tablets. His book *Kleinasien* served as a model for many subsequent publications. I am much indebted to this book, the more so as I have made a point of considering the works of art in close relation to the written sources, hoping thereby to convey a picture of Hittite art within the framework of Hittite daily life.

The present book is the first to publish a full set of photographs of Hittite art that do full justice to its quality, and I take this opportunity to express my thanks to Prof. Max Hirmer, whose discerning artistic sensibility enabled him to bring to life the treasures of a great civilization.

The new photographs were taken with the kind support of my colleagues. For permission to take these pictures, and for the release of unpublished material I am especially indebted to my Turkish colleagues Prof. Kemal Balkan (Ankara University), Director Halit Doral (Museum, Kayseri), Director-General Rustem Duyuran (Ankara), Director Dr. Hamit Koşay (Ethnographic Museum, Ankara), Prof. Dr. Tahsin Özgüç (Ankara University), Director Raci Temizer (Archaeological Museum, Ankara), Osman Sümer, Keeper of the Istanbul Museum, and Burhan Tezcan (Ankara). For the kind permission to take added photographs I owe thanks to Prof. Dr. André Parrot (Musée du Louvre, Paris), Mr. R. D. Barnett (British Museum, London), and not least to the President of the German Archaeological Institute Prof. Dr. Kurt Bittel of Berlin.

Captions for the plates and the Bibliographical Notes have been compiled by my publishers with the aid of material supplied by myself. The drawing of the main scene at Yazilikaya was carried out from my sketches by Refik Epikman.

EKREM AKURGAL

It is a well-known fact that the Hittites were the first Indo-Europeans to advance towards the South and found a remarkable civilization in the North Anatolian basin. Since the beginning of the present century investigations into the language, script, religion, art and culture of the Hittites have seen a steady development.

But in spite of many specialized publications the great achievement of Hittite art, an achievement which in many ways foreshadowed the development of Greek archaic art, is almost unknown to the general public.

To close this gap in literature and in our knowledge is the object of the present book. New photographs taken during extensive journeys in Anatolia, and in the museums of Ankara, Kayseri and Adana, of London and Berlin, supplemented by others from New York, Oxford and Paris present the bulk of Hittite art, including Early Bronze Age works created in the land of the Hatti several centuries before Hittite incursion. The period covered here extends from 2300 to the seventh century BC.

I wish to express my thanks to all those who have helped me in my task, chiefly the Director-General of the Department of Foreign Relations in the Ministry of Education at Ankara, Mr. Ferid Saner, the members of the Archaeological Museum of Ankara, Director Dr. Raci Temizer and Dr. Burhan Tezcan, the Director-General of the Archaeological Museum in Istanbul, Mr. Rüstem Duyuran and the Head of its Ancient Oriental Department, Mr. Osman Sümer; further the late Prof. Dr. H. Th. Bossert, Istanbul and his collaborator Prof. H. Cambel. Likewise I thank Mr. R. D. Barnett, British Museum, Department of Western Asiatic Antiquities, and the Director-General of the State Museum, Berlin, and Director of its Western Asiatic Department, Prof. Dr. Gerhard Rudolf Meyer.

The photographs were taken in collaboration with Frau Julia Petzi-Asen and my son, Albert Hirmer. Both deserve my sincere thanks for their ready assistance, especially the former for preparing the photographs for publication.

Not least I wish to thank Prof. Dr. Ekrem Akurgal for taking the trouble to accompany me on my Anatolian journey and introducing me to the artistic treasures of his country.

MAX HIRMER

Whenever possible existing English versions of Hittite texts have been used, i.e. those of O. R. Gurney for the Testament of Great King Tabarna and the Myth of Illuyanka in *The Hittites* (Pelican Books); the Prayer of Great King Mursili II to the Sun-Goddess of Arinna comes from the Annals of Archaeology and Anthropology (The University of Liverpool, Nov. 1940). Both are reprinted with the kind permission of the publishers. Albrecht Goetze's version of the Incantation of the Moon-God is reprinted in *Ancient Near Eastern Texts Relating to the Old Testament* by J. B. Pritchard (Princeton University Press, New Jersey). Prof. Kemal Balkan's rendering of the texts of Amun-Hirbi and Telepinu have been translated from the German.

CONSTANCE MCNAB

ACKNOWLEDGEMENTS

Acknowledgement is made for permission to reproduce line-drawings from the following sources (*see* list of abbreviations): H. Otten, 1955 (fig. 1, lower centre); C. Schaeffer, *Ugaritica III* (fig. 1, all except lower centre); Bittel, 1937 (figs. 16, 17); Bittel, 1957 (figs. 2, 3); Bittel/Naumann, 1912 (fig. 15); Bittel/Naumann, 1952 (fig. 4); Bittel/Naumann 1938 (figs. 5, 6); Bittel/Naumann/Beran/Hauchmann/Kurth, *Boghazkoy III*, 1957 (figs. 7, 8); Puchstein, 1912 (figs. 9, 10, 11, 12, 13, 14); OIC 14 (fig. 18, left); OIC 78 (fig. 18, right); Woolley, *Carchemish* (figs. 20, 21); AiS II (figs. 24, 25); AiS IV (figs. 22, 23).

The photographs of Max Hirmer have been supplemented by pictures from the following sources: Metropolitan Museum of Art, New York (plate 16); Dr Wolfgang Salchow, Cologne (plates 24, left, 44); Maurice Chuzeville, Paris (plates 34, 50, 53); Staatliche Museen, Berlin (plates 51, 130); Ashmolean Museum, Oxford (plate 52); Kurt W. Marek, Woodstock/New York (plate 141).

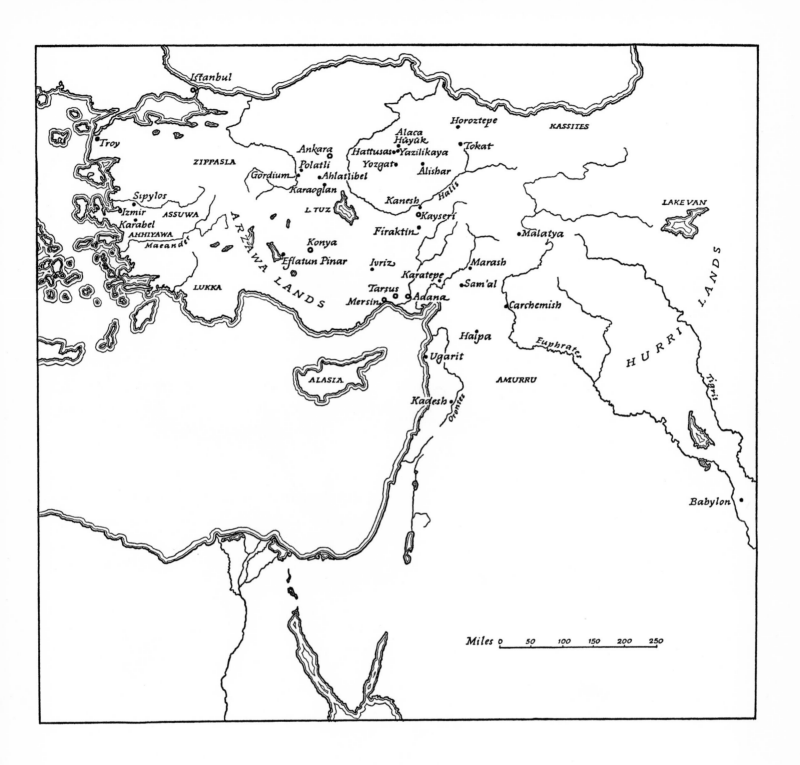

Asia Minor during the time of the Hittites.

Ancient names are used wherever they are known. Modern names of ancient sites are as follows: Halpa—Aleppo; Hattusas—Boghazköy; Kanesh—Kültepe; Malatya—Arslantepe; Sam'al—Zincirli; Ugarit—Ras Shamra

I

THE HATTIANS

THE PEOPLE AND THE LANGUAGE

When the venerable priests of the Hittite capital Hattusas conducted the ceremonies of their cult in the fourteenth and thirteenth centuries BC they sometimes recited ancient verses whose meaning was not altogether clear to them. In cuneiform texts these verses are inserted between the lines and furnished with translations. Where these passages in a strange tongue occur in the text, they are preceded by a statement that the priest is speaking Hattili, that is, the Hattian language.

If the first scholars working on the cuneiform tablets of Hattusas (Boghazköy) had seen these passages at the beginning of their attempts to decipher the Hittite language, they would probably not have called inscriptions of the second millennium Hittite, but would have reserved this term for the Hattian language spoken in the third millennium BC. The language now termed Hittite was known to the ancient inhabitants of Asia Minor as the speech of Nesa. On cuneiform tablets the adverb *nesili*, that is 'of Nesa' is attached to it. One ought therefore by rights to speak of a Nesian instead of a Hittite language. However, it does not really matter. For perhaps from the beginning of the Akkadian dynasty (about 2350–2150 BC) until the days of Solomon and the period of Assyrian kings of the late eighth century BC Asia Minor has, as we shall see, been called the land of the Hattians. Even the Hittites, the people of Nesa, called their realm the Hatti-country. The name of the Hittites and many other peoples was therefore predetermined by that of the Hattians.

It is true that in the modern philological publications the Hattian language mostly figures as '*proto-Hattian*'. But since this designation gives the impression that the Hattian was an earlier form of the Hittite language while in reality it was totally different, we have preferred to call it Hattian.

The valuable research of the French scholar E. Laroche has been a decisive step towards the study of the Hattian language. In recent years Annalies Kammenhuber has made important contributions.

Hattian differs from all other languages in Asia Minor and the Near East so far discovered. It is distinguished mainly by the frequent use of the prefix. For example the plural is indicated by a prefix: *Shapu*—god, *washapu*—gods.

The diffusion of Hattian cults shows that prior to the pre-Hittite period the Hattian people and their language were located in Central and Southern Anatolia. The leading divinities of the Hittite pantheon, the Sun-Goddess of Arinna (the Hattian Wurušemu), her spouse, the Weather-God, her sons, the Weather-Gods of Nerik and Zippalanda, her daughter Mezullaš and her niece Zentuhiš, are of Hattian origin. Also Telepinus, one of the most popular among the Hittite gods, and his spouse Hatepinus, the goddess Inaras and the group of Zithariyaš, Karziš and Hapantalliyaš, date from the Hattian age.

In the ensuing Hittite period Hattian influence can be traced especially in state religion, in court ceremonial and in the myth. The Illujanka-Myth and the so-called Telepinu-Myth stem from a Hattian prototype. But since these two mythical tales exist only in Hittite versions their Hattian character is only partially retained. The Hattian-Hittite bilingual story on the other hand of 'the moon which fell from the sky' gives a Hattian tale in its original form. The Hittite version is a faithful rendering of the original and, as A. Kammenhuber has pointed out, has retained much unusual grammatical construction which shows a slavish adherence to the original.

> The Moon-God fell down from heaven: he fell upon the *kilammar*. But no one saw him. The Storm-God sent rain after him, he sent rain-storms after him so that fear seized him and fright seized him. Hapantalliyas went and took his place at his side so as to bespeak him. Kamrusepaš saw what had fallen from heaven speaking as follows:
>
> 'The Moon-God has fallen from heaven. He fell upon the *kilammar*. The storm god saw him and he sent rain after him, he sent rain-storms after him, he sent the winds after him so that fear seized him and fright seized him.'
>
> Hapantalliyaš went and took his place at his side so as to bespeak him:
> 'What art thou going to do?'
> . . . long live king (T)abarna. Long live king Labarna.

A. Kammenhuber, who was the last to work on this bilingual story, declared the fairy-tale to be a lunar myth which owes its origin to a naïve combination of a lunar eclipse with a thunderstorm.

On Assyrian tablets from Kültepe of the nineteenth and eighteenth centuries BC, the Hattian personal and place names occur in great number. Hattusas too, the Hittite capital, is of Hattian origin and was first called Hatus. (The suffix 'as' or 'a' is the Hittite nominative ending.)

As we have pointed out, the Hattians are first mentioned in the texts of the Akkadian dynasty. The original inscriptions of the 'world conqueror' Sargon (*c.* 2400–2300 BC) give an account of his campaigns in the West country which must have extended to the confines of Asia Minor. In view of these reliable documents we must assume with Albrecht Goetze that semi-legendary chronicles of the later period also deserve a hearing. According to such texts Sargon embarked on a campaign in Asia Minor in the third year of his reign, obeying a summons for help from Assyrian merchants. About seventy years later we observe the same urge to move West in Naram-Sin, the third successor of Sargon. His inscriptions record warlike movements on the Anatolian border. In a legend dating from approximately 1400 BC, Naram-Sin figures as fighting against a coalition of seventeen kings, among them a Hattian ruler, Pamba. Huwartuwas, king of Amurru, whose name probably belongs to hieroglyphic Hittite picture-writing, is mentioned as another member of the rebel coalition. Much in these legendary records may be a subsequent addition, but it seems certain that the Hattians as a people were already known to the inhabitants of Mesopotamia in the second half of the third millennium BC. Otherwise they could not have given a pre-Hittite name to the peoples of Asia Minor.

The Hattian rulers were totally illiterate. Not even seals have been found in the graves. All indications point to an autochthonous Anatolian origin of the Hattian people and they must be considered as the numerically strongest layer of the population of Central and South-eastern Asia Minor during the early Bronze Age (2500–2000 BC). Some Hattian principalities retained their eminence even after the invasion of the Indo-Europeans at the beginning of the second millennium BC, and it will be shown in the next section that the Hattians continued to play an important part as an ethnic and cultural factor during the following Hittite period.

ART

THE HATTIAN STYLE

The material inheritance of the Early Bronze Age (2500–2000 BC) found in Central and South-eastern Anatolia appears to be connected with the Hattian people. Years ago Albrecht Goetze classified Hattian remains as belonging to the Early Bronze Age layers of Alishar and Alaca. Kurt Bittel too declared the said cultures to be Hattian.

Our present stylistic investigations show that this assumption is justified and may be supported by convincing archaeological arguments. In central Asia Minor the strata of this period have been rather thoroughly explored. The finds of the said area show a homogeneous character. The pottery of Ahlatlibel, Alaca, Alishar and other excavation sites of central Asia Minor is very similar in form and ornamentation. The handsomely proportioned long spouted jugs from Alaca, Alishar and Ahlatlibel with finely polished surfaces and the characteristic grooved decorations are beautiful copies of metal works from Alaca, Mahmutlar and Horoztepe. The elegant and slender gold cups from the *17* graves of Alaca are copies of ancient Anatolian models of a fruitstand which we shall find again later, during the Hittite period. A type of vessel of similar shape, this time a large fruitstand, appears in a princely grave of Horoztepe of the same period. It also occurs among Early Bronze Age pottery at Alaca.

The groove-pattern of Anatolian pottery used for the decoration of vessels from chalco-lithic times is a characteristic form of ornamentation for works in metal. The goldsmiths of the early Anatolian Bronze Age knew how to obtain a pleasing effect by treating the surfaces of their objects of art with a variety of grooved linear embellishments. These *V, VI, 14, 17* delicate gold objects with their elegant shapes and tasteful design give us a fair idea of the ordered feudal life of the times.

How closely related the contemporary pottery was to the goldsmith's work is shown *13* by a highly polished vessel of black burnished ware from a royal grave at Alaca. Its shape *14, 15* and decorations are identical with that of vessels of precious metal from the royal treasure.

The contemporary vases and stamp seals from Ahlatlibel and Etiyokushu likewise show incised designs identical with the ornamentation of vessels of precious metal. The idols *25* from the close of the Early Bronze Age are enlivened by handsome incised ornaments.

The magnificent metal work of Alaca, whose connections with neighbouring cultures have frequently been pointed out, has a homogeneous, purely Anatolian style. It is natural for decorative objects of the finest quality, destined for the homes of princes, to show a similarity with other courtly works of art of the period. But as Kurt Bittel, and lately Machtild Mellink, have shown, in these mutual relations Anatolia seems to have been at the giving end. The daggers from Alaca reminiscent of models from Cyprus differ from these latter by their oval double incisions which may be interpreted as peculiar to Asia Minor. Similarly incised daggers from Troy, the Cyclades and North Syria might have been inspired by Anatolian workshops. Apart from those found at Alaca, daggers of this type have been excavated in Tarsus. Still other types of daggers whose origin and developments stem from indigenous inspiration were in use in Anatolia during the third millennium BC.

Gold pins with double-spiral heads or other ornaments consisting of four spirals appear to have found their way from central Anatolian metal workshops to Troy and other cities of western Asia.

Their presence in north Syrian towns might be due to an inspiration from the Anatolian models. M. Mellink was probably correct in relating the clay 'frying pans' of the Cyclades to the bronze mirrors of Alaca. The graves of Alaca and Horoztepe contained several splendid examples of these mirrors. Originally they held a silver disk let into a depression in which the Hattian princesses looked at themselves. They are unwieldy objects, too heavy for the use of ladies, but of a grand and regal style.

1–12 The disk and animal standards too of central Anatolian priestly kings reveal an indigenous character deeply rooted in Anatolian soil. The open-work of certain standards *VII* with geometric decoration recurs in gold ornaments of Alaca. The wide gold diadem

II Ritual standard of a bull. Bronze and silver. Height 37 cm. (14½ in.).
From Alaca Hüyük—Ankara

from Alaca is fashioned in the same open-work of pattern composed of horizontal and diagonal bands, similar to those on geometrical disk standards found in the same graves. The same criss-cross pattern occurs at Alaca, on seals unearthed from layers of contemporary dwellings. A cruciform motif decorating the centre of an open-work standard recurs on a silver jug, and again as the base of a gold vessel; it is used in the ornamentation of contemporary seals from Alaca, Alishar, Ahlatlibel, Etiyokushu and Tarsus. The predilection for rows of dots which we find on the work of goldsmiths is repeated and applied in the same way on the standards. Thus the small needlepointed dots adorning gold plated twin idols, the gold pommel of iron daggers and the large gold diadem are found on a bull standard as a decoration distributed over the head and shoulders. Idols of Central Anatolia of the period were embellished by small punched dots. A decorative element of tiny balls seen on several bow-shaped standards recurs in the ornamentation of sceptre heads and necklaces. On female idols they mark the place of the breasts. The button-shaped tiny knobs which adorn the pinheads recur as an ornament on vases and other decorative objects. The points of the bull's horns on the standards are finished with similar knobs. The 'studs' which adorn two silver vessels from royal graves at Alaca are a form of decoration characteristic of Asia Minor. The same is used in different variations on the clay jugs from Ahlatlibel and Alaca. The studs encircled by grooved patterns on the pretty jugs from Ahlatlibel recur on a silver, half gilded vessel at Alaca.

The concentric rings which so effectively adorn some of the stag and bull figurines repeat a favourite indigenous motif used in the decoration of clasps, and of contemporary stone or clay idols in Central Asia Minor. It is repeated on a vase from Etiyokushu and a gold vessel from Anatolia, now in the Metropolitan Museum of New York.

The swastika, perhaps applied as symbolic motif in the open-work of a standard, adorns the bottom of a gold jug; incised like a whirl of hair on the crown of the head, it was frequently applied by the smiths of Anatolia.

The homogeneity of working method emerges clearly from the treatment of other details. The axe-shaped head of two figurines we find not only on gold plated idols, but on two disk standards of Alaca whose star-shaped ornaments are stylized according to the same pattern. The heads of several clay idols from Alaca, Ahlatlibel and Etiyokushu are the same shape.

It goes without saying that some of the above-mentioned motifs are not exclusive to the Anatolian Bronze Age. No doubt isolated examples appear in other centres of civilization and at entirely different periods. It is, however, important to note that a great many identical decorative elements can be traced simultaneously in pottery, on gold jewels and on standards. This simultaneous occurrence of motifs goes to prove that in the Anatolian Bronze Age a uniform style existed in all branches of art which might be termed as Hattian. It will be shown further on that all works of art of the same period reveal features of the Hattian style expounded in the present section.

18

III Ritual standard of a stag with twelve tines and two small panthers. Bronze with silver and gold. Height 22 cm. (8¾ in.). From Alaca Hüyük—Ankara

1–6　　The high artistic quality of the animal standards is astonishing. We refer to delicate
I, II　objects of an accomplished technique cast in bronze, inlaid with precious metals. The royal
standard of a bronze stag with a silver head and antlers and a body inlaid with a silver
pattern must have deeply impressed the worshippers of the Hattian realm during ritual
ceremonies performed under the guidance of priestly kings. The same technique is
observable on other animals whose heads or necks are plated with precious metal, while
their bodies are ornamented with silver inlay.

Characteristic of these animal figures are the sloping back, the long rump, and the
narrow, elongated muzzle. The forms may be stylized and abstract, but in their essential
features they remain naturalistic. A predilection for ornamental decoration lends to these
works of art a character of their own.

THE HISTORY OF THE FINDS

The splendid works of art of Alaca are the first fruits of modern Turkish archaeology
initiated by Atatürk. The first dig in 1935 resulted in valuable discoveries which eclipsed
Schliemann's 'Treasure of Priam' and placed the Anatolia of the third millennium BC in
the foreground of historical research. The first discoveries made at the beginning of the
excavation caused a great sensation. R. O. Arik and Hamit Koşay in charge of the excavations quickly uncovered the graves. They first struck a burial six metres deep, which
contained the large splendid standard of a stag. The other contents were amazing.
Breathlessly the workmen unearthed one peerless treasure after another. The first objects
revealed by their spades were the disk standards. With their open-work of fascinating
geometrical design, the strange, enigmatic and mysterious objects arranged in an almost
straight line stood out from the grey soil in a decorative pattern; at first no one was allowed
to touch them. The work proceeded with great care. After the large stag, more animal
standards, and a great many other objects of precious metal came to light. The gold jewels
shone impressively. The workmen, humble peasants from the small hamlet of Alaca
Hüyük, gathered with frenzied excitement round the unexpected hoard. They marvelled
and felt themselves transported to a fairy-tale world suddenly opened before their eyes by
some magic wand.

At first the copper and silver vessels seemed shapeless lumps. The former had acquired
a green, the latter a mauve patina which covered these decorative objects in several layers
so that their real shape could no longer be determined. A fine pin looked like a sceptre.
A few among the bronze standards had been so badly oxydized that they shattered to
fragments at the merest touch.

Other graves followed. One of them, to judge by its contents, was that of a woman,
probably a Hattian princess, as was indicated by a copper mirror, a silver comb, a bundle
of pins, three large clasps and several necklaces of gold and precious stones, as well as a
magnificent diadem, two gold bracelets, and one ear-pendant. To the left of the head a

copper stag was found which had apparently been mounted on a stick inlaid with silver. On the right side of the skeleton lay a disk standard. The person buried must have been a woman of distinction belonging to the court of priestly rulers of Alaca. The contents of another grave too indicated the presence of a woman rather than a man. The skeleton lay on its right side with the head to the west and the features facing south. A diadem encircled the skull. Gold and coral beads were wound round the neck and on the breast lay a gold clasp. To the left of the skeleton, at breast height, one could see a silver idol with breasts and shoes of gold and with blue inlaid eyes, also a copper idol, a silver spoon and silver spindle, both with gold handles, a gold cup, a pair of silver and a pair of gold bracelets, a silver pin with a gold head and a silver vessel inlaid with gold. In the foreground lay four handsomely decorated copper standards, and to the south-west of the grave a copper standard of a bull inlaid with electron, two gold baldachin handles and other objects in precious metal.

The graves attested to very curious burial customs. Each grave consisted of a trench from fifty to seventy centimetres deep, from three to eight metres long, and from two to five metres wide. The dead lay on their right side in the position of an embryo, the head pointing west, the feet pointing south-east and the face turned to the south. The corpse is invariably buried in a shroud and with his or her personal jewels. The ritual objects are usually laid before the dead person; divine symbols, stag and bull standards, were placed at a marked distance, often in the centre of the grave. The remaining objects, vessels of precious metal and clay, were scattered inside the grave. After the dead and his accoutrements had been laid in the ground the four sides of the trench were marked with stones. Wooden beams were pushed across the shaft and the whole covered tightly with earth. After the grave had been completed in this manner a funeral feast seems to have taken place, as is indicated by the heads and limbs of sacrificial beasts arrayed symmetrically at the head of the graves. In order to protect these sacrificial remains they were covered with a thick layer of earth.

To judge from the evidence of these excavations the royal graves of Alaca must have been situated outside the walls, or at least on the outskirts of the city, which was probably necessary for the protection of their valuable contents.

The thirteen graves excavated at Alaca were found at different depths of the soil. Each of the four levels of dwellings dating from the chalcolithic stratum contained one or more royal graves. This goes to prove that such burial customs continued to be used over a long period, lasting perhaps for 200 years. From some of the decorative objects found in them it is possible to ascertain stylistic variations that classify them as belonging to different periods. Grave H, for instance, which belongs to the most recent layer of dwellings of the *21 below, left* chalcolithic level, and bore marked traces of a conflagration, contained stylistically *21 below, right* evolved figurines, while grave L situated two levels below still yielded figurines shaped like primitive idols. A similar stylistic difference cannot be established between other decorative objects of the two levels.

The vessels found in the graves of Alaca are without exception examples of the older, hand-made type of an Early Bronze Age pottery. Among the disk and animal standards too no stylistic differences have been found which might be used for chronological classification. One would imagine grave K, in which a dagger with an iron blade has been found, together with a magnificent but unfortunately much damaged silver vessel adorned with a naturalistic snake relief, to belong to a later period. But according to the indications of the excavators this grave was situated two levels below grave H.

As Tahsin Özgüç has explained, the decorative objects in the grave of Horoztepe, on the other hand, differ in style from the examples of Alaca and may belong to a later period. The animal sculptures of this locality are more naturalistic than those of the Alaca graves. The occurrence of the sistrum, absent from Alaca, may indicate a later phase in which foreign motifs are more in evidence. The finds of Horoztepe are much closer to Caucasian examples, which constitute the only extant parallel to Central Anatolian works, than to the sculptures of Alaca. The Caucasian animal standards, however, are of an evolved, mannerist, almost playful style. If we are not mistaken they are of a later date than the finds of Horoztepe. It is possible that the marked resemblance between Central Anatolian and Caucasian decorative objects goes back to some sort of ethnic relationship, but the solution of this problem must be relegated to the future. At present it can only be said that the astonishing resemblance between Caucasian and Anatolian metal works can hardly be fully explained by trade relations.

The main bulk of the finds of Alaca shows a highly evolved, almost sophisticated technique of treating metal with gold, silver and electron inlay and gem encrustation. Hardly believable is the early production of iron used on the first ornamental weapons of the world. The splendid iron dagger with a wooden pommel shaped like a crescent moon and inlaid with gold may indicate Sumerian influence but, like another dagger from Khafaje in Mesopotamia, it is the product of an Anatolian metal workshop. One may assume on good grounds that the activities of these artistic centres of Asia Minor continued for at least two centuries.

The last phase of domestic culture of the Central Anatolian Early Bronze Age is characterized by the emergence of the so-called 'Depata', the double-handled Trojan vase, and of polychrome ware. As Miss Mellink has lately pointed out, the absence of these later characteristics from the graves of Alaca proves that their dynasties were extinct before the final destruction of the chalcolithic level. Within the Hattian period (c. 2500–2000 BC) the graves of Alaca may cover a period from about 2300 to 2100 BC.

Some scholars have proposed an earlier date (c. 2400–2200 BC) but the close stylistic affinities between the finds of Alaca and the decorative works of Karum Kanesh remove

IV Ritual standard of a stag with fourteen tines. Bronze. Height 22 cm. (8¾ in.).
From Alaca Hüyük—Ankara

their origin near the beginning of the twentieth century BC. It may therefore be preferable to date them about 2300–2100 BC.

The smaller settlements of Ahlatlibel and Etiyokushu near Ankara should be attributed to the last phase (*c.* 2100–2000 BC). The presence of stamp-seals indicates their late origin. The objects in question are hollow cylinder seals with surfaces loosely covered by geometrical patterns.

Compared with pottery from the royal graves of Alaca the monochrome ware of those two localities is more delicate and evolved.

During the last phase of the Anatolian prehistoric period Hattian culture achieved contact with the Mesopotamian world and received a fresh impetus. The emergence of cylinder seals marks the first step towards the beginnings of writing.

THE SIGNIFICANCE OF THE STANDARDS

The Hattian rulers, like the sovereigns of the following Hittite era, seem to have been the high priests of the realm.

12   Most of the objects found in graves were ritual implements. The rattle, the sistrum-shaped bullroarer and other objects shaped like standards from Horoztepe indicate their religious character. Similar implements are used today in the rites of the Orthodox churches. The priests of Hatti carried sistrums and used them during religious ceremonies as an accompaniment to their mysterious liturgic chants.

7–11   The disk standards were mounted on poles. They rested on crossbars inserted in the cleft of poles split at the top and probably fastened with thongs or ropes. The animal

1–6   standards or bulls and stags on the other hand were probably fixed onto baldachins or cult furniture. Almost all have wedge-shaped endings which must have been inserted in a cleft and were originally invisible. From the vantage point of the spectator the animal standards seemed to rest on bases shaped like human legs.

The ritual character of these impressive and mysterious works of art is particularly

8–11   striking in the disk or arch-shaped standards. The great bull's horns which serve as a

III, IV,   base, the halo and the spherical standards indicative of the celestial vault, can hardly be

10, 11   interpreted as purely ornamental compositions. The bull's horns are affixed to a frame so as to raise and support the standards. On some standards the disk's edge is adorned

7   with stars which, as it were, encircle the heavenly sphere like satellites. They are small models of the standards to whose periphery they have been added. The birds in flight

8, 9   which sometimes decorate the edge of the standards may be an indication of their celestial

III   significance. Flowers similarly attached could be a symbolic representation of plant-life

7   growing, reaching towards the sky. We cannot be sure whether the swastikas on a lozenge-shaped standard, revolving partly to the right and partly to the left, should be interpreted as the rising and setting sun; but the total aspect of these standards permits us to assume that it somehow represents the universe. The bull's horns which support this cosmic

24

symbol recall a Turkish fairy-tale which relates that the world rests on the horns of an ox. Every time the ox shakes his head, so the tale goes, the earth trembles. The precious implements of Hattian priestly rulers may be the oldest figurative representation of this concept. We find the same notion, that of a bull supporting the universe, later on in the various forms of Hittite symbolism. Nor is it accidental that the swift, lithe stag emerges from the solar disk, or that his antlers, which resemble a halo and the celestial vault, *10, 11* should reach to the limit of the heavenly sphere. On a relief of Jupiter Dolichenus, *III, IV* dating from the Roman period but representing an old Hittite motif, the spouse of the Weather-God stands, as has been pointed out by Hancar, on the back of a stag. The Hattians called this goddess Wurusemu, and her epithet of 'the Sun-Goddess of Arinna' defines her as the ruler of heaven and the universe. Considering that the bull is definitely to be understood as the attribute of the Weather-God we may endeavour to interpret the stag appearing in this context as a symbol of his spouse who invariably accompanies him. Certainly in the later Anatolian-Hittite period, the lion and the panther came to be the symbol of the great goddess, while the stag became the sacred animal of male tutelary *47* divinities. But it may be that the Hattian symbol of the great goddess was altered by the Hittites. On a standard from Alaca two panthers occur beside a stag. Perhaps the panther was the sacred animal of the chief goddess and became an object of worship as early as the third millennium BC. The fact that all the animal standards without exception represented either a bull or a stag compels us to interpret the bull as the attribute of the deity identical with the Weather-God. Drawing a parallel with contemporaneous Mesopotamian religious concepts the second deity of the Alaca standards could only have been a goddess. The Sumerian goddess Innini and the Semitic Ishtar combined feminine qualities with the characteristics of a warlike goddess and mistress of the sky, and played an important dominant part at the side of the principal male divinity.

The bull's horns and the halo are images derived from the religious concepts of Mesopotamian culture. Their figurative representation in the form of impressive symbols is an indigenous creation of artists from Hattian Anatolia.

THE SMALL-SCALE SCULPTURE

The idols and naturalistic female statuettes found in the royal graves of Alaca testify to a high standard of Hattian minor sculptures. A bronze statuette from Horoztepe and a *23* silver one with gold inlay from Hasanoglan near Ankara are two further magnificent *VIII, 22* instances of Hattian plastic art. An attempt at naturalistic representation can already be observed in the idols of Alaca.

Certainly the body and even more the head are still shaped like those of the idols. *21 below,* But an essentially realistic and life-like addition is the feet with meticulously rendered *right* shoes. The sculptor was obliged to conform to ritual custom and preserve the outlines of the idols, but he could not resist introducing a progressive style by rendering at least the

25

shoes in detail. The proportions of the body too, although they emulate the aspect of an idol, are naturalistic to a marked degree. The position of the arms, for instance, is identical with that which recurs later in an evolved form on lead idols of the eighteenth century BC *35* from Kültepe, Alishar and Boghazköy.

21, above   The most diagrammatic models are the violin-shaped twin-idols of gold leaf. It is true that they were found in the same grave as the naturalistic statuettes; but they had been sewn to the garments of priestly rulers, and therefore perpetuate the decorative and cultic ornamentation of the old style.

21, below, left   In the statuettes of Alaca, the abstract shape of the idols has been completely abandoned and the essential traits of the human body are reproduced in a natural manner. The semi-circular breasts and the pubic triangle are elements surviving from the older cultic art form. These objects belong to a grave situated in the most recent layer of the Early Bronze Age stratum. The idol-statuettes on the other hand come from a grave two layers below the first. The difference in style is therefore consistent with a lapse of time. The statuette of medium size carries vessels in both hands. The other two female statuettes raise their arms in similar fashion; they may therefore be interpreted as vessel bearers. We are dealing with worshippers, perhaps with Hattian princesses about to offer a libation to the goddess.

23   The large bronze statuette of a mother feeding her child, a magnificent sculpture from a royal tomb at Horoztepe, with its naturalistic treatment of the human form is a progressive work of art. Certainly, her breasts are still button-shaped and the pubic triangle is schematic, but the asymmetrical posture of the hands and arms and the almost naturalistic rendering of the face and shoulders indicate the beginning of a new movement. It is *21* more evolved by one degree than the figurines of Alaca. Perhaps the somewhat clumsy aspect of those figurines is due to their poor state of preservation. The bronze statuette from Horoztepe is much more mobile and alive than the Alaca figurines. Also she represents the style of the central Anatolian workshops. Her body is fashioned exactly like the Alaca statuettes. Her widely separated, parallel legs and thighs are treated like those of the vessel bearers of Alaca.

II, III   One is tempted to recall in both instances the stag or bull's legs known from the animal standards. That the mother and child and the animal standards were the products of the same metal workshops of Central Anatolia transpires from one detail. The feet of the large bronze statuette are cast from an almost identical mould as the bases of the *5, 6* animal standards shaped like feet. The bronze statuette of Horoztepe and the smaller figurine from Alaca have identical protruding buttocks. In both cases this part of the body is so prominent that when seen in profile they give the impression of seated figures.

Both the mother and child have abnormally big ears, like the larger of the two Alaca statuettes. Her deeply incised eye sockets, like those of the idols and statuettes from Alaca, were fitted with eyeballs of metal and semi-precious stones. She appears to be wearing a spiral of curls, of which two bronze examples were discovered in the graves of Alaca.

26

V Flagon. Gold. Height 15·3 cm. (6 in.). From Alaca Hüyük—Ankara

The bronze statuette of Horoztepe is the oldest naturalistic sculpture of a mother and child, which we find also in the idols from Kültepe of the period. We shall meet with the same artistic conception in the lead idols of the earliest historical period. The bronze work of Horoztepe might be somewhat more recent than the statuettes of Alaca and belong to the last phase of the Early Bronze Age, that is to say, to the end of the third millennium BC.

VIII, 22   The precious statuette of Hasanoglan near Ankara is a masterpiece of Hattian art. Its creator was undoubtedly one of the greatest artists of his time. Since the sculpture was found in an isolated provenance we are unable to determine an exact date for it, but its Hattian origin is certain. The characteristic pattern of the hair alone proves that *V, 14, 15* this magnificent silver statuette is closely related to the gold objects of the Alaca graves and the finds of Mahmutlar. The stylized way in which the hair is arranged round the top of the head recurs in almost identical form on the above-mentioned gold vessels. The technique of the sculpture, too, vividly recalls the metal work of Alaca. The small, ball-shaped breasts and the button-navel with gold inlay remind us of the idols and statuettes *21* in the Alaca graves.

    The manner in which the neck has been soldered with sheet gold recalls to mind the *II* animal standards whose necks were adorned in similar fashion. The Hasanoglan statuette as a whole combines modernity with the archaic style of idols. The triangular delineation and the punched dots on the pubic triangle, the cruciform bands across the breast and back, are other elements surviving from the idol sculpture. The neck is still abnormally long as was the fashion with idols found in Anatolia and the Cyclades. The modelling of the lower body and the gold anklets remind us of the recently excavated contemporaneous figures of the Dorak treasure from the shores of Lake Apolyont. It may be that during the late third millennium BC similar artistic centres existed in Anatolia. In any case the statuette of Hasanoglan proclaims a widely diffused homogeneous Hattian style.

    It shows a striking connection with the sculpture in stone of northern Mesopotamia. A head from Tell Brak with a similarly exaggerated neck strongly resembles the sculpture of Hasanoglan both in style and type of feature. The large, boldly curved nose, the marked brows and thick lips are almost the same. The statuette of Hasanoglan gives us a good idea of the ethnic type of the period. It may look like a Hattian princess. The statuettes of Alaca are of a related type. The likeness to the head of Tell Brak suggests a diffusion of the Hattian people as far as the North Syrian and Mesopotamian border. The same type of feature occurs later in the Hittite figures on Egyptian reliefs. The Hittite infantry which took part in the battle of Kadesh against Rameses II is represented there with a profile that bears an astonishing resemblance to the Hasanoglan statuette. It may be that at the time the main bulk of the population in Asia Minor still had a Hattian admixture.

    The silver statuette of Hasanoglan presents with its elongated fingers and numerous bracelets and the hands folded over the breasts, a beautiful, decorative aspect. The other ornamental elements, the slight swelling of the breasts, navel and the knees, and the punctured pubic triangle, the anklets and the precisely worked toes and hair, produce a nice contrast to the beautifully polished surface. The primitive form and naïve expression of the statuette is mitigated in a pleasant way by the clear precision of design and an accomplished technique. The modelling of the statuette, especially the rendering of the buttocks, is an artistic achievement, a successful attempt in the new naturalistic style. The humble posture of the hands indicates that the figure is a worshipper, probably a deceased Hattian princess. The assertion of the peasants that the statuette was found in a grave supports this view.

The progressive trend of the artist, who is making successful attempts at a naturalistic rendering of the face and form, gives an approximate clue for dating the statuette. It may belong to about 2000 BC.

To sum up our observations on the material heritage found in the Early Bronze Age stratum of the Anatolian city mounds we may conclude by saying that during the second half of the third millennium BC a unified style existed throughout Central Anatolia. This implies that the art of Central Anatolia and the language of this region were autochthonous. There thus appears before our eyes a people emerging from the depths of Anatolian prehistory of whose language and religion only minute fragments have come down to us, while their magnificent works of art exist in great quantity. Fortunately we know this race by name. They were the Hattian people who for many millennia to come gave the name of Hatti-country to Asia Minor.

II

THE EARLY HISTORICAL PERIOD

THE ORIGINS OF HITTITE CULTURE 2000–1700 BC

THE PEOPLES AND LANGUAGES IN EARLY HISTORY

The peaceful life led by the peoples of Asia Minor for nearly half a millennium, since the beginning of the Early Bronze Age, was ended some time about 2000 BC by a merciless invasion. In Alaca and Boghazköy the destruction in the respective levels is marked by signs of a great conflagration. During that period houses arose only on top of the citadel of Alishar, while building on the terraced city slopes was discontinued. The remaining centres of Central Anatolia excavated to date, Bitik, Karaoglan, Dündartepe and Karahüyük near Konya, fell victim to enemy attack. The settlements of Ahlatlibel and Etiyokushu near Ankara were totally abandoned. Violent fighting seems to have affected all of Central Anatolia.

The period after this burned level is characterized by a definite change in all departments of human activity. The causes of destruction can be attributed to the immigration of Indo-European peoples whose traces now appear for the first time in Asia Minor. But the newcomers were not the only carriers of the new culture; it was due in a large measure to indigenous Hattians.

Written documents and the material heritage of the early historical strata have been found in Central Anatolian dwelling mounds of the period, and above all in the ruins of contemporary trade settlements of Asia Minor built by Assyrian merchants.

ASSYRIAN TRADE SETTLEMENTS IN ASIA MINOR

Our main sources of information concerning the early historical period are cuneiform tablets and several kinds of archaeological finds discovered in Assyrian trade settlements. The latter were a foreign element in Asia Minor and have exercised almost no influence on Anatolian culture, but they furnish us with valuable, and what is more, chronologically classified material on the culture of the epoch. The most essential questions can therefore be discussed here.

The enterprising Assyrians had managed early to found commercial colonies, in the Hatti-country consisting of small principalities. Karums (autonomous commercial colonies) have been discovered in Kanesh (Kültepe) and Hattusas (Boghazköy). Altogether eight other commercial settlements existed in Asia Minor whose names are known to us, but whose sites have not been identified to date. Apart from these a small sort of settlement called Mabartum (station or colony) was recorded. One trading post lay near Alishar.

Trade between Mesopotamia and Anatolia began with the foundation of those trade settlements. Assyrian merchants bartered mainly tin and textiles for copper which was abundant and cheap in Asia Minor. The basic currency was gold and silver. The ratio of gold to silver was 1:8. Copper of good quality was worth forty-six to seventy times its weight in silver. For inferior grade copper the proportion was 105–200 its weight in silver. A metal called *amutum* fetched forty times the price of silver. It must have been iron. The means of transport was the donkey to which the adjective 'black' was regularly attached. On a casting-mould from Kültepe a donkey is represented with two divinities as the most important animal of the period. No roads existed for four-wheeled traffic. Trading was carried out on a big scale. Assyrian merchants derived more than 100 per cent profit from their import transactions. While they could buy up to twenty shekels of tin for one shekel of silver, the sale of one shekel of silver yielded from six to ten shekels of tin.

Karum Kanesh was the centre of those transactions. The other trade settlements were organized from there. The excavations directed by Tahsin and Nimet Özgüç and philologically covered by Kemal Balkan, have yielded excellent results. The Assyrian commercial colony of Kanesh was situated below the city mound inhabited by indigenous people.

The great importance of Karum Kanesh consists in the fact that this site shows four neatly distinguishable stratifications whose dates can be clearly determined. The discovery of seal impressions which name Ibbi-sin, the last king of the Third Dynasty of Ur, enables us to place the date of the foundation of Karum Kanesh in the first half of the twentieth century BC. It may be that the beginnings of trade relations with Assyria, as we have already shown in the foregoing chapter, go back even earlier, to the period of the Akkadian Dynasty. But since levels IV and III do not apparently cover a long period, they may have originated in the twentieth century BC.

From level Ib, which corresponds to the high period of Karum Kanesh, several thousand clay tablets were brought to light. According to the texts which mention the Assyrian ruler Irisum (1852–1813 BC) and his nephew Sargon (Sarrukin I) it can be dated approximately from 1850–1770 BC. The finest works of art in the locality date from this period. It came to a violent end. The enemy attack must have been so unexpected that the household implements and splendid clay vessels remained untouched in their respective places. The surviving spectacle gives a good idea of the daily life of the times.

The disaster had far-reaching results. It is generally assumed that the locality was abandoned for some time. The new level Ib is in every respect a continuation of the previous settlement and also contains cuneiform tablets of Assyrian business magnates. It was destined to last no more than thirty to forty years.

A letter found at Mari, addressed to Zimrilim of Mari, states that fifty donkeys are on their way to Kanesh. Heinrich Otten has pointed out the synchronicity and has dated the level Ib of Karum as belonging to the reign of Isme-Dagan I, a contemporary of Zimrilim and Hammurabi (1728–1686 BC).

The last level Ia contains no clay tablets. In many instances the inhabitants had repaired and used the houses of level Ib. It lasted at the most for one generation.

The excavators reported two separate strata with remains of burnt-out buildings on the city mound, the Hüyük of Kanesh, which correspond to those of Karum II and Ib. In the time preceding the formation of the Hittite state, warlike actions which caused this destruction were inevitable. It was a question of a shift of power away from the minor princes which we shall discuss further on.

The *Karum Hatush* mentioned on cuneiform tablets of Kültepe and Alishar has been located in recent years during the excavations at Boghazköy on the north side of the city, near the temple of the Weather-God of Hattusas. *Karum Hatush* and the Assyrian clay tablets of Alishar correspond to the period of the level Ib of *Karum Kanesh*.

The Assyrian commercial colonies could exist only at a time when numbers of minor kings ruled side by side. As soon as a central government was formed the business magnates of Assyria could no longer make their profits. The signs of a conflagration indicating the destruction in level Ib may be regarded as the first indication of the next period during which the Hittites gained the ascendancy in Asia Minor.

On examining the material inheritance one can observe that the great Assyrian merchants surrounded themselves exclusively with indigenous household implements and works of art. Their homes too were built in the local style. Without the ancient Assyrian texts and cylinder seals we should not have been able, by means of the existing archaeological material alone, to determine the ethnic provenance of these merchants.

THE IMMIGRATION OF THE INDO-EUROPEANS

On studying the history of Asia Minor one can ascertain that all peoples, regardless of their linguistic or racial group, have always retained the characteristics of the world from which they originally came to the peninsula. The Phrygians and the Celts came from the West, and the West determined their way of life. The Hittites, the Seljuks and the

Ottoman Turks reached Asia Minor from the East, and throughout their history remained dependent on the Orient. This process was determined by geography. None of these peoples, with the exception of the Ottomans, had been able to rule the entire peninsula, so that the point of gravity invariably rested with one half of Asia Minor; either in the West or in the East, and the culture of the respective Anatolian peoples was determined by the Orient or Occident. The markedly Mesopotamian character of the Hittites is proof of their Eastern provenance.

The Hittites arrived from their ancestral European home via the Caucasus and first established themselves somewhere east of Anatolia, close to the Mesopotamian world where they settled over a long period. Ferdinand Sommer has drawn our attention to a prayer of king Muwatalli in which the Sun-God is pictured as rising from the sea:

> O Sun-God of Heaven, my Lord, Shepherd of Mankind, you rise from the sea, O Sun-God of Heaven, and ascend to the sky.
> O Sun-God of Heaven, my Lord, daily you sit in judgement upon Man, Dog, Pig, and the wild animals of the fields.

That the sea should figure in a prayer otherwise largely influenced by Babylon may be a definite indication of the whereabouts of a former home of the Hittites. The sea in question will be the Caspian. It is a region conquered a thousand years later by other Indo-European tribes, the Iranian peoples. Like the Seljuks after three millennia, the Hittites may have set out for Asia Minor from there and covered the journey by slow stages.

The Hittite cuneiform script is paleographically much older than that of the Assyrian commercial settlements in Asia Minor of the nineteenth century BC. According to its style (ductus), Hittite cuneiform script can be traced to a yet undiscovered archaic Babylonian variant of dynasty III of Ur (app. 2150–2050 BC). Whether the Hittites learnt to use cuneiform writing before or after their immigration into Asia Minor is a controversial question. However, the general opinion is that the Hittites introduced writing only at the beginning of the Hittite Old Kingdom.

There are definite indications that the Indo-European peoples settled in southern and central Anatolia not later than the beginning of the second millennium BC. Sedat Alp was the first to point out the presence of the Hittites in Kültepe at the time of the Assyrian trade settlements. He has offered conclusive proof that the indigenous names in the Kültepe inscriptions ending with the suffixes 'ala', 'ili', 'ula', are the Hittite adaptations of the Hattian suffixes 'al', 'il' and 'ul'. He is inclined also to see a Hittite suffix in the genitive-endings of Hittite pronouns which cannot be explained as deriving from the Indo-European. He has correctly deduced that such a process would presuppose a long side-by-side existence of the two peoples. The successful excavations directed by André Parrot at Mari, a city on the middle Euphrates, produced a letter from an archive which indicated a long past of the Hittites of Asia Minor.

In this letter, whose beginning is largely lost, for which reason the names of the sender and the addressee are missing, it is written: 'I am a faithful servant of my master. Everything that is brought to me, treasures, works of art and precious objects from Kanesh, Harsamna and Hattusas . . . I will send you.' From an existing fragment of the first line of this inscription where the sender says: '. . . and the seam of the garment of . . . I touch' one may deduce that the recipient of the letter was probably king Jahdunlim, the father of Zimrilim of Mari. Jahdunlim of Mari was a contemporary of the Assyrian king Samai-Adad I and of the great Babylonian sovereign Hammurabi who ruled about 1700 BC. But it is most significant that in this letter the name of the Hattian city Hattus already figures in its Hittite form of Hattusas. Hattusas was therefore in the possession of the Hittites as early as 1700 BC.

Anitta, king of Kussara, who is mentioned on Assyrian cuneiform tablets of the eighteenth century BC of Alishar and Kültepe, and whose name appears on a dagger found in the city mound of Kültepe (Kanesh) is the author of the oldest known Hittite cuneiform inscription. It is true that the text from Boghazköy must be considered as a more recent copy, but as Heinrich Otten has explained, it is linguistically in old Hittite and should not be dated later than the will of Hattusili I. Whether this inscription is the original or a copy made soon after is an open question. In any case it gives us a lively picture of the political situation in Central Anatolia at the period. We cite its most essential parts, taken from the newest translation of the text (by Heinrich Otten):

Anitta, son of Pithana, king of Kussara. He was beloved of the Weather-God of the sky. The king of Kussara descended from the city with great might and took the city of Nesa by storm in the night. He captured the king of Nesa, but did no harm to the sons of Nesa, but treated them like mothers and fathers. Two years after Pithana, my father, I fought the battle. With the assistance of the Sun I conquered every country that arose against me.

. . . Pijusti, king of Hatti, came a second time, and I defeated all his allies near the city of Shalampa . . .

. . . Before that Uhna, king of Zalpuva, brought the statue of Shiushummi from Nesa to Zalpuva. Later on I, Anitta, the Great King, took Shiushummi of Zalpuva back to Nesa. And Huzziya, king of Zalpuva, I brought to Nesa.

When finally Hattusas was plagued by a famine, Shiushummi handed the city to the god Halmashuitta, and I took it by storm in the night, and on her site I sowed weeds. Whoever shall be king after me, and if he resettles Hattusas, he shall be struck by the Weather-God.

In the second part of the text Anitta goes on about his glorious deeds. He reveals himself an active patron of architecture:

. . . And in Nesa, I built fortifications, I built the house of the Weather-God of the sky and the house of Shiushummi . . .

VI Above: Vessel. Gold with carnelians. Height 5·8 cm. (2¼ in.). Below: Vessel. Gold. Height 8·2 cm. (3¼ in.). Both from Alaca Hüyük—Ankara

It is interesting to hear that Anitta favoured Purushanda, who had handed him his insignia of office:

> . . . brought me a throne and a sceptre of iron. So when I returned to Nesa, I took the man from Purushanda with me. As soon as he enters the inner chamber he shall sit down before me on the right.

The text is, as it were, the *res gestae* of king Anitta. His far-reaching policy of conquest aimed at supremacy in Central Anatolia which he of course failed to realize. The political structure of small states continued for a time.

A letter found on the city mound (hüyük) of Kültepe during the recent investigations of Tahsin Özgüç, affords an insight into conditions in the small states. Kemal Balkan has published this important document in a revealing dissertation. It is a letter addressed by king Anum-Hirbi of Mama to king Warshama of Kanesh. He announces:

> Anum-Hirbi, king of Mama, speaks as follows: Tell Warshama, the king of Kanesh. You have written to me: 'The man of Taishama is my slave.' I shall watch over him. But will you watch over your slave, the man from Shubbuha? Since the man from Taishama is your dog, why does he quarrel with the other princes? Does my dog, the man from Shibuha quarrel with the other princes? Shall a king from Taishama be a third king like ourselves? When my enemy conquered me and invaded my country he destroyed twelve of my cities. He drove away the cattle and the sheep belonging to those cities. He said: 'The king has been vanquished.'
> When your father Inar laid siege to the city of Harshamna for nine years, did my people invade your country? And was a single oxen or sheep killed? Today you write me thus: 'Why do you not clear the road for me?' I shall clear the road.
> . . . Now you write we should deliver an oath. Is the previous oath not good enough: Your messenger shall come to me and my messenger shall go to you. Instead of silver Tarikutana has left a sealed sack of stones. Are these things right before the gods? . . .

The three kings mentioned in the letter may be almost contemporaneous with king Phitana and king Anitta of Kussara. The name of king Anum-Hirbi now occurs in the text of Hattusas found during last year's excavations.

Half a dozen Central Anatolian City states ruled in the first quarter of the second millennium by petty kings are now known to us: they are Kanesh, Nesa, Kussara, Hattusas, Zalpa and Purushanda. To begin with they will have been small Hattian principalities of indigenous races, existing alongside many other, not yet rediscovered cities. With the immigration of the Indo-Europeans they fell into the hands of Hittite kings, one might almost be tempted to say according to plan. Since the Hittites preserved the personal and city names of their subjected peoples as part of their conqueror's policy, it is no longer possible to distinguish the small states according to their ethnic origin. But if one considers that the above-mentioned political development of the Hittite State led to the formation of the Hittite Empire we may regard the warlike actions of the period as struggles of the Indo-European invader against the indigenous rulers of Asia Minor.

VII Headband with open-work pattern. Gold. Diameter 19·4 cm. (7⅝ in.).
From Alaca Hüyük—Ankara

The philological investigations of the past decades have shown that apart from the Hittite several related languages were spoken under the Anatolian Indo-Europeans of the second millennium: Palaic, Luvian, and the language of hieroglyphic inscriptions. They are closely related to the Hittite language but have several peculiarities. The Pala country is mentioned in paragraph Five of the Laws, side by side with Hittite and Luvian territory, so that the Hittite Empire consisted in reality of three main sections. Under the Great Empire Pala was a border province which had to be periodically relinquished as a result of attacks by the Gasga (Kassites). It was evidently situated in Paphlagonia.

The Luvian language is the speech of Luviya which comprised the whole of south-western Asia Minor, together with Arzawa and Kizzuwatna. Luvian so closely resembles the language of the hieroglyphics that some scholars consider them to be identical. Anatolian picture-writing was diffused mainly in Central Anatolia. Under the Great Empire it reached to the Aegean, and in the south to the Mediterranean shores.

After the destruction of Hattusa, hieroglyphic writing was widely diffused in the southern part of Central and South Anatolia and in North Syria. Hieroglyphs were used for public and monumental inscriptions. As picture-writing they were attractive and of course meant much more to an illiterate population than the cuneiform script. It is therefore possible that hieroglyphs were used not only to convey a single idiom as has been generally assumed, but to communicate in several languages.

The oldest hieroglyphs that have come down to us originate in level Ib of Karum Kanesh belonging to the eighteenth century BC. A seal from the hoard of Soloi, a locality near Mersin, is apparently older still. According to Goetze the seal of Isputahsu from the period of the Hittite ruler Telepinu (c. 1550 BC) comes next. The Anatolian picture-writing may have originated somewhere in southern Anatolia and in connection with Cretan ideograms.

After the first attempts of the English scholar A. H. Says, it was due to the research begun around the year 1930 by scholars like Bossert, Forrer, Gelb, Hrozny and Meriggi that the first successes were obtained in deciphering the inscriptions employing a method based on combination. Ten years later H. G. Guterbock achieved important results whilst engaged on work on the Hittite seals from Boghazköy that bear the name of the king in cuneiform and hieroglyphic script. Sedat Alp made a significant contribution to the deciphering of personal names in Hittite hieroglyphic seals and inscriptions.

The study of the Karatepe bilingual inscriptions by Bossert and Steinherr confirmed the results achieved in the course of previous research by application of the combinatory method and yielded further information. The highly successful French excavations carried out under the direction of Claude Schaeffer brought to light a large number of Hittite seals. These formed part only of a wealth of finds. The research carried out by Emanuel Laroche using this material as a basis together with his other studies on Anatolian hiero-glyphic script represent a significant advance in the work of deciphering. The majority of the already mentioned scholars are still engaged on this work. In the most recent past other scholars—and more especially D. Kennedy—have reached valid conclusions.

As we have seen in the foregoing chapter, the indigenous population consisted in the main of Hattians, but also a large number of autochthonous races of whom as yet we know nothing. Relations between the conqueror and the subject peoples were close and harmonious so that a new nation was formed as a result of long and close proximity. The freshly arrived Indo-Europeans respected above all the religion and the manners and customs of the autochthonous population, and gradually adapted themselves to local conditions. The above-mentioned conservation of city names, and more still of proper names, is clear proof of the fusion of the Indo-Europeans with the Hattian people.

In the formation of the new Hattian-Indo-European culture Mesopotamia played an important part. The strong Babylonian influences noticeable in every department of intellectual and spiritual life of the ensuing Hittite era first reached Asia Minor at the beginning of the second millennium B.C. Even though Anatolia had been affected by the Mesopotamian world ever since the dynasty of Akkad, oriental influence assumed its ultimate importance only after the incursion of the Indo-Europeans. From a co-operation of these three components a new culture was born under the small states which developed further in the following period.

Especially in the domain of art the peaceful and harmonious co-existence of the invader with the autochthonous population produced outstanding results which we shall presently examine.

ART

Although they are derived largely from the Hattian tradition, the works of art familiar from various cities of this period show a marked change of style. It is true that the improvement of ceramic ware is to be attributed to the invention, towards the end of the third millennium BC, of the potter's wheel. But the new vessels show a striking transformation which may be interpreted as an indication of the arrival of the Indo-Europeans. It is most significant that about this time polychrome pottery appears in almost every city of [26, 27, 33, 34] Central Asia Minor. Albrecht Goetze has seen a connection between the prevalence of this ware and Hittite immigration. It is no coincidence that at the end of the third millennium and the close of the Early Bronze Age, richly decorated polychrome vessels suddenly appear where formerly only monochrome pottery was known. In Mesopotamia and Iran painted pottery had been in use since the fourth millennium BC. Since the Indo-Europeans came to Asia Minor from an easterly direction it is possible that the emergence of this kind of pottery was somehow connected with their arrival. Or it may be that the Indo-Europeans were merely an indirect instrument for the beginnings of painted pottery because the bonds between Asia Minor and the Orient had been strengthened through the invasion; for Anatolian polychrome pottery is inspired by oriental models, whether it originated with the Hittites or was stimulated by neighbouring influence.

The *depata* too, the double-handled chalice first known in Anatolia at the close of the Early Bronze Age, may, as has recently been suggested, be derived from southern Cilician models rather than from those of Troy.

The painted pottery which suddenly appears on the market at the close of the third IX, 26 millennium can be divided into three groups. The first type is best known under the term 'Cappadocian Pottery' or 'Pottery from Alishar III', distinguishable by a specific geo-X, 27, 33 metrical style. A second type, found chiefly at Kültepe, was developed from the first and is decorated in the main with undulating lines and aquatic birds. A third type initially discovered in Alishar and now in Polatli has been labelled by Osten as 'Intermediate Ware'. These should be the oldest of the three polychrome varieties. 'Cappadocian Pottery' and 'Intermediate Ware' are handmade. Among this painted pottery Syrian products have also been recognized.

Of the three above-mentioned varieties 'Cappadocian Pottery' deserves special attention. Its main characteristic is a purely geometrical ornamentation. It is represented by very beautiful vessels, chiefly from Alishar and Karum Kanesh. This kind of pottery was still made by hand, although the monochrome ware of the same period was fashioned on the potter's wheel.

The main subject of the evolved geometrical style is drinking vessels in the shape of 34 animals. These decorative objects, used principally as libation cups for religious rites, are known from the magnificent examples of level II at Karum Kanesh. In them we find the artist's pleasure in animal representation. Other drinking vessels have the form of 33 snails or upturned shoes. Two examples of the latter kind have recently been found in Mycenae. Their shape and geometrical design betray a strong Anatolian influence. They may have been imported from Asia Minor. Moreover, an Anatolian *rhyton* in the form of a stag of lead and silver has been discovered in Mycenae.

XII, 32, 34 Most popular were *rhytons* shaped like bulls. Lion and stag-shaped vessels, which we encounter in a great variety of forms, became the fashion at the time.

The high artistic standards of the early historical period can best be judged from the XI, 28, 32 monochrome ware. It represents the indigenous component in the new artistic movement. Even a brief examination shows that it perpetuates several types of Hattian pottery of the 29 third millennium BC. The fruitstands, beakers, spouted pots or 'tea-pots' and other types of vessels of the Hattian style revive in the new period under a perfected form.

The line of development leading from the Early Bronze Age to the Hittite period can be clearly traced through the so-called 'tea-pots'. The starting-point of this development

VIII Female statuette. Silver and gold. Height 24·4 cm. (9⅝ in.). From Hasanoglan—Ankara

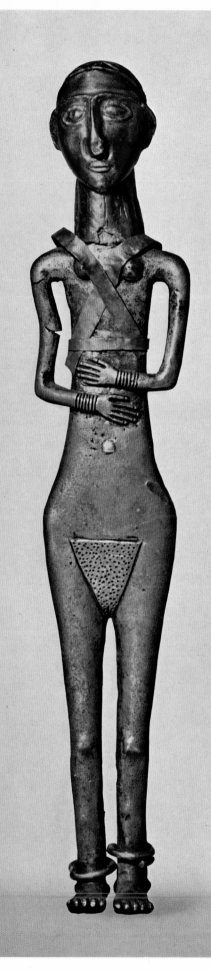

is an Early Bronze Age pot from Alaca. It is followed by a pot of similar shape from level IV of Karum Kanesh which is not burnished and is somewhat crudely fashioned. A model from level III of the same locality is burnished and polished, more disciplined in form and with a somewhat angular structure. The 'tea-pots' from levels II and Ib of Karum Kanesh have a brilliantly polished surface, sharply angular outlines, and an elegant shape. In levels II and Ib of Karum Kanesh new types of tea-pots have been found. They recur in Alishar, Boghazköy, Acemhüyük and Karahüyük near Konya, and date from the same period as the finds in level Ib of Karum Kanesh. To this latter type belong the models

36–39 of the Hittite Old Kingdom, but here they sometimes are of inferior quality. This fact will be discussed in the following section.

Apart from the perfected types of the Early Bronze Age, new forms appear in the era of small states which are quite alien to the tradition of Central Asia Minor. Among

39 these are pots with clover-spouts, double-handled goblets with pointed bases, cantharoi,

31–34 vessels shaped like grapes, clay shoes and *rhytons*—animal-shaped drinking vessels. The latter three seem to have been new inventions while the other types were inspired by contact with neighbouring cultures. But it is important that during this epoch even those vessels which were, as we have seen, inspired by foreign models are not copies: they are valuable re-creations.

Monochrome ware is much more frequent than the painted pottery and its diffusion was accordingly far wider. The pottery from the necropolis of Gordion, the Phrygian capital, belongs stylistically to the monochrome pottery of the small states. Characteristic for this period is a certain type of beaker-pitcher. Splendid examples are known from

XI, 30 Kültepe, Boghazköy, Alishar, Karahüyük near Konya and Acemhüyük near Aksaray.

The pitcher has a remarkable tectonic structure. The sharp arris of the belly makes a clear horizontal profile. The boldly elongated spout ending in a bird's beak and the two angular knobs on the shoulder produce similar attractive effects.

But these elements have a functional as well as an aesthetic purpose. The broad-bellied vase needs in fact a long spout, and the bird's beak is not only an attractive design but also a gutter preventing drops of liquid from running back on the spout. The two knobs on the shoulder likewise serve for supporting the vase with one hand while the other is holding the handle. This is the ultimate perfection of this type of pitcher. No further evolution follows, only imitation and degeneration.

Similar tectonic forms and definite outlines with boldly protruding spouts can be observed on other types of vessels of the period.

The animal vessels which we met in polychrome pottery are among the most important objects of monochrome ware. Plain drinking and libation vessels have been found on every excavation site of the period. They occur even where no polychrome ware existed. This means that the animal vessels were an invention of native craftsmen attached to workshops where monochrome pottery was made. The monochrome animal vessels are,

42

so to speak, continuations of the Hattian animal sculptures of Alaca, although conceived 31 ab.
in an entirely new style. The tradition of the Early Bronze Age survives chiefly in the
ornamentation of these monochrome animal vessels. As yet it consists in the main of small
incised circles which formerly adorned decorative objects of the late third millennium BC.
Some *rhytons* are engraved with small lines or incisions, like the traces of finger nails, that
is, with ornamental elements of Early Bronze Age terracotta ware. Most animal vessels 34
have tubular openings and a spout set inside the jaws. They were used for libations. This
religious significance of animal vessels goes back to a Hattian conception of the Early
Bronze Age which can be traced to the time of the small states.

In the period of the small states the anthropomorphous representation of the deity 31 below
appears side by side with its teriomorphous aspect. On a cup from Karum Kanesh we
see on the one side a male and on the other side a female head; both are depicted in full
face. The horns affixed to the belly of the vessel and below the mouth indicate their divine IV
nature. We are dealing here with a rendering of a pair of divinities, a schematic image
which we have met with earlier on Hattian disk standards with the stag and panther. 35
This representation of the divine couple is a theme exclusive to the lead idols from
Alishar, Kültepe, and Boghazköy, where it has become a stereotyped image. Seen from
the vantage point of the beholder the lead idols generally show the male deity on the
left and the female deity on the right. In the casting-moulds the scheme is naturally
reversed for the image to be cast in its correct position. This custom may have corresponded to a religious ceremony.

From the last paragraph of the text of Anitta quoted above we learn that the right
side was considered a place of honour. The motif of the wedded pair signifies the equality
of the male and female divinities. But it appears that the god compared to the goddess
is slightly raised. In the Great Empire this ceremonial custom became a fixed rule which
knew of almost no exception.

As has been pointed out by B. Landsberger, the female deity, who generally holds her
naked breasts, may represent the Mother Goddess. The god cannot be named with any
certainty. On the monuments of the Great Empire the male deity of this type is invariably
the Weather-God. But in these lead idols inspired by Mesopotamia the chief divinity may
not be a Weather-God. In the lead idols the three- or two-pronged fork is conspicuously
absent although this symbol as an attribute of the Weather-God appears on cylinder seals
of the period.

The goddess of the lead idols is not always the female divinity derived from Mesopotamian culture, depicted naked or holding her naked breasts. Some lead idols show a 35
goddess who is fully dressed holding a child against her breast. On other examples a
second child stands between the two gods. In this representation of the mother and child,
we recognize a further survival of native Hattian tradition. The bronze statuette of Horoz- 25
tepe, and still more the alabaster idols of religious significance from Kültepe belonging

43

to the end of the Early Bronze Age, already express the same artistic idea as the lead

76 above idols. On one mould a child leaning against the mother's breast wears a conical cap, like
its father. This is a motif repeated during the Great Empire in the principal scene of

Fig. 19 Yazilikaya near Hattusas where the divine pair is accompanied by their son wearing a
similar conical cap.

The lead idols of Alishar, Kültepe and Boghazköy are the works of indigenous artists.
The bulging, pointed cap of the male divinities seen on these sculptures occurs on a terracotta head of Karum Kanesh. The stuck-on slit eyes of the lead statuettes seem to have

32 been a peculiarity of Anatolian art during the time of the small states. The oarsman of a
ram-*rhyton* shaped like a boat from Karum Kanesh II has stuck-on eyes. A similar treatment of the eyes recurs on a sandstone figurine from Karum Kanesh.

31 above The type of feature found on the lead figures and the boldly arched nose are Hattian
31 below characteristics. A head on a sherd from Karum Kanesh Ib bears similar features. The heads
VIII, 22 of the above-mentioned vessels are of the same type. All these heads, as also the silver
35, above statuettes of Hasanoglan, may represent racial types of an indigenous Hattian population.

The seated ivory statuette from Karum Kanesh Ib, of a naked goddess holding her
breasts, is not of a type found from Asia Minor. She may, however, as the excavator has
pointed out, be a copy by a local sculptor. The bonnet-shaped headgear is found in two
bronze statuettes of Alaca and on the seated female deity of Eflatun-Pinar.

The extremely elegant golden headgear found in a grave of Karum Kanesh II on the
head of a skeleton is a sumptuous copy of contemporary Anatolian caps frequently
depicted on cylinder seals.

Although we do not possess any examples, large-scale sculpture seems to have already
existed during the era of the small states. In a record of his deeds Anitta, king of Kussara,
boasts of having 'returned the statue of Siusummi of Zalpuva to Nesa'. It may have been
a sculpture of the sort fashionable in the Mesopotamian cities. In the same text Anitta
relates that he built the house of the Weather-God of the Sky and the house of Siusummi at
Nesa. In the city mound of Kanesh (Kültepe) Tahsin Özgüç has excavated large buildings
probably belonging to the time of Pithana and his son Anitta. If Nesa was in fact identical
with Kanesh, as Güterbock has suggested, these buildings would correspond to those
mentioned by Anitta in his text. The monumental buildings rest on strong stone foundations and orthostats. Their walls are not made of unbaked bricks but of stone. Here the
emergence of a new architectural style parallel with the evolution of pottery and other
branches of art becomes apparent. In Karahüyük near Konya Sedat Alp laid bare a
palace which must belong approximately to the period of level Ib of Karum Kanesh.

In the same text Anitta records the construction of a fortress in Nesa. In Alishar and

IX Pitcher. Polychrome clay. Old geometrical style. Height 71·3 cm. (28 in.). From Kültepe.
18th century BC—Ankara

Karahüyük near Konya, important city walls have been exposed which emulate the box-wall system of Hittite fortifications at Hattusas. The fortress at Karahüyük, of which impressive remains have survived, is exceptionally large.

In Kültepe the excavators uncovered a large number of dwellings consisting of up to six rooms. The foundations are of stone and the walls of unbaked brick. Similar houses were found in Karum Kanesh where the four walls of every house faced paved streets, mostly with drains. The houses of Karahüyük of the same date as those at Hattusas are usually built on a megaron plan. Hearths, ovens, and large vats for provisions indicate the use of each room. Especially impressive are the handsomely ornamented hearths of which several examples were found at Karahüyük. The palace of this site includes a bathroom fitted with a hip-bath of clay.

The weak stone bases and thin walls of the houses belonging to this period indicate that they did not exceed one storey. The palace of Karahüyük near Konya, however, had two storeys.

Hittite glyptic too started under the small states. Level II of Karum Kanesh contains stamp seals with heraldic animals revolving round their own axis, that is, representational motifs which continued to be the fashion in the following Hittite period.

Through the discoveries in level Ib of Karum Kanesh the number of stamp seals has been largely increased and the choice of themes multiplied. Beautiful examples from Alishar, and lately from Karum Hattush, have been published. They are seals with cone-shaped, often grooved and faceted perforated handles. Their surfaces are invariably circular or clover-shaped. Specially popular were seals with the motifs of eagles or double-headed eagles. Animal contests and groups of three (twin animals standing on a prostrate animal) played an important part.

A number of stamp seals from Kültepe, Boghazköy, Alishar and Alaca are so similar in style that they must belong to the same glyptic workshops. A cylinder seal from Karum Kanesh should be included in this group.

On this kind of seal the human and animal figures have broad, smooth, rounded bodies of bulging proportions. Their arms and legs on the other hand are comparatively thin. It is one of their characteristics that human and animal shapes and the lower hem of garments are picked out in embossed lines.

Although in style they match the other pieces, the two stamp seals from Alaca may originate from the beginning of the Hittite Old Kingdom since Alaca does not seem to have existed at the time of the small states. If that was so this category of seals must have been made for several generations.

From level Ib of Karum Kanesh comes a golden stamp seal of a clothed and seated

X Vessel. Polychrome clay. Evolved geometrical style. Height 52·6 cm. (20¾ in.). From Kültepe. 18th century BC—Ankara

goddess in front of an altar with six loaves of bread. Nimet Özgüç has quite correctly compared this piece with later Hittite artefacts. It is a purely Hittite sculptural concept.

A number of achievements, the use of writing, the evolution of pottery, the appearance of monumental architecture and of fine, more evolved works of art testify to the high cultural standards under the small states.

Level II of Karum Kanesh has yielded the oldest and most beautiful products of this epoch. Similar and even more important works are expected to emerge from the corresponding level of the city mound of Kanesh. The ruined sites of Asia Minor which have so far been excavated produced no discoveries comparable to those of Karum Kanesh II. This indicates that the new culture began at Kanesh. The high period, however, seems to be *35* represented by the finds of level I which contained the most beautiful clay objects and lead idols. The centre of this culminating period was naturally the city mound of Kanesh where we must look for the residence of a ruler of Central Asia Minor of the period. The monumental buildings and important finds excavated to date give a vivid idea of the advanced cultural standards of the age.

Other discoveries contemporaneous with those of level Ib of Karum Kanesh were made at Alishar, Boghazköy, Karahüyük near Konya and Acemhüyük near Aksaray. Evidently by the second half of the eighteenth century BC the new culture had already spread throughout the length and breadth of Asia Minor. It is significant that polychrome ware disappears from level Ib of Kanesh and plain, highly polished vessels dominate the market. This change in fashion was the result of a rivalry between foreign and indigenous artistic movements, decided finally in favour of the latter. For a long time this pottery existed side by side with the native ware of Asia Minor; it was developed further, but in the end indigenous taste prevailed. The reason for this was that the Indo-European conqueror conformed to local conditions and adopted the superior culture of the vanquished Hattian population. The invaders submitted to a considerable degree to Hattian influence in language, religion, manners and custom. The new culture was founded on a groundwork of Hattian tradition. Its perfection, however, is the common achievement of the immigrant and the autochthonous races under the leadership of the Hittites. Several Indo-European people, some of whom we know at least by their languages, may have contributed to the formation of the new culture. The main contribution was however made by the Nesili—the race speaking the language of Nesa. We call these people the Hittites. They founded an Empire which survived for almost half a millennium. In the next chapter we shall see that the art of the Hittite Old Kingdom was merely a continuation of things achieved during the last half of this era. This enables us to declare that the first creations of Hittite culture originated in the final phase of the early historical period.

It is important to establish that the genesis of the Hittite state was due not only to political power, but also to the creation of a remarkable culture which was based on indigenous tradition and played a decisive part in its formation.

48

III

THE HITTITE OLD KINGDOM

ABOUT 1700–1450 BC

HISTORY AND CULTURE

Our knowledge of the history of the Hittite Old Kingdom is derived in the main from the so-called Text of Telepinu. This linguistic document of the fifteenth century begins as follows:

> Thus speaks Tabarna Telepinu, the Great King:
>
> 'Formerly Labarna was Great King; and his sons, his brothers, his kinsmen and blood relatives and his fighting men assembled round him.
>
> The country was small. But wherever he went to war he conquered the enemy country with a strong arm. Again and again he destroyed the country. And he made them neighbours of the sea.
>
> After him Hattusili reigned, and also his sons, his brothers, his kinsmen and blood relatives and his fighting men assembled round him. And wherever he went to war he conquered the enemy country with a strong arm. Again and again he destroyed the country. And he made them neighbours of the sea.
>
> But when the servants of the Princes rose, they began to throw down their houses, to plot against their masters and shed blood.
>
> When Mursili reigned in Hattusas his sons also, and his brothers, his kinsmen, blood relatives and his fighting men assembled round him. And he conquered the enemy country with a strong arm. And he made them neighbours of the sea.
>
> And he marched on Halpa [Aleppo] and destroyed Halpa. Prisoners from Halpa and their belongings he brought to Hattusas. After that he marched on Babylon and destroyed Babylon, he attacked the Hurri, and brought prisoners from Babylon and their belongings to Hattusas. . . .'

Later the word Tabarna (sometimes spelt Labarna) which we find in the Text of Telepinu as the name of the first Hittite king (who ruled approximately from 1680–1650 BC) became the title of all Hittite kings, as that of Caesar did, whose name, as the founder of the Imperium Romanum, survived in the title of the Emperor.

It is doubtful whether the stereotyped phrase 'and he turned them (the conquered domains) into neighbours of the sea' applies to this first king. But his successor Hattusili I (about 1650–1620 BC) was able to penetrate as far as Aleppo. In 1957 new tablets in an Akkadian and a Hittite version came to light in Boghazköy in which the king relates his exploits:

> Great King Tabarna, son of the brother of Tawananna, reigned in Hattusas. I marched on Shahuitta but did not destroy [the city] although I devastated their domain. I left my troops in two places and gave them leave to loot. I marched on Zabhar and devastated it. The gods [of the city] and three Majaltun-chariots I sent up to the Sun-Goddess of Arinna, and a silver bull to the temple of the Weather-God, and nine [other] gods I sent up to the temple of Mezullas.
>
> In the following year I marched against Alhalha [Alalah—Tell Atchana near Antakya] and devastated it. . . . In the following year I marched against the land of the Arzavi, I took their cattle and sheep. In [those] days he [Hattusili] set out, like a lion the Great King crossed the river Puran [Euphrates]. Like a lion with his paw he struck the city of Hassh[wa]. He heaped dust on it and filled Hattusas with its treasures.

They seem to deal with warlike actions which may be termed acts of robbery. In one place in the text describing the campaign to Arzawa, Hattusili admits that his conquests yielded no lasting results: 'Behind my back the enemy of the Hanikabat country invaded my domain and all the countries deserted me. Only the city of Hattusas was left.'

Also his campaign against Halpa (Aleppo) seems to have ended in a military defeat. As we have seen in the Text of Telepinu quoted above, what he was not destined to accomplish was achieved by his successor Mursili I (about 1620–1590 BC), who conquered first Aleppo and then Babylon and caused the downfall of the dynasty of Hammurabi.

According to the shorter chronology this event took place about 1531 BC but it might be more correct to date it from the beginning of the sixteenth century.

These successes obtained by Mursili I, however, were not of long duration. The enterprising early kings advanced too far. As conditions in their own country were not stabilized the hastily won positions had to be quickly abandoned. A period of internal difficulties followed. Already under Hattusili I conspiracies were afoot. The above-mentioned Text of Telepinu says:

> But after the servants of the Prince revolted, they began to betray their master.

The political testament of Hattusili I, which we shall quote in part, gives a gripping account of the details of this event. The crown prince had rebelled against the king. Hattusili proved strong enough to suppress the uprising and banish the heir-presumptive from Hattusas. But even though Hattusili mastered the situation and succeeded in placing his adopted son Mursili on the throne, the young king fell victim to an evil deed. In his

XI Jug. Clay with reddish-brown slip and polished surface. Height 39·8 cm. (15¾ in.). From Kültepe. 18th century BC—Ankara

victorious return from Babylon he was, so we are told in the Text of Telepinu, murdered by one Hantili, the husband of the sovereign's own sister.

At the close of the sixteenth century the internal difficulties were temporarily solved by Telepinu (about 1525–1500 BC) who was himself a usurper. He attempted to save the country from ruin by means of a law of succession. Fraternal strife and palace murders were to cease:

> Only a child by the first marriage, a son, shall be made king. If no prince of the direct line exists, a son of the second line shall be king. But if the king has no son, a daughter of the direct line, if she exists, shall take a husband, and he shall be made king.

But even this law of succession, which was still adhered to under the Empire, could not prevent the disintegration of the Hittite Old Kingdom. A dark age followed, extending over several generations. For a time supremacy in the Near East was seized by the kingdom of Mitanni.

The name of Hattusili indicates that he made Hattusas the capital of the country. In the voluminous inscription found in 1957 at Boghazköy from which we have quoted above, he calls himself 'Tabarna Hattusili, the great king of Hattusas, the man from Kussara'. The last word of this sentence indicates that Hattusili, like his predecessors Tabarna, Anitta and Pithana, lived in Kussara until he moved his Court to Hattusas. Consequently Hattusas became the capital of the Hittite Kingdom some time about 1600 BC.

Philologists are generally agreed that in spite of its archaic style (*ductus*) Hittite cuneiform script originated in the Old Hittite period. Hans G. Güterbock has pointed out that after the foundation of the Old Kingdom, Hittite kings imported scribes who wrote in the Old Babylonian style from a North Mesopotamian border province near the Hittite frontier. This is the most convincing explanation of the archaic character of Hittite cuneiform script; it does not of course exclude the possibility of other modes of writing being used occasionally during the period of the small states.

So far two very important documents in Hittite from the Old Kingdom are known to exist. The earliest is the political testament of Hattusili I, dating from about 1600 BC. This is followed by the Text of Telepinu which belongs approximately to the beginning of the fifteenth century. From the last-named text we have quoted extracts. The Hittite version of the newly discovered bilingual Text of Hattusili from Boghazköy is, as H. Otten has established, a later translation of the original text and cannot therefore be included here. In the opinion of H. Otten, who was the last to study this inscription thoroughly, the text of Anitta is, as we have said before, older than the testament of Hattusili and was therefore written before the foundation of the Old Kingdom.

At first the Akkadian text of the similarly bilingual testament of Hattusili was regarded as the original form to which a Hittite version had been attached, but a more recent investigation of the text has inclined us, as Heinrich Otten has recently said, to see the original text in the Hittite version while the Akkadian part shows every sign of the difficulties inherent in a translation.

The thorough study of both versions by Ferdinand Sommer and Adam Falkenstein is accompanied by an excellent translation which enables non-experts to appreciate the beauties of the Hittite language. The testament of Hattusili I is the best piece of literary work that we know from the Hittite world.

In his account Hattusili I enumerates the reasons why instead of his nephew, the heir-presumptive, he chooses as his successor his grandson Mursili I. As he is trying to justify himself before the assembly of nobles he describes the conditions in the royal family in great detail. From these frank and unrestrained words we learn not only of the king's relations with his family and the nobles, but many interesting details about the personal lives of the Hittites:

> Great King Tabarna spoke to the fighting men of the Assembly and the dignitaries, saying: Behold, I have fallen sick. The young Labarna I had proclaimed to you, saying: 'He shall sit upon the throne'; I, the king, called him my son, embraced him, exalted him, and cared for him continually. But he showed himself a youth not fit to be seen; he shed no tears, he showed no pity, he was cold and heartless. I, the king, summoned him to my couch and said: 'Well. No one will in future bring up the child of his sister as his foster-son! The word of the king he has not laid to heart, but the word of his mother, the serpent, he has laid to heart. . . . Enough! He is my son no more!' Then his mother bellowed like an ox: 'They have torn asunder the womb in my living body! They have ruined him, and you will kill him!' But have I, the king, done him any evil? . . . Behold, I have given my son Labarna a house! I have given him arable land in plenty, sheep in plenty I have given him. Let him now eat and drink. So long as he is good he may come up to the city; but if he come forward as a trouble-maker . . . then he shall not come up, but shall remain in his house.

After further accusations of his sister and her son, Hattusili announces his new decision:

> Behold, Mursili is now my son . . . my servants and leading citizens, must be at hand to help my son. . . .

Hattusili goes on to praise his new heir presumptive, and admonishes the Assembly of nobles to honour and obey the young king:

> He is the direct descendant of the king, the Sun! bring him up to be thy king, your hero! But you shall not be presumptuous. No enemy shall be among you . . . or my son will punish you.

Then Hattusili tells what happened to his son and daughter. He does not seem to have had a happy family life; he says:

> Till now no one of my family has obeyed my will; but thou, my son Mursili, thou must obey it.

53

We read of the advice given by the aged king to his successor:

Keep thy father's word! If thou keepest thy father's word, thou wilt eat bread and drink water. When maturity is within thee, then eat two or three times a day and do thyself well! And when old age is within thee, then drink to satiety!

The king recommends the same thing to the dignitaries and nobles of his realm:

Now you, who are my chief servants, you too must keep my, the king's, words. You shall only eat bread and drink water. So Hattusas will stand high and my land will be at peace. But if you do not keep the king's word . . . you will not remain alive, you will perish . . . you shall serve the gods humbly. Attend to their offerings of bread and wine, their broth and groats . . .

Then Hattusili turns once more towards his son:

I have spoken to thee, and this tablet shall be recited before thee every month. Thus thou shalt remember my words of wisdom in your heart. With my fighting men and my nobles thou shalt deal leniently. If one of them commits a wrong, either before a god or by uttering blasphemous words, then consult the *pankus* [the Assembly of Nobles], any dispute shall be referred to the pankus.

And in conclusion the mournful last words of his will:

Thou shalt wash my dead body according to the custom. Hold me to your heart, and holding me to your heart, lay me in the earth.

The signature reads:

Tablet of Tabarna, the Great King; when Great King Tabarna fell ill in Kussara and nominated the young Mursili as his successor.

ART

The art of the Hittite Old Kingdom keeps closely to the pattern set by the previous early historical epoch. The workshops were content to reproduce, or to vary, already existing trends. At the present stage of research it is therefore possible only in rare cases to make an exact distinction between the pottery and other decorative objects of the Hittite Old Kingdom and those of the preceding period.

The vessels from Alaca may be products of the Hittite Old Kingdom. For in this locality the finds characteristic of level II and Ib of Karum Kanesh, Assyrian cuneiform

XII Lion-*rhyton*. Clay with reddish-brown slip. Height 21·1 cm. (8¼ in.). From Kültepe. 18th century BC—Ankara

tablets, lead idols and painted pottery of the evolved geometrical style, are missing. It may be that phase II and Ib of Karum Kanesh in Alaca Hüyük are earlier by one generation.

37, 38   Part of the pottery from Alaca consists of brilliantly polished monochrome vases of a tectonic structure with handsome widely projecting spouts familiar from the previous period. But the remaining types of vessels from Alaca with their slender proportions express a new artistic sensibility. A vessel shaped like a crater from Alaca seems to belong to the Old Hittite period. In the vessels from Acemhüyük also, the predilection for slender forms can be observed.

36   The magnificent libation jug from Tokat, decorated with incised circles, now at the Hittite Museum at Istanbul, is an excellent example of the contemporary taste. The structure and the shape of the spout closely resemble vessels of the older period, but the slender form of the vessel seems to indicate an origin in the Hittite Old Kingdom.

Naturally, the best pottery is to be looked for in the capital of Hattusas (Boghazköy). During the excavations of the past years finds came to light which could be dated by stratification to the Old Kingdom. Similar vessels from the Old Kingdom were found XIII in Alishar. They no longer emulate the characteristic angular, sharply outlined shape of the early Hittite vessels. Gentle outlines and rounded shapes seem to be the guiding principle of the new movement. The technical finish of the goblets is excellent; their shining surfaces are effective. The jug with double handles is especially attractive, with its gay finely-polished ivory surface.

39   The remaining vessels from Alishar might belong to the time of the small states or to that of the Hittite Old Kingdom. One cantharos similar to that of Alishar has been found at Boghazköy in the level of the Hittite Old Kingdom; others occur in Alaca. The piece from Alaca might therefore well belong to the Old Hittite period. Vessels from the necropolis of Gordion in the early Hittite style might, at least in part, be reproductions from the Hittite Old Kingdom. During that time beautiful vessels were made and various new types invented or imported. Worthy of note are the pilgrim flasks from Boghazköy and Alaca also found at Troy VI, polished to look like ivory or painted in simple patterns. These date from the close of the Old Hittite era. A large number of clay hip-baths from Alaca and Boghazköy testify to the high standards of civilized living in the Hittite Old Kingdom. But vessels of that time show noticeable deterioration in quality which is even more marked under the Empire. The reason for this is that minor sculpture and the portrayal of the human form in general gained in importance while plain vessels slowly went out of fashion.

The ceramic artists were confronted with new tasks. During the Old Hittite period clay vessels shaped like animals and small-scale sculpture were favourite themes. Monochrome *rhytons* from Kültepe, known to have existed from the nineteenth century BC, were still very popular. They are distinguished works of art. In comparing these animal

XIII Three vessels. Clay with different coloured slips. Height of the vessel on the left including
the spout 32·8 cm. (13 in.). From Alishar. *c.* 1700 BC—Ankara

vessels with the examples of the eighteenth century BC one can see that they are far more naturalistic. The lion or bull sculptures which are still somewhat abstract in level II and Ib of Karum Kanesh, are now given a naturalistic likeness. A splendid bull-shaped *rhyton* from Tokat is a fine example of the new movement. It belongs to a new kind of the painted vessels which were an invention of the Hittite Old Kingdom. Fragments from Alishar of painted vases in relief may belong to the Old Hittite period. The most beautiful

XIV example of this kind, the vase from Bitik, and the newly-discovered sherds of Boghazköy, date from the beginning of the Empire. The fragmentary remains of a large clay statue of a bull, recently brought to light in the level of the Hittite Old Kingdom at Boghazköy, prove that the artists of the ceramic workshops made large clay sculptures as well. By means of these fragments, whose date has been determined from the stratification in which they were found, it can be asserted that the life-sized clay lion found in the citadel of Büyükkale near Boghazköy belongs to the Old Hittite period.

Monumental stone sculpture which we assign to the reign of Anitta, about 1800 BC, was known in the Old Hittite epoch. We have learnt lately that Hattusili I transported numerous statues of gods from the Hurrian country to Hattusas. We may assume that the Hittites copied these statues locally.

41 A lion's head from Alishar, part of a *rhyton*, initiates the type of sculptured lions familiar from the Empire. The gaping jaws, the hanging tongue folded over the lower lip, the U-shaped stylized cheekbones, the two knobs on the forehead, and the cubic shape of the head are the same as in the art of the Empire.

Fragments of vessels from Yazilikaya with a relief of five men offering gifts and the mould of a relief representing a battle scene cannot give us a real idea of plastic art in the Old Hittite Kingdom. Both are insignificant products of their time.

42 On the other hand the magnificent bronze statuette from the Vladimir Golschmann Collection in St. Louis is, as Hanfmann has pointed out, a work of art from the Hittite Old Kingdom. The position of the hands resting on the breasts and abdomen and the

VIII, 22 spindly arms of the bronze statuette recall the Hattian worshippers of Hasanoglan. The protruding buttocks and deeply carved eye-sockets, on the other hand, remind us of the

23 mother and child of Horoztepe. But the ethnic type of the Golschmann statuette is much closer to the Hasanoglan sculpture. It is of course far later than the two Early Bronze Age statuettes from Hasanoglan and Horoztepe. The long plaits falling over the shoulders indicate the evolved style of the artist. The bow-shaped ear-rings are not Anatolian. This detail may indicate the south-east Anatolian origin of the statuette. North Syrian and Mesopotamian influences have been noted on the silver statuette from Hasano-

43 glan. The worshippers of the Golschmann Collection show a remarkable likeness to a bronze statuette from Syria in the Museum at Istanbul. The profile is almost the same, with a long, pointed nose and an equally pointed angular chin. The devotional attitude of the hands resting, one on the breast and the other on the womb, is identical. Henri

Seyring has rightly declared the sculpture from Istanbul and a number of similar figurines to be Lebanese, that is Syrian, and has correctly fixed their date to the first half of the second millennium BC. The round ornament on the top of the head reminds one of the tassel found on the caps of Syro-Hittite divinities. The bronze statuette of Istanbul may be a Syro-Hittite sculpture from the fifteenth century BC; the sculpture from the Golsch-mann Collection, on the other hand, is a south Anatolian Hittite work with Syrian in-fluence from the sixteenth century. Entirely non-Hittite are the posture, dress and ethnic type of a small kneeling ivory statue found in Alaca. It may have been imported from the Syro-Phoenician area.

42

Early types of Hittite seals from the time of the small states survived in the Old Hittite period. Such stamp seals, indistinguishable in style or design from those of the foregoing period, were recently discovered in Boghazköy. It may be that the beautiful seals from Alaca mentioned above, which are stylistically related to the early Hittite seals, belong to a somewhat later period, to the beginning of the Old Kingdom.

The glyptic of the Hittite Old Kingdom consists of hieroglyphic seals with or without pictorial reliefs. The oldest hieroglyphic seal was found in Tarsus, outside the Hittite sphere. This is the seal of the Great King Isputahsu, the son of Parijawatri. Isputahsu was king of Kizzuwatna; he had concluded a treaty with the Hittite king Telepinu who ruled in the second half of the sixteenth century BC. Naturally similar stamp seals were custom-ary in the Hittite country. Recently a seal of the pommel-cone type with a hieroglyphic inscription in the centre field has been discovered in the levels of the Old Kingdom at Boghazköy. It may belong to the beginning of the Old Hittite period.

45, above

The seal with a flat cylindrical surface and a cone-shaped pommel handle and with centre fields encircled by plaited or spiral bands can be assigned to the period before the Empire, as also several other outstanding pieces with figured designs.

During the past two years German digs in Hattusas under Kurt Bittel have brought to light levels of the Old Kingdom in two places on the towering fortress of Büyükkale and on the north side of the lower town. Architecture continues in the style of the pre-ceding period but an advance in technique and design is unmistakable. One of its characteristics is the use of large blocks of stone. Public buildings continue to have stone foundations and walls of unbaked brick, but the walls are stronger, with clearly balanced façades. Private houses too are carefully built and indicate a high standard of civilized living. A partly excavated house of the lower city contained a room with a clay hip-bath.

On the acropolis, the seat of the Old Hittite kings, several palaces like those of the last phase of the small states must have arisen. The layout of fortifications over eight metres deep with a box-wall system, follows its precursors in Alishar and Karahüyük near Konya.

The latest excavations proved that tunnels under the ramparts used for defensive sorties during the Empire were known in the Old Hittite period. On the south-west side of the royal palace a postern gate thirty-four metres long has been laid bare, with a corbel vault which is similar to those of subterranean gates of later days.

IV

THE PERIOD OF THE EMPIRE

ABOUT 1450–1200 BC

HISTORY AND CULTURE

After the Hurrite Kingdom of the Mitanni had lost some of its power, the reascendance of the Hittites began. The great Syrian campaigns of Thutmosis III fall approximately within this period. About 1450 Tudhaliya mounted the throne at Hattusas. He was a monarch of unknown descent and the founder of a dynasty which ruled the Hittite Kingdom for over 250 years. We can see that already at this time the Hittites were interested in North Syria. By then they were sufficiently strong in their own country to follow the old political tradition and advance on the south-east. The next kings, Arnuwanda I, Hattusili II, and Tudhaliya III, persevered in the attempt to establish Hittite supremacy in North Syria. However, the kingdom of Mitanni was as yet far stronger than the Hittite State. Towards the end of the reign of Tudhaliya III (1400–1380 BC) the enemy invaded the country on all sides. The Kassites conquered the northern provinces and were even able to set fire to Hattusas.

His son Suppiluliuma I (1380–1346 BC), who was an impressive sovereign, quickly mastered the situation. Within a short time he seems to have restored order in Anatolia. Soon after we find him establishing vassal states on the south-eastern border. He then defeated the king of Mitanni, Tusratta, after an initial setback, and conquered his country. He did not, however, cause the total downfall of the Mitanni kingdom but placed the son of Tusratta, Hattiwaza, on the throne and turned the large kingdom of Mitanni into a buffer state, intending to avert the danger threatening from Assur. The chiefs of the border states were won over to the interests of the empire by means of marriage to Hittite princesses. Thus he made the king of Arzawa in the south-east his son-in-law. The small states of Carchemish and Halpa (Aleppo) which he had conquered he handed over to his sons Pijasili and Telepinu. The remaining border states, Hajasha in the north-east, Kizzuwatna in the south, and Amurru in Syria, were attached to the Hittite Empire by means of clever treaties. In this way the border states ruled by small kings, dependent on the Hittite State, came into existence and served as buffer states against Assur, Babylon

I. Seal impressions of kings of the Great Empire
Above, left: Suppiluliuma I and Queen Tawananna. *Centre:* Mursili II. *Right:* Hattusili III and
Queen Puduhepa
Below, left: Hattusili III and Queen Puduhepa. *Centre:* Urhi-Teshup (Mursili III).
Right: Tudhaliya IV and his tutelary deity (right) and female divinity (left)

and Egypt. This southern frontier created by Suppiluliuma remained the outermost demarcation line of Hittite expansion in the south. To later Hittite kings fell the task of holding and defending this frontier. At this time the north of the peninsula was held by Troy (settlement VI) and the south-western peninsula probably by Ahhiyawa. Suppiluliuma's only causes for anxiety were the Gasga in the north with whom he fought a war lasting twenty years. During the reign of Suppiluliuma we find that Ahhiyawa is already mentioned in the texts. Relations seem to have been friendly. As yet the West constituted no danger.

During his long reign Suppiluliuma, the greatest strategist and most important statesman of the Hittite dynasties, created a great power on a par with Egypt and Babylon. The prestige of the Hittite king was so great that the widow of the Pharaoh Tutankhamon, who had died young, begged him to give her one of his sons for a husband. The royal widow of the otherwise highly exclusive Egyptian Court wrote to Hattusas: 'My husband has died. I have no son. They say that you have many sons. If you would send me one of your sons, he could become my husband.' The Hittite Great King was somewhat taken aback by this unusual proposal. He hesitated. The disappointed and slightly offended queen wrote again: 'Why do you say: "they want to deceive me"? If I had a son, would I write to a stranger and let him know my need? You distrust me. My husband is dead, and I have no son. Shall I marry one of my subjects? I have written to no one but you. Everybody says that you have many sons. Give me one, he should be my husband and rule over Egypt.' At last Suppiluliuma was forced to comply with her demand. But the Hittite prince never reached his goal. What Suppiluliuma had feared came to pass. In the meantime an Egyptian had mounted the throne. He informed the Hittite Great King of the death of his son. Suppiluliuma was appalled. He wrote: 'You have murdered my son.' He asked his son and co-regent Arnuwanda to avenge him. King Mursili II recounts that his father attacked and punished Egypt. He is probably talking of a campaign against Egyptian vassal states in Syria.

45, *Fig. 1*   Several royal seal impressions of Suppililiuma on lumps of clay are preserved. A handsome seal impression comes from the French excavations of Ras Shamra. The seal also bears the name of the reigning queen, Tawananna.

In the cuneiform legend on the seal we read: 'Seal of Suppiluliuma, the Great King, the king of Hatti, beloved of the Weather-God. Seal of Tawananna, the Great Queen, daughter of the king of Babylon.' In the centre ring is an *aedicula* containing the names of the king and queen in hieroglyphs. The cone-shaped sign to the right signifies 'King', the volute placed above it, 'Great', together, 'Great King'. The woman's head to the left signifies 'Queen', the volute above, 'Great', together, 'Great Queen'. The winged sun above is the symbol of royalty. The four signs to the left correspond to the term Tawananna and the upper of the three hieroglyphs to the right, (although they have not yet been read ideographically), together with the third syllable 'ma' have been interpreted as

62   Suppiluliuma. The boustrophedon inscription from Nisantas begins on the top right with the cartouche of Suppiluliuma. The same hieroglyphs can just be discerned in the original as identical with the two seal impressions of Suppiluliuma from Boghazköy. The signs to the right and left, of a dagger and blossom, are titles of the Hittite Great King, like the cone and volute discussed above.

Suppiluliuma died of a plague spread in Hattusas by prisoners of war from Palestine. His eldest son and co-regent Arnuwanda (1345 BC) mounted the throne; but a few months later he succumbed to the same malady. He was followed by his brother, Mursili II (1345–1315 BC), who is considered one of the greatest monarchs of the Hittite Kingdom. To begin with he had to retain and consolidate the conquests of his father. He installed his brother, and after the latter's death his son, as kings of Carchemish and his nephew Rimisharma in Halpa (Aleppo). He also attached the remaining border states to the realm.

XIV Vessel in relief with polychrome slip. Fragment. Height of the fragment 36·5 cm. (15⅜ in.). From Bitik near Ankara. *c.* 1400 BC—Ankara

During his conflicts with the renegade kingdom of Arzawa the question of Ahhiyawa arose. The fallen prince of Arzawa was seeking asylum with the king of Ahhiyawa. But the latter gave up the fugitive. From now on the Hittite kings begin to have dealings with the West.

The politically successful king Mursili II had an unhappy private life. The plague which had killed his father, whom he revered deeply, and his elder brother continued to devastate the country. Within the royal family his mother-in-law made his life very difficult. His wife allegedly died from a curse prepared by his mother-in-law. In addition to all this he suffered from a nervous impediment in his speech due to being struck by lightning, which tormented him even in his dreams. He himself writes about it: 'A thunderstorm broke. The Weather-God shook his fearful bolt, and I was terrified. Words failed me, and the words came haltingly. As the years came and passed away, this condition began to play a part in my dreams. Then the hand of god struck me in my dreams, and I lost the power of speech. I consulted the oracle. . . .' According to the Hittite faith this misfortune was due solely to the wrath of god. The text goes on to say that the Weather-God demands burnt offerings, which were made at once, with due observance of all the rules.

Mursili believed that the impediment in his speech and the awful disease in the country were the result of a sin committed by his father; we learn this from a prayer for the cessation of the plague, the melancholy, woeful address of a passionately moved, sensitive man:

> 'Ye gods, my Lords, because you would avenge the blood of Tudhaliya, know that those who killed Tudhaliya have atoned for the crime. And this crime has ruined the land of Hatti once again; the land of Hatti has atoned for it. Because this crime has now come upon my head, I and my family will atone and make amends. And may ye gods, my Lords, soon be appeased. Be once more kindly disposed to me, ye gods, my Lords. And I will appear before you. And because I pray to you, hear me. For I have done no evil. Because among those who were at fault and did evil none survive; they are long since dead. But all the same my father's deeds have come upon my head, behold on account of the plague upon the land I will make a propitiatory sacrifice to you ye gods, my Lords. And because I appear before you as your priest and servant, be (kindly disposed) towards me. Drive out the pain from my heart, and from my soul lift fear.'

Fig. 1 The beautiful steatite seal of Mursili was brought to light during French excavations of Ras Shamra (Ugarit). This is the only actual seal of a Hittite king that we possess. So far only seal impressions on lumps of clay have been found in the Hittite sites. It is therefore interesting to learn how a Hittite king's seal came to be in Ugarit. Claude Schaeffer believes, and is probably right, that an ambassador sent by the king carried this seal with him, to use in the king's stead. It may have been lost in Ugarit. The cuneiform legend of the large seal with a circumference of five centimetres runs thus: 'Seal of Mursili, the Great King, king of the Hatti-Country, the hero'. The inner circle surrounds an *aedicula* which consists of two contrasting signs signifying Great King. In the centre of the *aedicula* are three signs: hieroglyphs of the king's name. Below are a small vertical line and a knife topped by an elongated triangle. The knife corresponds to the sound 'li', and the whole group of signs signifies 'Mursili'.

The Hittite advance in the south came at a time when Egypt under the reign of Amenophis III and Amenophis IV (Akhnaton) was inactive in its foreign policy. Under Haremhab (1345–1318 BC) the Egyptians became once more interested in the small states south of Palestine and in Syria. By the time Muwatalli (1315–1282 BC) ascended the throne after his father's death, the Egyptian danger made itself felt once more. Seti (1317–1311 BC) had advanced as far as Kadesh, where he was able to erect a stele commemorating his victory. Muwatalli's brother, Hattusili III, relates that Muwatalli had removed the seat of government, together with the images of the gods, from Hattusas to the city of Dattassha. At this close range he could keep the rebellious border states more easily in check. The site of the town is unknown but it can hardly have been far from the Syrian battlefield. The rock relief of Muwatalli in Sirkeli, north of Adana on the River Ceyhan, *XX, 98* the ancient Pyramos, is perhaps an indication that his headquarters were in the vicinity.

The inevitable clash between the Hittite Empire and Egypt took place in the fifth year of the reign of Rameses II, in 1286–1285 BC. The king of Egypt started from the Nile valley with three large army divisions and marched north. Muwatalli, who had also amassed a large army and had at command over 3,500 horse-drawn war chariots, planned to annihilate the enemy in a surprise attack. By means of spies who pretended to be messengers from their own ranks, he let it be known to the Pharaoh that the Hittite king was encamped in the vicinity of Halpa (Aleppo) and did not dare to advance towards the south. In reality he took up his position close to the city of Kadesh on the Orontes, southwest of Homs. He hid his divisions behind the various hills by the Orontes. When Rameses approached Kadesh and learnt of the Hittite ruler's ruse from two prisoners, he was with the Amon-division at the head of his troops. The two remaining divisions followed at wide intervals. The Pharaoh ordered the vizier to bring up troops from the south with all possible speed. But Muwatalli attacked at once. He dispersed the central division which was about to arrive. He and his charioteers advanced like lightning and attacked the leading division commanded by the king, which had marched past in the direction of the north, and had already pitched camp. The Egyptians record: 'They attacked the Re-division in the centre as it marched past, suspecting nothing and not prepared for battle. The army and the charioteers of His Majesty were subdued by them.'

The crew of the Hittite battle chariots consisted, as the Egyptian texts point out, of three men to each chariot, one driver and two warriors. Hittite chariots are generally depicted thus on Egyptian reliefs. This tactic gave the Hittites a superiority over the Egyptians who manned their chariots with two men only, one driver and one warrior. Senseless confusion arose in the Egyptian ranks. The plan of the Hittite king had succeeded so far; the two divisions were actually routed. But then something untoward happened. A well-trained unit, perhaps a cadet corps, arriving from the sea, intervened in the battle and saved the Egyptian army from total destruction. The stages of the battle are represented in great detail in the writing and hieroglyphs on the temple walls of Egypt, in the Rameseum, at Karnak, Luxor, Abydos and Abu Simbel where the Egyptians figure as the victors. The fact that after the battle of Kadesh the disloyal state of Amurru returned to the Hittite fold, and also that in Syria no more was heard of the Egyptians for a time, indicates clearly enough who was the real victor.

In Anatolia Muwatalli had to ward off violent attacks from the Gasga. From a treaty concluded by him with Alaxandus we learn that he led a campaign against the provinces of Arzawa.

King Muwatalli, the successful strategist, has left no record of his deeds. In the annals of his brother Hattusili we find him as a mild and lenient man. He seems to have countered the cunning schemes of his evil brother with kindness and good nature.

XX, 98   The oldest monumental image of a Hittite king which has come down to us is of him. It is not a portrait. He is merely shown in the pictograph of a Hittite Great King. On stamp seals he appears again as the same pictograph. Only the Egyptian sculptor who represents him in his war chariot seems to have attempted an individual likeness. Unfortunately his features are much damaged on the Egyptian relief but the ample figure suits the mild character of the ruler.

45   Several impressions of royal seals are preserved on lumps of clay. We print a reproduction of the best among them. On the outer circle of the stamp seal we can read in cuneiform script '. . . Great King, son of Mursili, the Great King, the hero'. As the sequence of kings of the Hittite Kingdom is well known from inscriptions, the missing name here can only be Muwatalli. The inner circle, also in cuneiform script, runs thus: 'Sun-God, Teshup-hellipi, Sarruma and protective deity.' These are the names of Muwatalli's favourite gods. The hieroglyphs above the left hand of the god give only one divine name: above a volute, in the centre the sign of the Weather-God, and underneath a crescent moon in which Sedat Alp has recognized the sky. The complete hieroglyph means 'Great Weather-God of the Heaven'. Beneath the left arm of the divine image the cartouche of the king is discernible. It consists of two Great King signs topped by a winged sun. In the centre of the *aedicula* is the sign for 'Great King' with the Weather-God sign and a W above it. This does not signify a name but is an indication that royalty was somehow related to the Weather-God. The signs on the left of the image correspond to the four syllables 'mu-wa-ta-li'. Admittedly so far only the sign for knife, the last syllable 'li', can be interpreted with any certainty. The above mentioned rock relief of Sirkeli contains the same signs as this seal.

Since the Egyptian danger was over, Urhi-Teshup, who adopted the name of Mursili after his accession (1282–1275 BC), was able to transfer the seat of government back to Hattusas. He did not pursue a very active foreign policy. His greatest anxiety was

XV Hattusas. View from Büyükkale towards the 'Narrow Defile', the rocks of Büyükkaya and the country to the north-west

Hattusili. The latter, who had not dared seize power at his brother Muwatalli's death, rebelled against his nephew Mursili III and usurped the throne. Urhi-Teshup was banished.

The only source of information concerning the reign of Mursili III comes from inscriptions of Hattusili in which he speaks of his brother as Urhi-Teshup, but makes no mention of his royal name of Mursili. That Urhi-Teshup adopted the name of Mursili after he mounted the throne we glean from the study of his seal impressions. An impression of one *45* of his seals is preserved on a handsome lump of clay. In its centre is the *aedicula* with the king's name in hieroglyphs: a triangle with diagonal lines above a small vertical line and a knife. This is the hieroglyphic spelling of Mursili which we have met with above. In the cuneiform legend we read as follows:

'Seal of the Sun . . ., of the Great King, the king of Hatti, the hero, grandson of Mursili, king of Hatti, the hero, great-grandson of Suppiluliuma, king of Hatti, the hero.' We can fill in the name of the owner of this seal from picture writing and the unequivocal genealogy of Mursili III. H. G. Güterbock has been able to establish from the seal of Mursili II of Ras Shamra that the Prince known on cuneiform tablets as Urhi-Teshup adopted the name of Mursili after his accession to the throne. Another seal impression (found in 1953 in Boghazköy) on which the king's name happens to be missing, but with Mursili written on the margin, furnishes conclusive proof of the identity of Urhi-Teshup with Mursili III *Fig. 1* which was originally pointed out by Güterbock. We reproduce the design restored by H. Otten. Without the discoveries at Ras Shamra (Ugarit) and Boghazköy we might never have learnt the royal name of Urhi-Teshup. These small finds throw a vivid light on an obscure affair which was the work of the evil Hattusili III. Urhi-Teshup was not the son of a queen but of an Esertu-woman, the first lady of the royal harem. He ascended lawfully to the throne because his father had no son by his first marriage. This means that the law of succession passed by Telepinu was still in force. But Hattusili seems to have spoken of this succession in such a derogatory way that Urhi-Teshup discarded his Hurrite name and, in order to stress his rightful descent, adopted that of his grandfather. It is significant that on his seal he traces his genealogy to his great-grandfather Suppiluliuma, while the other sovereigns confined themselves to listing their fathers and grandfathers. If Hattusili calls him Urhi-Teshup in his own inscription he does so with the intention of belittling him. The hostile uncle who deprived his nephew of the throne begrudged him his royal name too.

Hattusili III (1275–1250 BC), who had coveted his brother's throne during the latter's reign, became an important king of the Hittite dynasty. While still a prince he governed the North Country and was under-king of Hapkis, whence he ruled over Nerik, the most important religious centre of the Hittite Empire. He earned fame through his successful campaigns against the Gasga. At the time of the war in Kadesh he pursued his intrigues with the Amurru Prince Bentesina whom he reinstated on the throne of Amurru after his own accession.

68

XVI Hattusas. The Lion Gate on the south-west side, seen from without

As Great King he pursued an intelligent foreign policy. His negotiations with Babylon created a common bloc of power against Assur. But Hattusili acquired his greatest merit by concluding a treaty with Egypt in 1269 BC which ensured a lasting peace between the two states.

This treaty was equivalent to an official recognition by Egypt of the Hittite victory of Muwatalli at Kadesh. We possess two texts; one is an Akkadian translation of the Egyptian version found in Boghazköy (Hattusas). The other gives the Egyptian translation of the Hittite version written on a silver tablet. It is engraved on the temple walls of the Rameseum and Karnak. This treaty is a non-aggression pact in which both partners pledge themselves to support each other in war and to exchange prisoners. This is the oldest treaty in history signed between two great powers.

The beginning of the treaty consists of titles, preambles and the mention of previous friendly relations. These are followed by a definition of the points contained in the treaty. In the Egyptian translation of the Hittite version the preamble runs as follows:

'The treaty engraved on a silver tablet by Hattusili, the great prince of Hatti, the powerful, grandson of Suppiluliuma, the great Prince of Hatti, the powerful, for Rameses II, the great ruler of Egypt, the powerful, the son of Seti I, the great ruler of Egypt, the powerful, the sound treaty of peace and brotherhood which establishes peace between them for all eternity.'

Hattusili continued to maintain friendly relations with Egypt. He gave one of his daughters to Rameses as his chief wife. She adopted the Egyptian name of Maatnefrure. Egyptian sources describe the arrival of the Hattian princess: 'Her face was fair as that of a goddess'. She brought countless gifts for His Majesty. The Egyptian Pharaoh sent an army and a body of nobles to meet the Hittite princess at the frontier. 'His Majesty was full of joy. The Master of the Palace was glad when he heard of this extraordinary event. It was a great and wonderful, hitherto unheard of marvel.' No greater joy and honour could befall a ruler of the south than to have a princess from the north, perhaps a fair-haired beauty, for a wife. With this *mariage de convenance* Hattusili ensured the hegemony of the Hittite Empire in the Near East.

In his above-mentioned inscription, the oldest autobiographic document in world literature, Hattusili speaks with great pride: 'The rulers who were in agreement with the Hittite country before my accession are in agreement with me now. They show themselves willing to send me their ambassadors, they show themselves willing to send me gifts. The gifts they send me they had not sent to my fathers or forefathers. The kings who had to swear allegiance to me swore allegiance. Whoever was my enemy I have conquered.' He was strong enough to refuse brotherhood to the Assyrian king: 'Are we born of the same woman?' he asks. The golden age of the Hittite Empire continues.

Fig. 1 The excavations at Boghazköy and Ras Shamra have brought to light several royal seal impressions of Hattusili III. We reproduce two examples from Ras Shamra. In both

70

cases we are concerned with different seals on clay tablets of Hattusili III and his wife Puduhepa. The first clay tablet, whose seal impression comes from a carelessly engraved model, mentions an agreement between Hattusili, the Hittite Great King, and king Niqmepa of Ugarit concerning the merchants of the town of Ura. The second clay tablet, with a seal impression taken from a finely engraved model, talks of an obligation of Hattusili to return deserters from the domain of Habiru. The cuneiform legend of the first seal runs: 'Seal of Tabarna Hattusili, the Great King, the hero'. The queen's name appears only in picture writing on the left side of the *aedicula*. This is the same as on the seal of Suppiluliuma: the sign for 'Great Queen' on one side and on the other the sign for 'Great King'. The hieroglyphs of Hattusili consist of a combined sign, the trident with the knife. We have met the knife earlier in the name of Mursili. The same combined sign *62* appears in the above-mentioned genealogy of Nisantas as the name of Hattusili II, the grandfather of Suppiluliuma. It also occurs on a monument of Fraktin, together with the *101* signs of the queen. That Hattusili consists of four syllables but is expressed by two hieroglyphic signs suggests the idea that this spelling was an abbreviation; 'ha-li'. The hieroglyphic signs of the queen read from the top downward have been interpreted from cuneiform legends as Puduhepa. We shall find the second sign in Tudhaliya, the last two *Fig. 19* signs in the name of the goddess Hepat at Yazilikaya. The queen owned other seals that contained her name only. We have already seen the name Puduhepa in cuneiform and *45* hieroglyphs on the seal impressions from Tarsus.

Important documents were signed jointly by the king and queen, as the Egyptians state at the end of their translation. The silver tablet engraved with a Hittite version of the treaty between Hattusili and Rameses II contained on one side the seal of Hattusili, on the other that of Puduhepa. The description of the seal on the silver tablet given by the Egyptians corresponds closely to that of Hittite royal seals. On the seal of the silver tablet Hattusili is seen in the embrace of a god. It is true that the Egyptians speak of Seth, but in *45, Fig. 1* reality he is the Weather-God, as on the seals of Muwatalli and Tudhaliya. The Egyptians record that Puduhepa too is embraced by a deity. They do not give it an Egyptian name but call it a goddess from Hatti, and give a verbal translation of the cuneiform legend on the margin of the seal. It says: 'Daughter of the land of Kizzuwatna, priestess of Arinna.'

It corresponds to Hittite custom that Tawananna too, the reigning queen, is found in the embrace of a deity. But to date no such pictorial representation has been discovered.

Of his marriage to Puduhepa Hattusili writes in his autobiography: 'On the command of the deity I took the daughter of Pentipsarri, the priest of Ishtar of Lawazantiya, as a wedded wife. And we had sons and children.'

Puduhepa seems to have been the outstanding woman of the Hittite ruling dynasty. We shall see further on that Tudhaliya IV mentions his mother Puduhepa in his genealogy. On a relief at Fraktin she performs a sacrifice at an altar before a seated goddess. It is *100, 101* perhaps not accidental that Hattusili, who officiates beside her, occupies a much smaller space than the queen. Tawananna cannot have had as much influence as Puduhepa, the priestess of the indigenous Hattian goddess Arinna. Hattusili III appears on the walls of the temple in Abu Simbel where he is depicted with his daughter. It is significant that, in contrast to several Hittite portraits on Egyptian reliefs, he is represented with a regular and handsome profile.

The reign of Tudhaliya (1250–1220 BC), the son of Hattusili III, still belongs to the golden age of the Great Hittite Empire. The Hittites continued to maintain their gains; they had not yet lost an inch in Syria. The Amurru country, now as ever, remained a vassal state of the Great Empire and formed a barrier between the Egyptian and Hittite zones of influence. It is true that a great danger arose for Tudhaliya in the person of the Assyrian king Tikulti-Ninurta I (1243–1207 BC), but the Great King mastered the situation and was able to forbid the king of Amurru to trade with Assyria. 'No merchant from your country shall go to Assyria, you must not allow a merchant of that country to enter your country, and he shall not pass through your country.'

As transpires from a newly discovered seal from Boghazköy, Tudhaliya was the first Hittite king to be addressed as 'King of the Whole'. This Assyrian title was revived in Assyria with Adad Nirari I (1297–1265 BC). In asserting his claim to supremacy in the Near East Tudhaliya IV seems to have deemed it necessary to use the same title as the Assyrian kings.

XXII, 102 Tudhaliya IV also secured the borders of the realm in the west. Hittite texts record the annihilation of the Assuwa country by Tudhaliya. A rock relief in Kemal Pasha (Karabel) near Izmir, which seems to bear the name of Tudhaliya in hieroglyphs, may be an indication of his victorious advance to the west. This monument showing the king who conquered Assuwa confirms the assumption that Asia, the geographical term used by Greeks for the central part of western Asia Minor, is derived from the term Assuwa.

Tudhaliya seems to have been quick to recognize the danger threatening his country and to take the measures necessary for defence. His military orders, as Sedat Alp has pointed out, show his efforts to keep discipline in the armed forces of the empire. 'If officers or men desert from the army it should be immediately reported to the palace. And if the king himself goes into battle the soldiers shall fight with all their might. And if a task has to be performed it shall be done conscientiously and well for the sake of the future.'

Tudhaliya was a great king. As we shall see at the shrine of Yazilikaya he reformed the religious cult. Sculpture reached its highest point during his reign. Of no other regent do *XIX 78, 85* we possess so many handsome portraits as of Tudhaliya IV. At the shrine of Yazilikaya he is depicted twice. Probably a statue of Tudhaliya which no longer exists stood in the side chamber of the same shrine, beside his cartouche on the wall. Numerous handsome seal impressions survive with his name. On one seal from Ras Shamra he wears a

XVII Hattusas. The right-hand lion of the Lion Gate

Fig. 1 sacred cap and stands in the embrace of a tutelary God, Sarruma. The *aedicula* shows the same pattern as that of Suppiluliuma. It consists of symmetrical 'Great King' signs and contrasting hieroglyphs, the dagger and blossom, that form part of the titles of Hittite Great Kings. Of the signs in the centre the upper one has been read as Mount Tudhaliya. The names Tudhaliya, Arnuwanda, and Ammuna, were originally those of sacred mountains revered by the population. We have met with the lower sign in the hieroglyphic spelling of Puduhepa as the syllable 'tu'. The identification of the two hieroglyphs with Tudhaliya happened originally because of the genealogy of Suppiluliuma in the re-

62 peatedly mentioned Nisantas inscription. Later Güterbock established that a Mountain-

78 God Tudhaliya existed. On two cartouches of Yazilikaya and several seal-impressions we do in fact find sacred heights accompanied by the syllable 'tu'. Since other mountain divinities existed, the sculptor has added the sign 'tu' beneath the mountain to let the beholder know that in this instance he meant to represent the Mountain-God Tudhaliya. The most beautiful cartouche of Tudhaliya is in the monumental picture writing of Karakuyu where the composition of the seal of Ras Shamra is repeated. There too Tudhaliya names his father Hattusili III. The central hieroglyphic inscription in the *aedicula* of the

Fig. 1 seal from Ras Shamra is a human body without head, interpreted as the god Sarruma. At the bottom of the seal the cartouche of the king recurs, this time with an additional sign which is symmetrically repeated. Laroche has read the entire hieroglyph as 'the Life of Tudhaliya'.

Under the next Great King, Tudhaliya's son Arnuwanda III (1220–1190 BC), political events in Western Asia Minor developed rapidly to the detriment of the Hittites. From the indictment against the rebellious Madduwatta of Zippasla we learn of the difficult position of the Hittite Great King. Zippasla must have been somewhere in the centre of Western Asia Minor. Madduwatta of Zippasla, originally an insignificant vassal of the Hittite Empire, succeeded in extending his sphere of influence bit by bit, and finally in conquering the southern part of the peninsula. Arnuwanda says: 'And Madduwatta broke his oath to the father of the Sun and seized the entire land of Arzawa.' By now Madduwatta was strong enough to attack Alasia, the island of Cyprus. From the same indictment it transpires clearly that other vassals too rebelled against the Hittite Empire, and that in the west a coalition had formed against the Great King.

Conditions in the east and south-east were favourable. After the murder of Tikulti-Ninurta Assur constituted no danger for a time. The imminent downfall of the Hittite Empire was therefore caused by warlike actions initiated in the west.

The next texts of Boghazköy, published by Kemal Balkan in 1948, proved that a Suppiluliuma II ruled as Great King in Hatti. The French scholar Laroche showed subsequently that a number of texts formerly assigned to Suppiluliuma I belonged in reality to Suppiluliuma II, who was a brother of Arnuwanda III. The reign of the last king of the Hittite dynasty cannot have been of long duration. Egyptian and Assyrian sources give a

clear picture of the time and of events which caused the downfall of the Hittite Empire. On the inscriptions at the temple of Medinet Habu, Rameses III states that the people from the north destroyed Carchemish, Arzawa and Alasia (Cyprus). The said events took place in the eighth year of Rameses III. This is the year 1190 BC. The Assyrian king Tiglath-pileser I (1122–1074 BC) records that he was forced to fight against 20,000 Mukshi led by five kings who had appeared, fifty years before the beginning of his reign, on the Upper Tigris, the northern frontier of Assyria. The Mukshi were the precursors of the Phrygians. They may have formed at least part of the peoples from the north mentioned by the Egyptians. The date 1160 BC, derived from the record of the Egyptian king, may be too early; the fifty years he mentions are probably to be understood as an approximate figure. For Hittite sources from the end of the Hittite Empire tell of a king Mita of Pakhuwa. O. R. Gurney, who was the last to work on these texts, points out that the Mukshi were settled in Asia Minor at a time when the Hittite Empire had not yet been overrun. If king Mita of the Hittite texts, who lived 400 years earlier, is in fact the ancestor of the Phrygian king Mita mentioned by king Sargon (721–205 BC), the peoples of the north, who destroyed Arzawa, Alasia and Carchemish, must have started their first migrations in Asia Minor at a period when the heart of the Hittite Empire was still intact. One may visualize the drama which unfolded at that time in the Anatolian zone as follows: After the destruction by the Achaeans of the mighty citadel of Troy about 1240 BC the door was opened to the small Thracian tribes avid for land in Asia Minor. At first they settled in north-western Asia Minor and later set out from there to occupy new sites in the peninsula. During these attempts they advanced as far as Syria and Assyria, without apparently stopping to deal with the Hittite Empire which was in its last stages of resistance. They settled in eastern and south-eastern Anatolia, where their presence is recorded by the Hittites and the Assyrians. After having encircled the Hittites they annihilated the Empire. The date of this event may be fixed approximately as 1180 BC. Since, according to Egyptian sources, the above-mentioned destruction of Arzawa, Carchemish and Alasia took place about 1190 BC, a somewhat later date for the fall of Hattusas is easily justified.

RELIGION

The federal system which was the Hittite form of government is undoubtedly the reason why the Hittites did not achieve a unified conception of their gods. The nature of their religious attitude is a phenomenon which has no parallel in history. In this lies the special character of Hittite religion. Tolerance in religious matters and the marked realism of the Hittites determined the religious life of the Empire. 'No fusion of cults and sacred myths but a spiritual federation' is the excellent definition of Anton Moortgat. The Hittites speak of the 'thousand Gods' of their realm. Considering the long list of deities in their writings this is no exaggeration. At the time of the Empire the Hittites practised an extreme form of polytheism like that of Anatolia under the Roman Empire. Actually their gods are merely local variants of a few main deities. Also, the various divine families, the Hattian, Luvian, Palaic, and the Hurrian and Mesopotamian gods were similar and parallel types which merely bore different names but performed identical functions. Thus the Weather-God and goddesses like Hepat and Ishtar existed under many local names which in ultimate analysis could be traced to one Weather-God and one Great Goddess. This the Hittites knew; occasionally 'all Weather-Gods', 'all Hepats', 'all Ishtars' are merged. This tolerant attitude enabled the Hittite ruling caste to safeguard their hold over the small tribes. Theirs was neither a syncretistic nor an eclectic religious policy but a conscious, politically conditioned religious tolerance. Personal preferences mingled with political considerations. In his capacity as king Hattusili III was the priest of Ishtar (Saushga) of Samuha, a Hurrian rather than a Semitic goddess. His wife Puduhepa, whose name implies that she was a devotee of Hepat, was the daughter of a priest from Lawazantiya in the Hurrite Kizzuwatna country. She caused clay tablets from Kizzuwatna to be copied for the Hisuwa festivals. Consequently Tudhaliya IV was introduced early to the Hurrian religion in his parents' house. Later he reorganized the state cult according to the Hurrian rite. The sanctuary of Yazilikaya near Boghazköy (Hattusas) where all the gods bear Hurrian names in hieroglyphic script, testifies to this innovation.

    If one analyses the at first confusing spectacle of the Hittite gods, one can see that the thousand gods of the Hittite pantheon are basically the local subsidiary types of a few important deities. We shall now consider the religion of the Hittites as it was after the reformation of Tudhaliya IV.

THE WEATHER-GOD

The chief divinity of the Hittites is the Weather-God. In conjunction with the principal female deity he is the greatest binding factor in the federal Hittite Kingdom. He is the common god of the autochthonous section of the people and the newly arrived Indo-Europeans of Asia Minor. In the texts he is invariably represented by the ideogram of the Meopotamian Adad. His Hittite name is as yet unknown. We know merely that it ends with 'una'.

    In the Hurrian idiom the Weather-God is Teshup, in Luvian he is Data. The hieroglyphic ideogram reads Tarhund. He corresponds to the Greek Zeus. In Hittite texts he is generally 'the Weather-God of Hatti', 'Weather-God of the Heaven'. There are dozens of Weather-Gods distinguished by their special functions: 'the Weather-God of Hattusas', 'the Weather-God of the Palace', 'the Weather-God of the Army', 'the Weather-God of the Rains'. Besides the usual divine ideogram he is characterized in picture writing by the sign of lightning which means Weather-God. If the Weather-God has a special name a third hieroglyph is added. Thus the main Weather-God of Yazilikaya bears a divine sign and the sign for lightning (No. 42), while at the same shrine a special abridged hiero-glyph of his name is added to that of the Weather-God of Hattusas (No. 41).

In the art and writings of the Empire the Weather-God stands on a mountain peak. From Hittite texts we know that mountains were objects of worship. The mountains of Hazzi (later Mons Cassius on the Syrian coast, close to the mouth of the Orontes) and Nanni (whose whereabouts are unknown) are sacred heights connected with the Weather-God. Holy mountains like Tudhaliya, Arnuwanda and Ammuna may be mentioned in this connection. In one Hittite text describing a figurative representation, the Weather-God of the Heaven strides across two mountains represented as men. A figurative render-ing of this conception has come down to us in the principal divinity of Yazilikaya. If one *76, Fig. 19* observes the tunics of the Mountain-Gods, one will see that they are adorned with cone-shaped ornaments. Identical decorations can be seen mainly on the Mountain-God Tudhaliya (in the cartouche of king Tudhaliya). They may stand for isolated peaks. *78* One of the Weather-Gods of Yazilikaya stands upon two such cones stylized to represent *XIX, Fig. 19* mountains.

The proper attribute of the Weather-God is the bull. The religious conception which venerated gods in the form of animals was still alive in the Empire. We have seen that these zoomorphic notions of gods were characteristic of the Hattian people during the Early Bronze Age. The animals originally revered in the Hittite Kingdom had become the *I, II, 1–6* constant companions of deities that were now depicted in human form. Hittite gods generally stand on the back of their sacred animals. The likeness of a god mounted on a bull is probably a creation of the North Mesopotamian-Anatolian cultural sphere. Edith Porada has observed that the figure of a god on the back of a bull in the Old Babylonian style appears late. This may be attributed to contact with Anatolia. Deified animals stand- *III, IV, 10,* ing between bulls' horns and worshipped as divinities of the Hattian Anatolian period may *11* be regarded as a first phase of the idea of the god mounted on a bull. Examples from Kültepe are contemporaneous with those in the Old Babylonian style. It is significant that the motif of a god mounted on a bull survived in this region throughout the age of the Mitanni kingdom, and during the Empire can be traced at Carchemish in South-east Anatolia. During French excavations at Ras Shamra a cylinder seal of king Ini-Teshup of Carchemish was found on which the Weather-God is mounted on a bull or ox, as on the seals of Kültepe.

It has always been noted that the motif of the Weather-God on the bull is totally absent from the art of the Hittite Kingdom. Texts too make no mention of this form of the Weather-God. This may be due to the fact that the Hittites continued to worship the bull as a deity. In the texts he figures as the symbol of the god. In a relief on an orthostat from *92* Alaca showing a bull enacting the part of the Weather-God, we even possess a naturalistic representation of the bull cult.

In Yazilikaya the Hurrian bulls Hurri and Serri appear with the chief god and goddess. *76, Fig. 19* On the rock relief of Imamkulu and the orthostat relief of Malatya the Weather-God *105*

77

mounts a chariot drawn by two bulls. This concept too is, however, absent from the texts known up to date.

THE CHIEF FEMALE DIVINITY

In Anatolia the cult of a female divinity as an expression of the matriarchal system dates from the Stone Age. English excavations carried out during these past years in Hacilar, south-west Anatolia, have brought to light the remains of an ancient Anatolian culture of the fifth millennium BC in which the naked goddess must have played an exceptionally large part. The Sun-Goddess originating in the Hattian period of the third millennium and the Hurrian Hepat are the younger types of the Stone Age Mother of the Gods of the newly discovered prehistoric cultures in Anatolia. Kupaba of the late Hittite period and the greatly honoured Cybele of Graeco-Roman Asia Minor are late forms of the same goddess.

Although in the ritual sacrificial lists Hepat and the Sun-Goddess of Arinna figure as two distinct goddesses, they were, at least in the state cult of Tudhaliya IV, regarded as the same deity. 'Sun-Goddess of Arinna, my Mistress, Queen of all Countries. In the land of the Hittites you bear the name of Sun-Goddess of Arinna, in the far country, that which you made the land of cedars, you assumed the name of Hepat.' This part of the text says clearly enough that in the figure of Hepat represented in the main scene at Yazilikaya we have before us the Sun-Goddess of Arinna. The Hurrian Hepat is the spouse of Teshup. The Sun-Goddess of Arinna has a Hattian Weather-God for spouse whose special name we do not know. Accordingly, in Yazilikaya we see the Sun-Goddess of Arinna as the wife of the Weather-God of the Heaven.

76, Fig. 19

In the shrine of Yazilikaya the chief goddess stands to the left of the Weather-God. When looking at the early lead idols of Kültepe we saw that on images of the divine pair the god compared to the goddess is in figurative representations slightly raised; but in the texts the goddess sometimes takes precedence over her partner, the Weather-God. She is the principal divinity of the state. From the hymn we learn of her characteristics and her great power over the faithful:

35

> Thou, Sun-Goddess of Arinna, art an honoured deity.
> And thy name is honoured among names, thy divinity
> is honoured among the gods; nay, among the gods
> thou alone, O Sun-Goddess of Arinna, art honoured. Great also
> art thou alone, O Sun-Goddess of Arinna; nay, compared with thee no other deity
> is honoured and great. Of sure
> judgement thou art lord,* and kingship in heaven
> and earth thou controllest,
> thou settest the boundaries of the lands;
> and it is thou that hearest the prayer.

* (In the English translation of the tablet the Sun of Arinna is a goddess, but throughout this section her attributes are masculine. She is a divine hermaphrodite. *Translator's note.*)

78

XVIII Hattusas, Büyükkale. South-west view of building E and the north-west wall of the
royal palace

Thou, O Sun-Goddess of Arinna, a merciful god art thou,
and it is thou that takest pity. The uplifted
man is dear to thee, Sun-Goddess of Arinna,
and thou, Sun-Goddess of Arinna, exaltest him.
Within the circuit of heaven and earth thou, Sun-Goddess of Arinna, art the source of warmth.
Among the lands thou art the deity whose cult is most celebrated,
and thou art the father and mother of every land.
The inspired lord of justice thou art untiring.
Among the Ancient Gods thy cult is celebrated, and to the gods the sacrifices thou,
O Sun-Goddess of Arinna, allottest; to the Ancient Gods also
Thou allottest their portions.
To thee in return they open the door of heaven,
and thou, O celebrated Sun-Goddess of Arinna, dost pass through the gate of heaven.

The Hattian name of the Sun-Goddess was Wurusemu. Her Luvian name is not yet known, nor do we know her Hittite name, as it is always written ideogrammatically. *Fig. 19* Apart from the sign for 'god' the main goddess of Yazilikaya has three hieroglyphs which Bossert has deciphered as Hepatu. The two lower signs we have met with in the name of queen Puduhepa. The second sign read from above corresponds to the sound 'ha' or 'he'.

76 In the shrine of Yazilikaya Hepat stands on a panther which appears as her sacred animal, but so far no panther has been known to figure in the texts as the attribute of any god. Lion-shaped *rhytons* are mentioned only in the cult of Zababa and the Ishtar of the fields. Lions, however, appear in Hittite art as the attributes of various deities.

The Sun-Goddess of Arinna entered the Hittite pantheon from Hattian religion together with her sons, the Weather-Gods of Nerik and Zippalanda, her daughter Mezullas, *76, Fig. 19* and her niece Zentuhis. On the other hand we see that in Yazilikaya the family of a Hurrian divine pair is represented. The young god standing on a panther behind the great *84, 85* goddess is the Hurrian god Sarruma, the son of Hepat, and we know him from the texts. The hieroglyph of marching limbs above his right arm was read by Güterbock as 'Sarruma', not only because this figure *is* most probably Sarruma, the son of Hepat, but because the two parallel strokes on either side are to be read as 'ma'. It should be remembered that the four identical strokes occur as the last syllable of the hieroglyph of Suppiluliuma.

The great Babylonian goddess Ishtar was worshipped in Anatolia. Her Hurrite name was Saushga. She is the sister of Teshup and is the goddess of both love and war. As the *79, below centre* Hurrian War-Goddess she appears at the shrine of Yazilikaya, together with her attendants, the Hurrian goddesses Ninatta and Kulitta.

Apart from the Sun-Goddess of Arinna the Hittites worshipped a Sun-God called Sun-God of the Heaven. His Hittite name is Ishtanu, in Hattian Eshtan. The Moon-God, Arma *79, below, left* in Hittite and Kuwu in the Hurrian idiom, was a Hattian divinity called originally Kasku. *116* Both gods appear frequently together, the Sun-God following in the Moon-God's wake.

One text describes the 'Protective deity of the Fields' of Viyanavanta. He is shown as

a male figure holding a bow in his right hand and an eagle and hare in his left, armed *47, 104*
with a sword or dagger, and standing on a stag. Similar divine figures existed in great
numbers both in the time of the Empire and in the late Hittite period.

Images of gods have come down to us in art for which we find no evidence in the texts. *79, above; 87*
Especially the twelve gods represented twice at Yazilikaya, who recur once more under
the Roman Empire, do not exist in the texts known to date.

MYTH

The myths of the Hittite people, like their religion, derive partly from Hattian and partly
from Hurrian sources. The Myth of the vegetation god Telepinu and that of the Weather-
God and the dragon Illujanka are Hattian. The Myth of Telepinu contains magical
elements. In this tale the narrator wants to show that with the help of an effective rite
divine wrath can be appeased. The Illujanka Myth exists in two versions. The older one
recounts how the Weather-God, at first defeated by the dragon Illujanka, kills the
monster with the help of the goddess Inar. The goddess Inar invites Illujanka to a feast:
'So up came the dragon Illujanka with his children and they ate and drank, they emp-
tied every barrel and quenched their thirst. And they could no longer descend to their
caverns. Hupasaya came and bound the dragon with a rope. The Weather-God came and
slew the dragon and the gods were with him.'

The later version has the character of a moral tale:

> The dragon Illujanka vanquished the Weather-God and took his heart and eyes away from
> him. The Weather-God sought to revenge himself upon him. He took the daughter of a poor
> man for his wife and he begat a son. When he grew up, he took the daughter of the dragon
> Illujanka in marriage. The Weather-God instructs his son: 'When thou goest to the house of
> thy wife, ask them for my heart and mine eyes.' When he went there he asked them for the
> heart and they gave that to him. Later he asked for the eyes, and they gave him those too.
> He brought them to the Weather-God, his father. Thus the Weather-God got back his heart and
> his eyes. When the frame had been restored to its old state, he left for the sea for battle. When he
> had engaged the dragon Illujanka in battle, he came close to vanquishing him. But the son of
> the Weather-God, who was with Illujanka, shouted up to heaven to his father: 'Count me as
> with him! Spare me not!' So the Weather-God killed the dragon Illujanka and his son too.

An orthostat relief from Malatya depicts the Illujanka Myth. The presence of a second *104, below*
Weather-God proves that it is based on the more recent version of the myth.

This ancient Anatolian legend survived into classical times. A tale of the battle between
Zeus and Typhon from the *Bibliotheca* of Apollodorus, dating from the Roman period,
states the Illujanka Myth in its essential points. In the Myth of Typhon Zeus loses not only
his heart and eyes in the struggle with the monster, but the sinews of his hands and feet.
In the Illujanka Myth the lost members are restored through the intervention of the

divine son of the Weather-God and his spouse, the dragon's daughter. In the Myth of Typhon it is Hermes who steals the sinews, while Aegipan distracts the attention of the virgin entrusted with guarding the dragon. The geographical names indicate an Anatolian origin of the Typhon legend. Mons Cassius, mentioned there, is situated in Syria. The dwelling of Typhon in the Corycian Caves lies, as the legend says, on the Cilician coast. In Aeschylus and Pindar too the legend of Typhon is laid in Cilicia. From this we conclude that the version of the Typhon legend as found in the *Bibliotheca* of Apollodorus derives from old Anatolian sources.

The representation of the Illujanka Myth, of which we have so far only the above-mentioned Hittite example from Malatya, seems to have served as a model for the Greek representations of Hydra. But we must assume that the Greeks were familiar with other oriental representations of the combat with the dragon Illujanka, some of which we know from Mesopotamia.

The Hittite myths of Hurrian origin are epic works of unusual importance. Especially worthy of mention are the Epics now known as 'The Divine Kingship' and the 'Song of Ulikummi'. They are Hittite translations of Hurrian originals. The first Epic is a theogony which distinguishes three generations of gods: Anu, Kumrabi and Teshup. Anu is the Babylonian Sky-God, and in one of the lists of gods Alalu figures as his father. Kumrabi is the Hurrian name of a deity who resembles the Sumerian Enlil. Kumrabi emasculates Anu by biting off his genitals. He swallows the seed but brings it up again when Anu tells him that by doing so he has conceived three awful deities. 'You are glad that you have swallowed my manhood. Do not rejoice in your heart. Three fearful gods I have placed inside you. You will end by beating your head against the rocks of the mountains. . . .' The earth became pregnant from the seed spat out by Kumrabi. In the following, very fragmentary passage on the clay tablet there is a vivid description of how the earth gave birth to the Weather-God Teshup and two other gods. From parallel texts we finally learn that Teshup became king instead of Kumrabi. It has long been recognized that the *Theogony* of Hesiod is derived from this Hurrian Myth. Hesiod too tells of three generations of gods: Uranos, Kronos and Zeus who ruled the sky in succession. Here too the first god is emasculated by his son. Hesiod recounts that when Uranos embraced his wife Gaia in the dark, Kronos came and severed the phallus of his father with a gigantic sickle, throwing it over his shoulder. From the drops of blood spattering the earth's surface she conceived the giants. But from the phallus long tossed by the waves of the sea arose the foam-born Aphrodite.

The 'Song of Ulikummi' relates how Kumrabi fashioned Ulikummi, a gigantic monster made of diorite, in order to win back supremacy over the sky from his son Teshup. But Teshup vanquished the stone monster after a long combat and regained the kingdom of the sky for all eternity. This epic chant too seems to have influenced Greek mythology. In the *Theogony* of Hesiod we are told that after his victory over Kronos and the Titans

Zeus was attacked once more by the monster Typhon. The sequence of happenings coincides. In both versions the site of the epic is the same, namely Mons Cassius, the Hurrian Mount Hazzi which has repeatedly been mentioned.

FOREIGN COMPONENTS AND ELEMENTS IN HITTITE CULTURE

During our examination of Hittite religion in the second section of this book we saw that Hittite culture rested solidly on the indigenous Hattian tradition. In the same place we pointed out the influence coming from Mesopotamian countries. Under the Empire they were strongly felt in several spheres of life. The most important factor linking the Asia Minor of the Hittites with Mesopotamia was the cuneiform script used in Hattusas from the time of the Old Empire. The study of cuneiform writing presupposed a certain knowledge of the Akkadian language. The Hittite scribes were so deeply influenced by their Mesopotamian prototypes that for the words most frequently occurring in their own language they used the corresponding Akkadian, and sometimes even Sumerian signs. Whoever did not know these Mesopotamian ideograms could of course not understand the Hittite text. The Akkadian language was used for diplomatic correspondence and state treaties. Among the tablets from Boghazköy are fragments of dictionaries in the Sumero-Akkadian-Hittite language. Several hundred texts written entirely in the Sumerian or Akkadian language, or containing large sections in the two languages, have been found on the same site. The legendary text of the battles between Sargon and Naram-Sin in Asia Minor and the Epic of Gilgamesh should be mentioned here. A preoccupation with prophecy and magic were Babylonian characteristics adopted by the Hittites. The Babylonian influence is especially apparent in naturalistic art and we shall have more to say on this subject later on. Let us at present discuss the question of Hurrian components in Hittite culture.

During our recent survey of the history of the Great Empire we came across the kingdom of Mitanni, the greatest state ever founded by the Hurrians. We first meet with the Hurrians on the tablets of Kültepe of the nineteenth and eighteenth centuries BC, where they appear as isolated foreign traders. Under the Hittite Old Kingdom the Hurrians were a considerable section of the people in cities like Ugarit (Ras Shamra) and Alalakh (Tell Atchana). In Halpa (Aleppo) there must have been a similar ethnic situation. Pilliya, king of Kizzuwatna and a contemporary of Idrimi of Alalak, bears a Hurrian name. It is therefore quite possible that the Hurrian element played an important part in this country, even at the time of the Hittite Old Kingdom. In any case, at the beginning of the Empire Aleppo and Kizzuwatna already belonged to the kingdom of Mitanni. In Mari, a town on the Middle Euphrates, Hurrian influence can be traced in some religious texts in the Hurrian idiom.

As transpires from the Hittite texts several minor Hurrian States must have existed. In the fifteenth and fourteenth centuries BC the country extended from Lake Van to Assur in the south as far as Carchemish, Aleppo, Tell Atchana, and to Ras Shamra in North Syria. The most important state founded by the Hurrians was, as we have said, the kingdom of Mitanni. King Shausshatar of Mitanni, the son of Parashatar, ruled about 1450 BC over Kerkuk as far as Aleppo in North Mesopotamia. The kingdom of Mitanni therefore marked the furthest extension of the Hurrians whose original home lay further north, in south-east Anatolia. In the fifteenth century BC Assyria was subjected to the Mitanni kingdom. The text of Mattiwaza from Boghazköy records that Shausshatar was able to carry off a gold and silver door from Assur and set it up in his palace in Wasshu-kanni, the capital of Mitanni, which lay in the vicinity of the present Ras Shamra el Ain on the Khabur. Suttarna II, the second successor of Shausshatar, sent the image of the goddess Ishtar from Nineveh to Egypt to heal the Pharaoh. But as we saw above, Suppiluliuma I put an end to the kingdom of Mitanni. Kizzuwatna had ceased to be a political power, and was incorporated in the Hatti country. But Hurrian influence was even more apparent under the reign of Suppiluliuma I. The occurrence of Hurrian names given to princes, and above all to the female members of the Hittite royal family, is significant. From the time of Tudhaliya III (at the end of the fifteenth century BC) the reigning queens of Hattusas bear almost exclusively Hurrian names. They are Nikalmati (the wife of Tudhaliya III), Asmunikal (the wife of Arnuwanda I), Puduhepa and Hinti (two successive wives of Suppiluliuma I), Manlikal (the third wife of Suppiluliuma I), Tanuhepa (Tawananna of the reign of Mursili II, Muwatalli and Mursili III) and Puduhepa (the wife of Hattusili III). Several princes bore Hurrian names. The best known among them are: Sharru-kushuh, son of Suppiluliuma I who was king of Car-chemish, and Ini-Teshup and Talmi-Teshup, two later kings of Carchemish. We have seen earlier that Mursili III while still a prince bore the Hurrite name of Urhi-Teshup.

Attempts have been made to explain the Hurrian names of members of the Hittite royal family by the Hurrian origin of the dynasty in power during the Hittite Empire, but it was simply a matter of fashion, due to the strong influence of Hurrian culture. This culture was then at its height; the Old Kingdom had been destroyed by the rise of the kingdom of Mitanni, but all that was of value in it, and the wealth and wisdom of the Mesopotamian world, reached the Hittites through Hurrian intervention. Moved by similar feelings the Seljuk Turks, centuries later, when they settled in Asia Minor, showed a preference for Persian names. The Hittites were a self-confident people. They did not object to adopting alien manners and morals which they added to their own cultural in-heritance. By this method they won the confidence of their subject peoples. In the same

XIX Yazilikaya. King Tudhaliya IV standing on the mountain peaks. In front of him the cartouche with his name. Relief on the east wall of rock chamber A

way they had adopted Hattian names directly after their immigration into Asia Minor. In this bold liberal policy of the Hittites lay their strength. Their power of adaptation, and respect for the politically vanquished, enabled the Hittite royal house to secure its ascendancy. In spite of the introduction of foreign manners and alien concepts the Hittites lost none of their racial characteristics. Many scribes and several authors of magical texts from Hattusas bear Hurrian names. Four clay tablets from Boghazköy contain translations of a Hurrian text on the training and acclimatization of horses. The author of this text was a man called Kikkuli from Mitanni.

The Hurrian is one of the most original languages of the Orient. It differs markedly from the Indo-European and Semitic languages which use the suffix and from the Hattian with its use of the prefix, and shows an agglutinative character.

Hurrian culture itself was open to Indo-Aryan and Luvian influences; all the Mitanni kings bear Indian names. In Kizzuwatna too Indo-Aryan kings with names like Pariya-vatri, Suna-sura and Pattatisshu came to the throne. The technical terms used on the text of the horse trainer Kikkuli mentioned above include Indian numbers. We know that the kings of Mitanni used to invoke the Indian gods Indra, Mitra, Varuna and the Nasatya in their oaths. The Hurrian people were therefore ruled by an aristocracy of Indo-Aryan descent. To this not very numerous caste of nobles belonged the knights called Marianni who bred horses and fought from war chariots. No doubt it was they who introduced the breeding of horses and chariotry into the Near East.

In the South Anatolian and North Syrian provinces the Hurrians seem to have produced a mixed culture with the Indo-European Luvians and it has been established that the idiom used in hieroglyphic inscriptions is probably not Hurrian but Luvian.

THE SPECIFIC CHARACTER OF HITTITE CULTURE

In spite of strong Anatolian-Hattian, Mesopotamian and Hurrian influences, the Hittites created their own particular culture on Anatolian soil. It is altogether amazing that a people as strongly influenced by Mesopotamian civilization as the Hittites could show totally different features from their oriental neighbours in several branches of their cultural life and a genuinely occidental philosophy.

The most important characteristic of the Hittites is their sense of loyalty to a state governed by law. In spite of hereditary kingship the ruler is merely *primus inter pares*. The Hittite Empire remained aloof from oriental absolutism and the idea of the divine rights of kings. Only towards the end of the Empire do we find the Hittites inclined to tolerate some specifically oriental feature. But this tentative appearance of orientalization of fundamental concepts could not really affect the character of Hittite culture. In the testament of Hattisili I we read that the nobles had to be referred to the *pankus* (community of nobles) and in the law of succession passed by Telepinu the rights of nobles are highly respected. The king is admonished: 'You shall not kill one of the kinsmen, that is not right.' Or: 'Whoever becomes king and plans evil against his brothers and sisters, and if you sit in the *pankus*, then tell him this: "How deeds of blood shall be dealt with, see from the tablet." Whoever commits evil among brothers and sisters answers for it with his royal head. Call the Assembly, and if the thing comes to a decision he shall pay with his head.'

It was the king's duty to attend to the welfare of his realm, to wage war and, as high priest, to conduct religious ceremonies. We have seen in the Text of Telepinu that the founder of the Hittite dynasty had spelt his name Tabarna or Labarna. This is a Hattian term, and was adopted as a title by the later kings.

As we can see from the study of royal seals, in time the Hittite kings felt obliged to adopt grandiloquent titles that corresponded to oriental custom. This was inevitable if their prestige was not to suffer *vis-à-vis* their vassals. But these were merely the first steps in a process of orientalization accelerated in the late Hittite period. Albrecht Goetze says that royalty in the time of the Hittite Kingdom had become theocratic and he cites a text: 'The country belongs to the Weather-God, heaven and earth and the people belong to the Weather-God. He made Labarna, the king, his regent and gave him the entire land of Hatti. Thus Labarna shall rule the entire country.' This formula introduces an essentially oriental idea into the Hittites' concept of a king.

We know of no inscription in which a Hittite king was deified in his life-time, as was the case with oriental rulers. The Hittites admit only the deification of deceased kings. Of the dead king the texts say: 'He has become a god.' But it seems that at the end of the Great Empire the oriental custom of deifying the king in his lifetime was introduced into Hattusas. In the large rock chamber at the shrine of Yazilikaya Tudhaliya IV had himself *XIX* depicted as a god standing on the mountain peak. As this relief was probably cut during his reign we are faced here with an oriental kind of apotheosis. It is striking that on his seal from Ras Shamra this king is wearing a sacred cap with horns. A limestone stele *Fig. 1* with the name of Tudhaliya in hieroglyphs, probably Tudhaliya IV, found in the shrine of Büyükkale is one more proof of his fondness for putting up his cartouche in places of worship. These are clear indications of the process of orientalization of the Hittites towards the end of the Empire.

One of the most important features of the Hittites, which distinguishes them from their oriental neighbours, is shown in the humane character of their laws. Albrecht Goetze has pointed out: 'a higher evaluation of human life and the rights of the individual. Humiliating punishments like mutilation, applied under Assyrian law, are almost wholly absent.' The killing and burning of the enemy, the erection of skull pyramids, impaling and flaying of the enemy, all the atrocities customary with the Assyrians were unthinkable in Hittite Asia Minor. Neither the texts nor the sculptured monuments give evidence of such cruel deeds. The treatment of slaves was very humane. Albrecht Goetze writes: 'The law permits a slave to marry a free woman legally, without the latter thereby losing the rights of her free birth, provided always that the slave pays the price for the bride. If such a marriage is dissolved, the fortune and the children are distributed according to the same principles as those applied to marriage between free men. Evidently slavery did not prevent the amassing of a private fortune, and its possession began to raise the barrier between free men and slaves.'

Marriage between brother and sister frequent among orientals was punishable with death. This transpires from the unequivocal words of Suppiluliuma I in the Hukkanas-Treaty:

> 'My sister, whom I, the son, have given you in marriage, has many sisters of various degrees. They have now become your sister too because you have married their sister. There is one important law for the Hatti-Country. The brother may not have sexual intercourse with his own sister or his cousin. Such is the custom. Whoever disobeys it, shall not live in the Hatti-Country. He should be killed, but since your country is immoral it is your custom to let the brother sleep with his own sister or his cousin. This is not permitted in Hattusas. If a sister, a half-sister or a cousin of your wife comes to stay, give her to eat and drink. Eat and be merry. But do not allow yourself to desire her. That is not permitted, that is punishable with death.'

The superior social position of women is another Hittite characteristic which distinguishes them from the people in some parts of the Orient. In our chapter on political history we saw that the position of the Queen Tawananna was strong. She remained Queen even as a widow, throughout the reign of her son. Her daughter-in-law inherited the rank of Tawananna only after her death. Since Tawananna is a Hattian term, the superior position of the queen, almost equal to that of the king, may be a custom of indigenous Hattian origin. Only the reigning king had a harem. The people do not seem to have practised polygamy. As for the rest, family life was organized on a patriarchal pattern.

These characteristics and basic concepts grant the Hittites a special place in world history. For over 500 years they stood for a humane outlook surpassing that of their immediate neighbours. In this lies the greatest merit of the Hittites. Few people in the history of the world so ably combined their arts of war with a successful diplomacy. Thanks to their extraordinary ability and unparalleled power of adaptation based on tolerance and good sense they could, for a half a millennium, unite numerous races of different languages and culture under a common rule.

ARCHITECTURE

The greatest artistic achievements of the Hittite people lie in the field of architecture. The well preserved ruins of Hattusas near the present-day hamlet of Boghazköy, with their grandiose architecture, still convey the living atmosphere of a past age.

THE BUILDINGS ON THE CITADEL

The large fortress of Büyükkale was the seat of the Great Kings. Since the beginning of *54* this century the nearly intact foundations of buildings erected there in the fourteenth and thirteenth centuries have been uncovered by German excavations. Let us now *Figs. 3–6,* examine the main features of these buildings. Structure A excavated between 1931–1933, *70, above* when excavations in Boghazköy were resumed after the First World War, served as a deposit for clay tablets, that is, for archives. The main building is approximately thirty-two metres long and consists of store-rooms on the first floor which is still standing, and a long lateral corridor. In the four rooms to the west double rows of rectangular limestone bases for pillars have been found, some of which have since disappeared. These pillars supported the upper storey. The outermost and narrowest room on the east side contained no stone bases; it was probably the place where the staircase was located.

Most of the 3,350 best preserved clay tablets, found either whole or in fragments in the archives, came from the three southern rooms. It is possible that the upper storey too was used for storing tablets. They stood on wooden shelves along the walls, like modern books. As all the clay tablets from Boghazköy were flat on one side and slightly concave on the other they could be easily taken down and put back, which would have been impossible with tablets flat on both sides. Labels were found consisting of small rectangular or oval blocks, six or seven centimetres long and four or five centimetres wide, which must have been propped up against the clay tablets or lying on the slightly protruding edge of the shelves. They indicated the contents of the tablets, for instance: 'Tablets concerning the deeds of Mursili', or 'Thirty-two tablets concerning the *Purulli* festival of the city of Nerik'. Catalogues were added. They contained entries such as 'Complete' or 'Incomplete' or 'Complete, first tablet has not been found', etc. The texts were not arranged according to their contents. Clay tablets dealing with totally different matters stood side by side.

The scribes of the clay tablets were among the most honoured citizens. In Hattusas during the Kingdom they were reduced to a few families. The profession passed from father to son. The scribes name themselves and their fathers in the colophon of the text, i.e. at the bottom of the tablets. One of them boasts in the colophon: 'When queen Puduhepa charged Urmahlu, the chief scribe, to find some clay tablets from Kizzuwatna in Hattusas, he copied these tablets concerning the Hisuwa festival on that day.' Among the scribes are some with Hurrian and Luvian names.

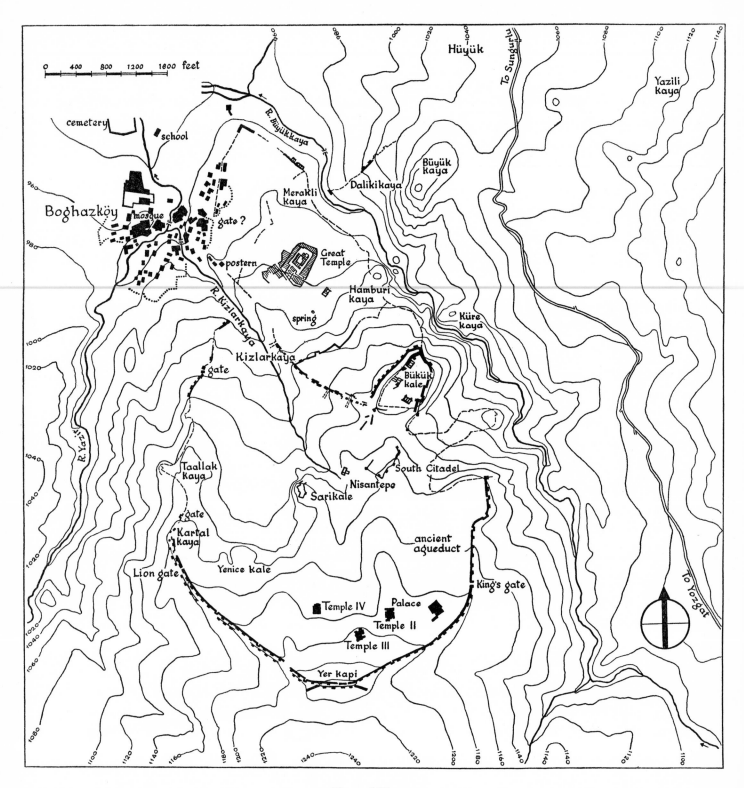

2 Plan of Hattusas

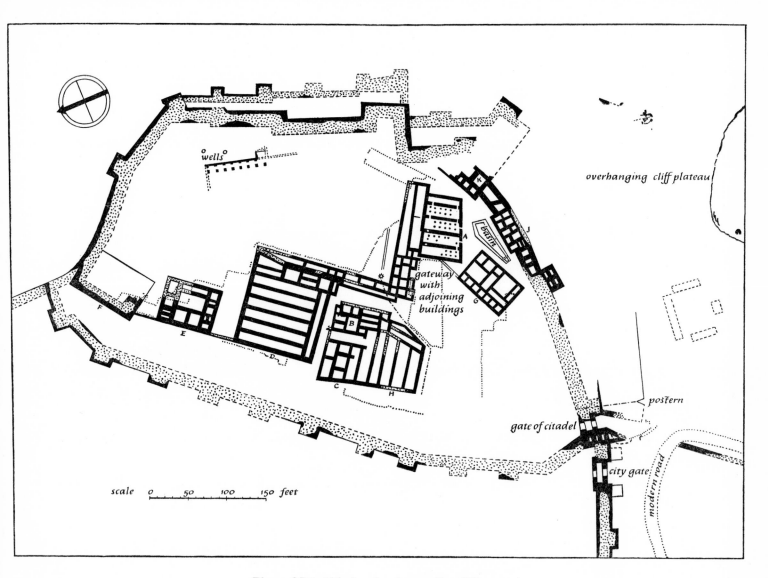

3 Plan of Büyükkale, the Acropolis of Hattusas

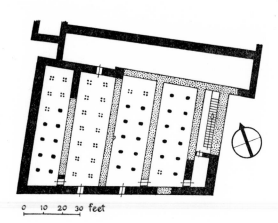

4 Hattusas, Büyükkale. Building A

5 Hattusas, Büyükkale from the east

XVIII   Two rooms of building E on the western slope of Büyükkale and the store rooms 10–12 of the temple of the Weather-God of Hattusas served as archives. The first excavators working in Boghazköy, Hugo Winkler and Theodor Makridi, have discovered great numbers of clay tablets in both places. In building D too there were many fragments strewn over the floor.

Fig. 4   The archives of Hattusas form the oldest library in history. The next oldest collection of records of the Ancient Orient known to date was found in Assur. It belongs to the time of Tiglathpileser I (1112–1074 BC). More important still was that of Asshurbanipal (668–626 BC) containing five to ten thousand clay tablets, found at Nineveh in the early years of archaeological research in Mesopotamia.

A notable collection of clay tablets with literary texts brought to light in Nippur does not, as was first assumed, come from a temple library but from the living quarters of a priestly scribe, although it must originally have formed part of a library.

Some archives with a number of clay tablets of the eighteenth century BC were found in Kültepe. As we saw earlier, the tablets were kept in the houses of Assyrian merchants, in earthenware vessels or baskets standing on the floor, and are almost exclusively business accounts stored in the homes as private records.

Private libraries existed in the Ancient Middle East. One is known from Assur, from the reign of Tiglathpileser I, and another from south-east Asia Minor, discovered in Sultantepe near Urfa. In the latter locality stood the house of a rich man, with a collection of clay tablets with literary texts. It had been destroyed in 610 BC. The tablets lay on a low brick platform surrounded by empty wine jars.

Figs. 3, 7   As Rudolf Neumann has rightly seen, building B forms the portico to complex A B D, with rooms that were probably destined for the palace guard.

6 Hattusas, Büyükkale from the north-west

Building C may be visualized as a small shrine. In the centre apartment of a six-room building a quantity of jugs, plates, beakers and shells, probably votive offerings, were found. A channel served to drain these rooms. The adjoining eastern room contained a limestone stele with the hieroglyphs of 'Tudhaliya, son of Hattusili'. As the name of the grandfather is damaged one cannot say with any certainty which Tudhaliya is meant. Probably it was Tudhaliya IV because in these ruins of late imperial times it is more likely to have applied to a late than an early king. Because of it the excavators have thought that the central room was a 'Stone House', a burial chamber. As no other burial chambers exist inside the royal palace they are inclined to regard it as a minor shrine.

Building H too has a ground plan closely resembling that of the archive-room, A. Rudolf Neumann suggests that this building, which should be thought of as having two storeys, housed tailors, tanners and goldsmiths who worked and stored their materials here.

Building D, a rectangle of thirty-nine by forty-eight metres, is the largest construction *Figs. 7, 8* in the citadel. The lower storey, which is still preserved, was a house. At the western end of a long south room a great number of seal impressions on lumps of clay were found. From the plan of the vanished upper storey Rudolf Neumann has convincingly reconstructed an audience hall. The position of the site dominating the entire landscape with the temple of the Weather-God of Hattusas bears out this reconstruction.

We might visualize a small guest house in building E. With its symmetrically laid-out *XVIII,* ground plan it is entirely different from the other sections of the palace. A circle of *Fig. 3* smaller rooms surrounded a large central hall. The east side with the portal recalls the Bit-Hilani type of building, characterized by a hall with two columns or pilasters at the front. The poor state of preservation has prevented a corresponding reconstruction in the small room. The upper storey must have been planned like the lower. In the two central rooms of the west front many clay tablets were lying. The building must therefore have had an official character. The hall measuring twelve by seven metres may have been a minor audience chamber; as we saw, another probably existed on the first floor.

On account of its isolated position Rudolf Neumann has regarded building F at the north-west corner of the citadel as the private apartments of the king from which gardens of modest proportions may have extended to the hall of pillars east of the rock plateau. Its dominating position above the highways to the capital and the magnificent view across the country in three directions, including that of Yazilikaya, made it a fit private residence for the Great Kings.

70, below

Building G in the south-west part of the citadel occupies a particularly important site. The arrangement of limestone and granite orthostats, the painted wall, the hall of pillars and the large rooms show that it was an official residence. The broad, well-paved road following the fortifications on the inside, and so far uncovered for a length of forty metres, leads past building G. The basin which, to judge from votive offerings, fulfilled a ritual function was, together with building G, somehow connected with building J. The complex to the east, on the highest point of the rock plateau of which only the part built into the rock has survived, was the royal palace proper. But the entire plan makes it clear that the remaining, previously discussed buildings were various sections of the royal palace. It should not be overlooked that this edifice, which dominates the site of the fortress, occupied a special position in the whole palace complex. At this point the summit has been levelled off in a wide circuit. The holes in the rock mark the position of pillars; on one rock ledge the wall pilasters corresponding to the pillars are still visible, so that the ground plan of a hall of pillars can be traced. The length of this wall is approximately twenty-four by twenty-seven metres. The entire building occupied part of a site visible today, while the other part served as a courtyard. Buildings A to F and the palace itself were grouped round the courtyard to the East. As the ground rose to the east and south-east, the buildings facing the courtyard had one storey on that side and two storeys on their outer front.

Before the royal palace to the south-west lay an open square. A path must have led from the palace doors to the west of Building A. Structure H has an intentionally sloping eastern wall which takes into account the position of building G. The square, surrounded on three sides by buildings, may have been a meeting place in the open sky. The axis of the portal is not in the centre of the walls but gives on the path skirting the buildings H C D E and F. The interior of the courtyard was connected with this path by separate lanes.

As Rudolf Neumann has pointed out, during the Empire the citadel of the Hittite capital, Büyükkale, was the chief residence of the Great Kings, and also the administrative centre. The sequence of squares, doorways, and large and small courtyards was excellently suited to Hittite ceremonial. The more private palaces might be looked for outside the citadel, in the lower city.

94

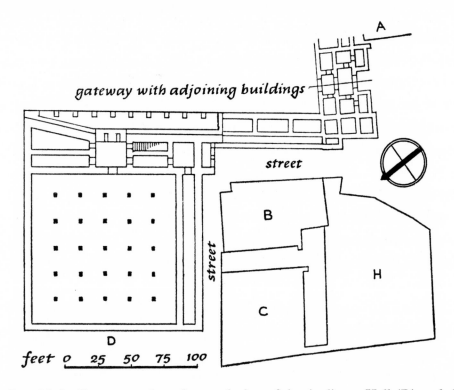

7 Hattusas, Büyükkale. Reconstruction of ground plan of the Audience Hall (D) and the Gateway

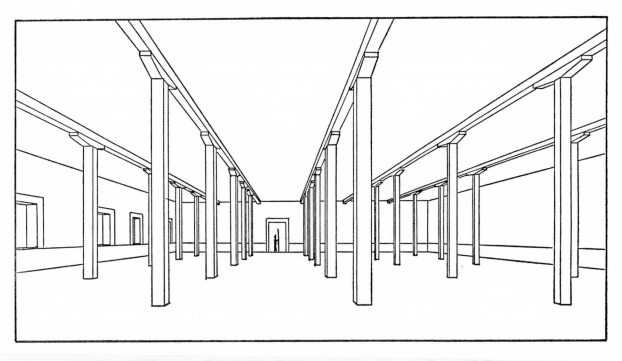

8 Hattusas, Büyükkale. Reconstruction of the Audience Hall

Unlike the great palace enclosures of Mesopotamia and Crete, the citadel of Hattusas is not designed on a homogeneous plan with buildings grouped round numerous courtyards, but consisted of a number of isolated constructions. The palaces of Mycenae differ from the Hittite royal palace although they too are an agglomeration of single buildings. It is true that the megaron-shaped houses of Mycenae stand each by itself, but they give the impression of being laid out according to a single plan, as they adjoin or are enlarged by subsidiary buildings. The citadel of Hattusas, on the other hand, reminds one much more of Troy VI, where we find the same arrangement of strictly isolated buildings set out in circular fashion round the hillside. What is so surprising is that no megaron-shaped houses existed in the citadel of Hattusas, the more so as this type of long-house occurs in the early historical period of Anatolia at both Kültepe and Karahüyük.

THE CITY

Fig. 2 The earliest Bronze Age settlement of Hattusas was in the lower city, below the temple of the Weather-God. Excavations during the last few years have laid bare the strata of the Karum Kanesh and of the Old Hittite period.

In the same district excavators have proved the existence of two habitation levels from the Hittite Empire. The oldest belongs to the fifteenth–fourteenth centuries BC, the more recent to the thirteenth century. The private houses on these levels have yielded handsome objects which we shall discuss later.

Under the Empire the city was considerably enlarged. The southernmost part, on raised ground, with the small palaces and the temples II–IV, was built during the period. So was the large temple to the North, rising in the centre of the old settlement in the lower city. Kurt Bittel records that all additions to the city and the walls in the south were finished by that time and that the temple of the Weather-God was already completed by about 1400 BC.

THE FORTIFICATIONS

Fig. 9

XVI,
XVII, 63

46

The fortifications of the city consisted of a strong main wall, with a small outer wall on slightly raised ground below it. Both were equipped with jutting square or rectangular towers. The lower 'cyclopean' part of the walls was built of huge blocks of stone. Blocks more than two metres were combined with smaller ones. Some were roughly hewn and taken straight from the quarry, but in most cases their surfaces were smoothed and they fitted closely together. The surfaces of the blocks, however, show their natural convexity. The largest gaps were filled with small stones. The stone-block base of the towers reached a height of six metres while the upper part consisted of flat, square bricks. What a wall and tower were like we learn from two fragments of a vase or incense burner. The protruding towers of the fort of Hattusas may have had the rectangular windows and crenellated crown of the clay model.

9 Hattusas. The City Walls near Yerkapi

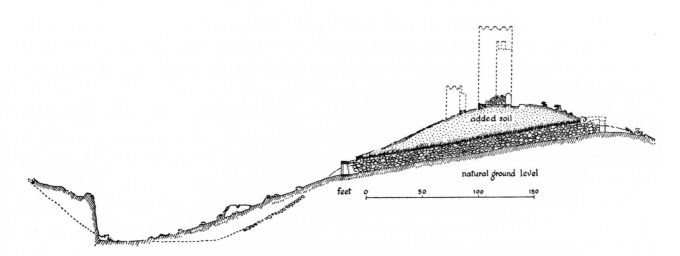

10 Hattusas. Cross section of the City Wall and Postern Gate near Yerkapi

11 Hattusas. Reconstruction of the City Gate, seen from the inside

Fig. 2   At the southernmost point of the city the fortress was comparatively vulnerable, because there the enemy could not be kept off by a steep slope as on the east and west. Consequently the city walls in this place formed a strong bulwark for offensive sorties. On this weak section of the fortifications the defenders, after having assembled in the space between the inner and the outer walls, could descend the steep and narrow stairway and

73   meet the enemy troops on open ground outside the city. A postern gate seventy metres long served as an outlet for sorties against the enemy. This subterranean tunnel with a

72   corbel vault could be held and blocked by a few men. One of the towers attached to the main wall stood within the axis of the postern, flanked by double sphinxes on the inner side.

XVI, 63   The remaining gateways of the city, the King's Gate and the Lion Gate, are well preserved and represent the most remarkable remains of Boghazköy. The Lion Gate opened

XVII   from the western walls. The lion to the right, almost intact, is a magnificent example of Hittite sculpture. The head of the second lion has been severely damaged, perhaps during the siege by Thracians about 1200 BC. Like the apotropaic dogs mentioned in the texts, these lions with their gaping jaws were meant to keep evil powers at bay.

63–65   The King's Gate was on the eastern wall. A relief of the God of War, the protective deity of Hattusas, was carved on the inner side of the gateway monolith; it is now at the Museum of Ankara and is the best piece of Hittite sculpture in existence.

A fourth gate existed on low lying ground to the north where the walls have been destroyed. These four gates were built to a single plan. A gateway with double doors was

Fig. 11   framed on the outer and the inner sides by strong monolithic pillars ending in a curve. Massive towers flanked the gates to the right and left.

The outer line of defence was supplemented by several barricades within the city. This system enabled the defenders to close the city quarters one by one and hold them, even after the enemy had occupied other sections of the town. Several small forts within the city housed members of the royal family or the chief nobles. A few were handsomely situated and their ruins still convey an idea of the feudal atmosphere of their time. One of them,

Fig. 2   Yenice Kale (the New Castle) still shows large sections of the walls. The castle south of Büyükkale, whose excavation may give interesting results, must have been an important seat. Fine, typically Hittite ashlar walls are standing on the site of Sarikale (the Yellow Castle), but the remains of dressed stone here date from Phrygian building alterations and reconstructions.

To the west of the southern citadel and the modern path across the city ruins rises Nisantepe, the 'Hill of Signs' where an imposing castle must have stood. A weathered

62   hieroglyphic inscription of eleven lines, eight and a half metres long, on the sloping eastern wall of the north valley, can be seen from the path. Thanks to the seals found at Büyükkale at least the names of kings have been deciphered there. Apparently the inscription, starting from the top right, dates from Great King Suppiluliuma, the son of

Great King Tudhaliya, grandson of Great King Hattusili. Since the two kings called Suppiluliuma happened to have the same genealogy as far as their fathers and grandfathers we cannot say with any certainty which of the two is meant, but we think that it was Suppiluliuma I. The size of the inscriptions indicates a great ruler rather than the last king of the Hittite Kingdom.

The city wall of Alaca Hüyük belongs to a different type of fortification. The orthostats *92–93* in relief along the base of the walls are so far the only ones of their kind in Central Asia *94–96* Minor. But in the late Hittite Empire they were generally in use and can be considered a peculiarity of the Hurrian or Syro-Hittite cultures of the second millennium BC. As for the rest, the technique is similar to that of the walls of Hattusas; it is even more evolved because the stones fit better, with straight joints throughout. More advanced still is the technique at the sanctuary of Eflatun Pinar where stones are cut in squares of equal size. *XXI* They are carefully treated and have bosses with a broad edge. But it should be noted that the symmetrical joints of the blocks were originally foreign to Hittite building technique.

THE TEMPLES

The most important edifices of the capital were doubtless the imposing temples. Up to now *Figs. 2,* five of them have been excavated. The building at the upper southern section of the city, *12–16* first believed to be a palace close to three temples, was later recognized as another temple (temple V).

The largest among them, the temple of the Weather-God of Hattusas, is well preserved *55–60* and impressive. The entire complex, comprising the storehouses, is 160 metres wide. The temple is rectangular, with an inner courtyard and an annexe with ritual chambers to the *Figs. 12, 15,* north-east. The storehouses form an enclosure, like the Greek *temenos* walls. The sanctuary *16* in the south-east was approached through a monumental gate whose monolithic doorway and two sentry rooms to the right and left of the outer entrance are still intact. The door frame and the hinges are partly discernible. On the north-west and south-west were two additional entrances for temple servants. The narrow store rooms seem to have had a second storey. Rooms 7 and 8 allegedly showed traces of stairs. These rooms evidently served to keep provisions and the temple treasure. In the rooms facing north and west double rows of massive *pithoi* were found, like those in Cretan and Mycenaean palaces.

A large number of clay tablets came to light in rooms 10–12 of the southern stores. The temple had a monumental portal, more grandiose than the entrance to the store rooms of *56, above* the south. One crossed a monolithic threshold leading to a small vestibule with two open *57, below* rooms with low windows in front. The entrance proper follows, with rooms for sentries right and left. It leads to a further vestibule with rooms on either side lit by windows that open on to the courtyard.

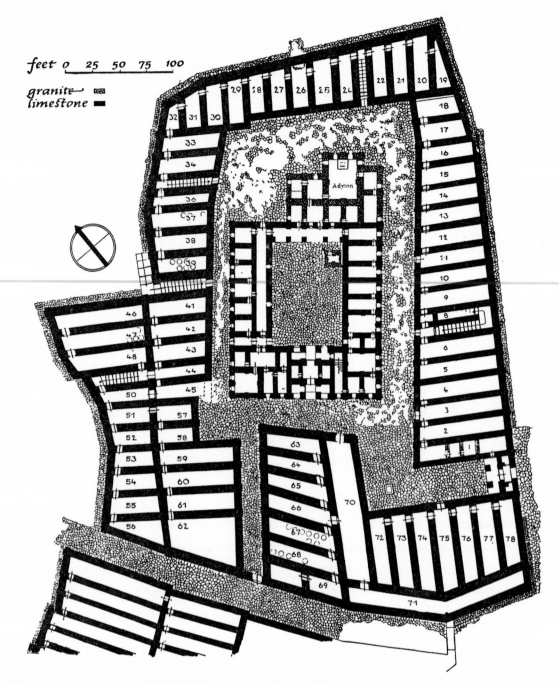

feet 0 25 50 75 100

granite
limestone

12 Hattusas. The great Temple of the
Weather-God. Ground plan of the Temple
and the surrounding store rooms

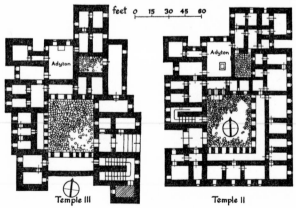

feet 0 15 30 45 60

Temple III

Temple II

13 and 14 Hattusas.
Ground plan of Temples II and III

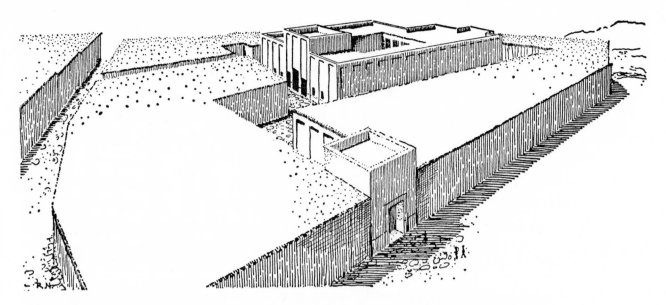

15 Hattusas. The great Temple of the Weather-God and the storehouses

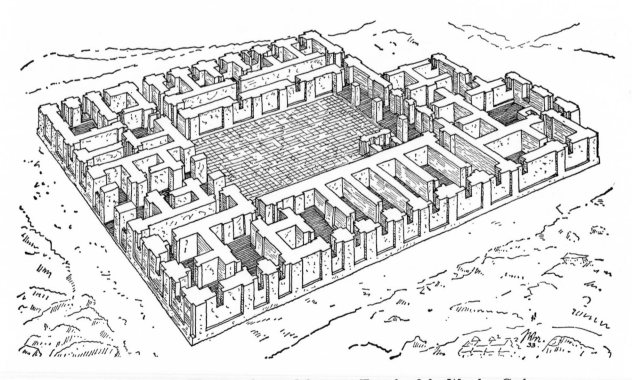

16 Hattusas. The stone bases of the great Temple of the Weather-God

This portal of temple I shows the best type of Hittite gateway, characterized by its plan of three sections extending across and lengthwise. The asymmetrical rooms to the right and left of the portal belonged to the storehouses rather than to the façade. Along the lateral sides are six narrow adjoining rooms; the same number lie to the north, but these are separated from the courtyard by a narrow corridor running the entire length of the walls. The round bored holes often observed in rows on the surface of the stone blocks served also to mortise the wooden panelling of brick walls in the temple.

The paved courtyard was sealed on the further end by a hall of pillars which gave access to the ceremonial halls. In the north-eastern corner of the courtyard are the remains of a sacred fountain-pavilion which served for lustrations before entering the ritual chambers.

These chambers are of granite on the north-east side while the remainder are built of limestone. This differentiation between the ceremonial buildings proper and the structure with the courtyard is repeated in the arrangement of the plan as a whole. In the largest *59, above* room of this annexe stands a stone pedestal which might have supported the statue of the Weather-God. This would mean that it was the part in which the most solemn religious ceremonies were held.

We might visualize the Hittite temple more vividly by reading the text describing a royal feast. Here it is, in the words of Albrecht Goetze:

The usual royal feast begins in the morning with the opening of the 'Halentuwa-House', perhaps best translated as the 'Rest-House' where the king has apparently been staying. He goes to the 'Wash-house' to prepare himself and put on his robes of office. He returns to the 'Halentuwa-House' from whence the procession to the temple sets out. It leads through the gateway (*hilammar*) into the court (*hilas*). There the ceremonies of purification are carried out: washing the hands and lustrations with a liquid called *tuhhuesar* which has not yet been identified. Only then does the king enter the holy of holies where he performs the proskynesis and ascends the throne. The flesh sacrifices and libations for the 'sacred places' follow. The king performs a second proskynesis and sits down on the throne. The insignia of his office are produced and set up or laid down in certain places. Now begins the main part of the ceremonial, consisting of a ritual meal. It is inaugurated by a second washing of the hands, and then a cloth is placed across the king's knees to protect his garment. A table with the sacrificial loaves is brought in. The nobles, the dignitaries and the priests are admitted according to their rank, and directed to their allotted places. While this goes on the king breaks a loaf with a spear. After this the meat and drink are distributed to the assembled community. The king removes the cloth from the table set up in front of him; he throws it among his retinue who pick it up and put it away. After the meal the ritual chamber is swept. Before the next part of the ceremonial the king again washes his hands. Bread and drink are brought and he breaks loaves for the various gods and pours out libations, after which the priests leave the room, the assembly dissolves, and the king leaves the temple.

We can see clearly that this account of a royal feast accords largely with the plan of temple I. The mention of the courtyard and of lustrations before entering the ritual chambers is a description of the temple of the Weather-God of Hattusas. Eight small rooms, together with the larger one with the god's statue, served for the ceremonies described in the texts. However, one misses a mention of the statue of the Weather-God.

The remaining four temples of Hattusas have a ground plan similar to that of temple I. But in temples II–IV the inner sanctuary consists of more and bigger rooms than in temple I. It may be that in time the comparatively small number of rooms in the large temple proved insufficient, and that this was taken into consideration in later building. *61, Figs. 13, 14*

A sixth temple belonging to the Empire was laid bare by Kurt Bittel on the slope in front of Yazilikaya, about two kilometres from the capital. It is a sanctuary open to the sky, with four outcrops of stone that formed a natural setting for ceremonies of the cult. The temple which was erected later in front of this rock shrine shows traces of three different periods; in the first period a wall separated it from the outside world. In the second period the building assumed the canonical aspect of a Hittite temple. An additional annexe can be assigned to this period and might be regarded as a gateway to the temple. In the last period the east wing was altered. The gateway follows the plan of the storehouses near temple I. The temple includes a courtyard with a 'fountain-pavilion' and a hall of pillars giving access to the holy of holies. *74, 75 Fig. 17*

Whoever wished to enter the rock shrine had to pass through the temple. The large room A with rock reliefs was its ritual chamber. Ceremonies of the cult, which in the temples of Hattusas took place in closed rooms before the statue of the god, were here performed under an open sky, below the rock relief representing the entire Hittite pantheon.

The monumental building of Alaca Hüyük too, with a courtyard eighteen to twenty metres wide and eighty metres long, flanked on two sides by porticos with pillars, we suspect to be a temple rather than a palace. A study of the architecture of Hattusas tells us that in Hittite society the large buildings served religious purposes while the palaces were comparatively small. *89*

THE TOMBS

The Hittites burnt their dead. The earliest cremation grounds in Anatolia have been found during the past few years at Boghazköy. The oldest graves containing ashes known to date, at Troy VI, belong to the last layer of houses of this Trojan period, that is to say, the close of the fourteenth century BC. The newly discovered necropolis of Osmankaya shows that during the Hittite Old Kingdom the Anatolian peoples burnt their dead and buried the ashes in various kinds of vessels.

Osmankaya lies to the north of the rock massif of Büyükkaya, half right of the path to the rock shrine of Yazilikaya. Below an overhanging rock a burial ground three metres wide and twenty metres long has been examined and found to contain fifty graves with ashes and twenty-two containing skeletons. Several urns were discovered on flat rocks and in niches, some leaning against the rock or pushed underneath it. The majority were

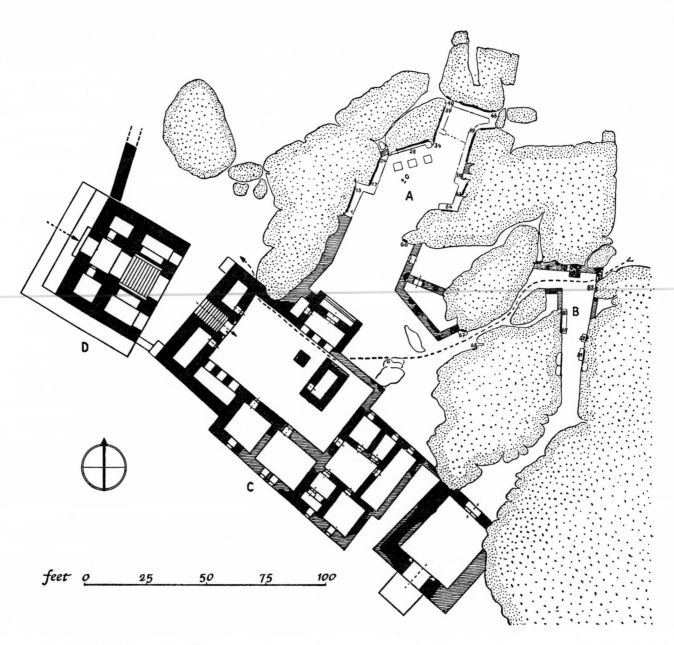

17 The Rock Shrine of Yazilikaya with the Temple and Gateway. The numbers 1–83 on the surfaces of
rock chambers A and B refer to the entire sequence of gods, daemons and kings depicted there

buried in the ground below the rock. After the inhumation all the urns were covered
with gravel and earth.

It is important to note that the contemporary necropolis of Gordion, in which typically
Hittite vessels were found, contains no graves with ashes. From this one may conclude
that burials at Gordion were not Hittite, but that it is simply a question of imported
Hittite vessels used in the graves; perhaps an indication that the Hittites did not come to
Asia Minor from the west.

As was said earlier, in the burial ground of Osmankaya a large number of ordinary
graves was found. We venture to assume that these belonged to the indigenous population

of Boghazköy. This fact may indicate the co-existence of both the ethnic elements which created Hittite culture. But cremation was unlikely to inspire the erection of monumental tombs. The custom of imposing tombs, generally diffused in the second millennium BC, with which we are familiar chiefly from Mycenae, Crete and Ras Shamra, cannot have been without repercussions in the Hittite cultural sphere.

Hittite texts describing detailed burial rites relate that after cremation the bones of the dead were deposited in the 'Stone-House'. Since there is mention of a couch and bedroom, this burial place must have had a proper chamber. The subterranean chamber of Gâvur-kalesi, which is a characteristic example of the Isopata type of grave, can be regarded as a grave monument of the Hittite Empire.

99, Fig. 18

On entering the subterranean chamber of this grave which measures three by four metres and is supported by false vaulting, one is reminded of the tomb of Tantalus and the graves of Ras Shamra. Similar graves must have existed in Western Asia Minor, and have served as models for this monument.

Gâvurkalesi, the 'Castle of the Infidels' (from Giaourinfidel) lies to the south-west of Ankara, on the way to Haymana. During the Hittite era a rounded peak rising about sixty metres above the valley was smoothed to form a plateau measuring thirty-five by thirty-seven metres and fortified by cyclopean walls. The front facing the valley is adorned with a relief of two marching gods before a seated goddess. The burial chamber which we have discussed lies parallel with the relief. The cap of the foremost male figure bristles

99, above

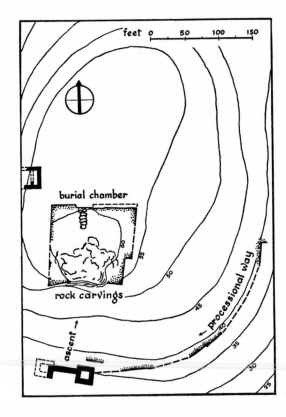

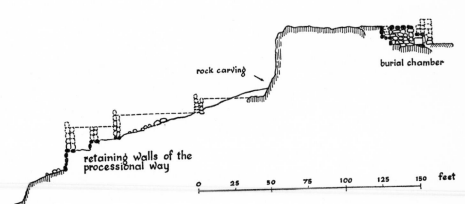

18 Left: Gâvurkalesi in Hittite times
Below: Gâvurkalesi. Cross section of burial chamber, cliff and retaining walls

with six horns; three horns only are attached to the front of the second figure. Although on a seal of Ras Shamra Tudhaliya IV wears a cap with four horns, owing to their many horns the figures of Gâvurkalesi may be gods rather than kings. The foremost figure might be the Weather-God followed by his son. Together with the goddess they may represent the greatest Hittite deities as in the main scene of Yazilikaya. The reliefs and the tomb were probably a sanctuary connected with the cult of the dead kings.

Fig. 17　　Yazilikaya near Hattusas must have been a similar shrine for the cult of the dead kings. The excavators of Yazilikaya were correct in seeing in the stone base at the far end of the side chamber (B) a socle for a statue of Tudhaliya whose cartouche adorns the rock wall immediately beside it. They have noted that the figure representing a mountain in this *80–87* cartouche faces south while the other reliefs on both walls of the side chamber without exception are directed north, towards the statue. From their position it is clear that the side chamber was intended for the king's worship.

Kurt Bittel and his colleagues are of the opinion that the shrine was dedicated to the cult of the dead king, namely Tudhaliya II or III. But we believe that it depicts the apotheosis of the king in his lifetime. The same king is seen in the small eastern chamber B and again in the main chamber A. The differences in style between the three reliefs may have no chronological importance as they were probably carved by different artists and may have been completed at different periods of the monarch's life. We believe with Laroche that the reliefs in the two chambers date from the reigns of Hattusili III and Tudhaliya IV. Building C in front of the rock shrine and the additional building D must belong to the era of Tudhaliya IV. Perhaps he erected the side chamber B during his life- *XIX, 78* time, intended to have a 'Stone-House' ready after his death. The great relief of Tudhaliya in the main chamber (A) must belong to this time. Several details from the life of this monarch which have come down to us show that he had a marked inclination towards the oriental concept of kingship. It is therefore possible that he allowed himself to be venerated as a representative of the god, perhaps during his co-regency with his widowed mother, *80, 81* Tawananna Puduhepa. The two rectangular niches of the side chamber may have con- tained the urns of the last kings of the Hittite dynasty beginning with Hattusili III or his *XXI* wife Puduhepa.

We have still to discuss the interesting monument of Eflatun Pinar which seems to have been a shrine attached to a sacred spring. It lies to the south-west of Konya, not far from Lake Beyshehir in Isauria. A spring gushing from the soil is dammed up to form a pond of thirty by thirty-five metres. On its northern shore stands a square monument of blocks seven metres long whose rockface is adorned with reliefs. A winged sun occupies the upper part, upheld on either side by two hybrid demons, one standing on the shoulders of the other. Below the great winged sun disk are two lesser winged sun disks supported by six demons arranged in superimposed pairs. The lesser suns crown two seated deities: to the left a god with a peaked cap, and to the right a goddess coifed with the disk of Hathor.

106

By seeing in the male figure a Mountain-God, and in the female a divinity of the spring E. Laroche may have made a correct guess. Nor need we stress what water meant to steppe and desert peoples. It is therefore most likely that the figures are source and mountain divinities rather than a pair of Sun-Gods. The god symbolizes the earth; the goddess, water; on the façade are thus represented the three basic elements of fertility in nature, sun, earth and water. Over 1,200 years later the same theme was treated by Horace and a sculptor working on the Ara Pacis in Rome. As E. Laroche assumes, the shrine by the spring must date from the reign of Tudhaliya IV.

THE BASIC CHARACTERISTICS OF HITTITE ARCHITECTURE

The distinguishing feature of Hittite architecture is the total asymmetry, not only of the *Figs. 2–4,* ground plans of individual buildings but also of city planning. In looking at the arrange- *12–14, 17* ments of the temples one can see that individual tracts or parts of façades have totally divergent plans, the only exception being the severely symmetrical gates. One wonders whether these are perhaps of oriental origin. The same is true of building E at Büyükkale.

Specifically Hittite is the preference for diagonal walls resulting in irregular outlines. We have already pointed out the similarity between Hittite store rooms and those of Cretan palaces. In both cultural centres the narrow proportions of the stores were determined by the building technique. They had to be planned as narrow passages, and these substructures supported the upper storeys. There is a marked similarity between the city plans of Crete and Hattusas.

The use of space in Hittite building, however, differs fundamentally from that of Cretan palaces in that it is based on the principle of encirclement. In the big temple district of the Weather-God of Hattusas the temple proper, as has been observed by Rudolf Neumann, *55, Fig. 12* the paved roads and storehouses surround the courtyard which here almost gives the impression of a *cella.*

The strict isolation of single buildings may therefore be regarded as a peculiarly Hittite *Fig. 3* characteristic, but one which occurs in Troy VI, and was to become the rule in Greek city planning.

The use of large blocks of stone, which can be considered as an expression of primitive *63, XVI,* monumentality, is a custom found in Anatolia after the Hittite immigration. We meet with *XVII* the same 'Cyclopean' style in the contemporary buildings of Mycenae, while at the same time only small and medium sized stones were used in Troy and Crete.

The box wall system predominates in Hittite fortifications. The outer and inner front of the walls, up to eight metres wide, are joined on the inside by crossbars and filled with rubble. It is most impressive on the south wall of Hattusas but has, as we have seen, pre- *Fig. 9* cursors in Alishar and Karahüyük, near Konya.

The Hittites were the most skilful fortress builders of the Ancient Middle East. The strategic adaptation of the walls to the difficult terrain and the layout of the defence make of the city walls of Hattusas the most grandiose fortification in the ancient world.

73 The Hittites were masters in the building of postern gates and corbel vaults which are the oldest known in history. The well-proportioned parabolic corbel vaults of Hattusas are an original creation of Hittite architecture which still commands our admiration.

89, below   The column was not known; the Hittites used square pillars instead. Characteristic and unique are the large windows with low window sills opening, not on to the court-

59 above; yards, but from the external temple walls. These outside windows facing the open road are
Fig. 16   unthinkable in the Mesopotamian world and represent a characteristic of Hittite architecture, which differs totally from that of the rest of the Orient. The room containing the statue of the god projected in such a way as to receive light from three windows. This love of light suggests that originally the religious ceremonies of the cult were held under an

74, 75   open sky, as we can still see at the shrine of Yazilikaya.

SCULPTURE

Hittite art reached its peak in the time of the Empire. Monumental sculpture did not fully develop until this period. The erection of large temples and palaces led to the adoption of a type of sculpture which was eventually accepted as the official imperial style in all parts of the Hittite Federal State.

Hittite sculpture may have originated at the beginning of the Empire, together with large monumental buildings. It is true that a number of motifs originate from the early Hittite period, but the style of the Empire has an entirely different character. Concepts like the god standing on a bull, the protective deity holding a bird and mounted on a stag, and the god with a bull-drawn chariot go back to models of the early historical epoch. The peaked cap and the symbolic thunder brandished by the Weather-God appear in the glyptic of Kültepe. All these motifs were transformed into an entirely new style.

44   The small bronze statuette from Tokat shows us that the type of Hittite god of the Empire was not unknown in the Old Kingdom. Although we are dealing with an Anatolian work the way in which the horns are attached, not to the peaked cap but to the skull, is not Hittite. Entirely non-Hittite too is the position of the right arm, the hand lifted

47, 52, 76, level with the head which formerly held a weapon. Hittite gods invariably shoulder their
77, 101   weapons on their symbols. This type of raised arm is seen in the glyptic of Mitanni and Syria and on statuettes found in Syria. The peaked cap too is affiliated to that of Syrian figurines although it occurs in similar form in Hattusas.

50, 64   It should be noted that on this statuette the characteristic male costume, the richly adorned skirt and the diagonal sash-belt, are missing. Stylized muscles occurring on most sculptures of the Empire were unknown to the maker of the bronze statuette. The broad *50, 51, 64, 84* square face shows, however, that it is the work of a metal workshop of Central Anatolia. The sphinxes of the gate and other sculptures of Hattusas have similar features. Like its *50, 51, 53 below left, 69, 65, 86* Syrian models the bronze statuette of Tokat may date from the sixteenth or fifteenth century BC. It is therefore significant that this specifically Hittite type of god had not yet been conceived at the end of the Old Kingdom.

The oldest figurative representations dated by their inscriptions are from the reign of Muwatalli (1315–1282 BC). These are several fine seal impressions and the relief of Sirkeli. *XX, 45, 98* The next oldest relief with an inscription that determines its date is the monument of Great King Hattusili III and Great Queen Puduhepa at Fraktin near Kayseri. But since *100* the city wall of Hattusas was already standing in 1400 BC, the sculptures of the three gates, the lions, the God of War, and the sphinxes must be considered as the oldest known monu- *XVII, 64–69* mental sculpture of the Hittites. The last named works of art are the most beautiful and significant creations of Hittite sculpture. They may come from the same workshop.

The sculptures at the gates form a special group. They are the only Hittite sculpture in the round that have been preserved. The God of War too gives the impression of free *64, 65* sculpture as he is worked in a pronounced high relief. His head emerges almost three-quarters from the background and his body is moulded like the lions and the sphinxes. Perhaps the bare chest and feet are a further indication that we are dealing with the representation of a god. He wears a pointed helmet with cheek and neck flaps. The helmet has a plume reaching down to the elbow. A similar peaked helmet with a band worn by king Mardukbalidin II is seen on a *Kudurru* from the end of the eighth century BC. The god's hair shows below the neck flap and hangs down in a long plait below the helmet. The brief skirt is fastened with a belt from which a long diagonal sash reaches down to the right knee. On the left side the god carries a sword with crescent-shaped pommel and a strongly curved blade. In his right hand he holds an axe with a long handle with a dangling tassel. The figure may be a God of War guarding the gate of the capital. The relief is worked with great care, the ornaments are finely chiselled. The minute details go so far as to include the cuticle of the nails. The modelling of the face and body, the rendering of the collarbones and the muscles is masterful. The sculptor must have been one of the greatest artists of his time. By representing the right leg full face and the left in profile, and by raising the ground below the advancing leg, he has given his work a mobile and lively aspect which creates the impression of a marching figure.

The lions and the sphinxes are of the same artistic quality. As we have said, they and the high relief on the King's Gate may originate from the same workshop. The well-preserved lions of the other gate display the same technique in the carving and detailed *XVII* modelling as the head and body of the War-God. A similar neat and precise technique is found on a double-headed duck from Boghazköy which can be dated from the fifteenth *48, 49* century BC. In the sphinxes, on the other hand, we recognize a slight deviation from the manner of the same workshop. Their head-dress shaped like a tree with six spiralling branches is, as Friedrich Matz has proved, a motif which occurs in Mycenae.

This style, which began about 1400 BC, with the gate sculptures of Hattusas, remained almost unchanged until the decline of the Hittite Empire. If one studies the iconographic and stylistic details of all Hittite sculpture, one can see that the artists worked according to a set convention. Not only the details of the headgear, the hair and dress, but the parts of the body are represented according to an established scheme. The rendering of the features, eyes, brows, mouth and ears, one would almost be inclined to say, follows a norm as in hieroglyphs. The unity of style indicates that sculpture as we know it from the time of the Empire was a unique creation of a few workshops, and covered a comparatively brief period. Had many centres contributed to the creation of Hittite sculpture, and manifold foreign influences been at work, the art of the Hittite Empire could have included a variety of parallel styles as was the case in the late Hittite period.

THE HUMAN FORM IN HITTITE SCULPTURE

76–86
Fig. 19
It is characteristic for the male to wear one large ear-ring and sometimes a beard, but never a moustache. The men wear their hair long or short. In the former case the plait reaches down to the elbow and ends in a slight curl.

Whether the figures carry something in their hands or not, the position of the arms is always the same. Seen from the beholder's viewpoint the male figures keep one bent arm pressed against the body and the other arm extended. Both hands are clenched; the hand in the background held level with the breast shows the palm; that seen in the foreground the back. Female figures hold the further hand in the same way, but the one in the foreground at an angle of ninety degrees. The hand in the foreground is shown level with the neck, with raised fingers forming a sort of pincer.

XIX, 78
The gods are mainly recognizable by their horned caps. In the sculptures of the Empire the unusually tall cap ends in a point or in a rounded form. The Mountain-Gods wear special caps whose peaks bend over the front. This kind of headgear is familiar from Ras Shamra.

The horns attached to the divine cap are, so to speak, insignia which indicate the rank of Hittite gods. Those belonging to a higher sphere wear caps with a multitude of horns. The Weather-God of the Heaven for instance wears a cap with six horns to the front and *85* back. The god Sarruma who embraces king Tudhaliya on one relief, and on another follows the goddess Hepat, is wearing six superimposed horns in both cases. That a difference in rank is indicated here hardly needs to be stressed. More striking still is this *99* difference on the rock relief of Gâvurkale where the foremost god wears a headgear with three horns to the front and three behind, while the god in his wake has only three horns to the front. The same differentiation in rank confronts us at Yazilikaya. It is hardly accidental that the figures at the rear of the procession of divinities wear caps with one horn *79* only. Thanks to these differences we are in a position to clarify the hierarchy of Hittite gods up to a point.

19 The Rock Shrine of Yazilikaya. The meeting of the gods. North wall of rock chamber A

The horns also appear on the head of fabled beasts and hybrid creatures and other *66, 69, 93* divine figures. The Hittite peaked cap with horns goes back to Mesopotamian models, but those that we find on the gods of the Empire are an original Hittite creation. On sculptures in the round they are attached to both sides of the cap. On the reliefs they adorn the front, and sometimes the back of the cap. Only the relief of the War-God wears *65* a horn attached to the side of the helmet, as for sculptures in the round. These details are a further confirmation that the relief at the King's Gate is older than the other known sculptures of the Empire. It would appear that the horns were originally attached to the side of the relief. Later they were placed on the front and back of the cap for the sake of simplification. This change lends to the Hittite peaked cap a special and original character.

A further differentiation in rank is made possible by the halved ellipses which adorn the caps of high-ranking deities. They are arranged symmetrically to the right and left of a *85, Fig. 19* line dividing the divine caps, like the horns to which they correspond in number. Outside Yazilikaya they occur only in Malatya.

The halved ellipses are merely the divine ideogram which we know from picture-writing. That this adornment of the caps is a privilege of the highest gods is indicated by the fact that none but the Weather-God of the Heaven in the main chamber of Yazilikaya wears this sign. It is interesting to observe that in the main scene at Yazilikaya the god Sarruma does not wear a divine ideogram on his cap in the presence of the highest gods, but in the relief depicting king Tudhaliya IV in his embrace, he does wear it. The *85* Sword-God in the side chamber seems to have been an important deity, since he too wears *83* a peaked cap with the divine ideogram.

The usual dress of the gods consists of a tunic with short sleeves ending just above the

64 knees in a straight or slightly undulating line. Sometimes the gods wear a cloak over the tunic; they are usually armed with a sword which has a crescent-shaped pommel and a

86 curve at the end of the blade. The twelve gods of the side chamber at Yazilikaya carry a sickle each which is their special attribute. The other weapons, lances, bows, axes and maces, are to be regarded as special attributes of various gods.

101 Female deities wear either a polos or a flattened, cone-shaped cap. The latter head-

92 gear is seen in the goddesses of Fraktin, Gâvurkale and Alaca Hüyük, and on a seal im-

76, Fig. 19 pression of Tudhaliya IV. Poloi are either high or low. In Yazilikaya they are made like

XXIII a city crown. The seated goddess of Sipylos wears a city crown similar to that of the goddess of Yazilikaya. On the original the remains of the joining line above the left ear can still be discerned.

The goddesses wore their hair long. The plaits are much longer than those of the gods and tucked into the belt. Female figures are clad in long gowns with wide sleeves. The

79 below right tunic is belted, and the skirt falls in vertical or handsomely draped folds. Pleated robes are a speciality of female figures in Hittite art. Shaushga who, as the Goddess of War, wears the horned cap of the gods and takes part in the divine procession at Yazilikaya, is recognizable as a female deity by her pleated gown and bare leg. Her attendants Ninatta and

79 below centre Kulitta wear identical long gowns with vertical pleats. Some female figures are clad in a thin cloak thrown over the head which leaves the face bare, partially covers the body, and reaches down to the feet.

In the art of the Empire the kings invariably appear with a round skull-cap, the

92 above 78 best examples of which are found on the reliefs of Alaca Hüyük and Yazilikaya. As the texts tell us, the kings are entitled to wear horns only when depicted as deified rulers after their death. But there are indications that the kings were venerated as representatives of a god in their lifetime. It is very unusual for a king to wear the same horned peaked cap as

101 above the god before whom he officiates, as is the case with Hattusili III on the rock relief of

98, 45 Fraktin. The kings are clad in the short tunic of the gods. It is characteristic for the king to wear a cloak of specifically Hittite cut. Muwatalli wears such a cloak on the rock relief

XIX, 85 of Sirkeli and on several seal impressions. Tudhaliya IV wears it on two sculptures at

92 above Yazilikaya and so does a king in Alaca Hüyük.

The most important symbols of regal dignity are the winged suns and the *Kalmush*. We learn from the texts that in the Empire the king apostrophizes himself as 'my sun'.

45, 78, 85 The winged suns of the royal cartouches, or wings placed above the heads of kings, are their hieroglyphic titles. Sedat Alp has identified the *Kalmush* with the long pastoral curved

XIX, 53, 85 staff held by the Great Kings. He observed that the crook-like pieces of metal from Early

92, 98 Bronze Age graves at Alaca Hüyük were probably the lower heads of such royal staves. It may well be that the Hittites, who drew much inspiration from the Hattians, adopted this symbol from their kings.

The Hittites wore up-tilted boots. This form of footwear known in Anatolia since the *33*
Early Historic period appears on both male and female figures to protect the feet among
rocky mountains.

ETHNIC TYPES

On studying the heads of human figures in Hittite sculpture we can determine several
types of features. The true Hittite is probably represented by the God of War at the King's   *65*
Gate, the gate sphinxes, the twelve gods from the side chamber of Yazilikaya, and by a few   *69, 86*
bronze or gold statuettes. All share a square face with high cheekbones, protruding eyes   *50, 51, 53,*
and a hooked nose. The bodies are squat.   *below centre*

The ethnic types of some gods and of the two well-preserved portraits of Tudhaliya IV,   *78, 85*
on the other hand, show almost idealized features with a straight, handsome nose. The
king's figure is slim and well made. The best preserved examples of this type are, in
addition to the Tudhaliya portraits, the two statues of the god Sarruma, the male divi-   *85*
nities in the main chamber of Yazilikaya, the figures on the rock reliefs of Fraktin,   *76, 77, 100*
the gold leaf figurines of Carchemish, the ivory figurine of a Mountain-God, and male   *53*
heads incised on a clay tablet.

A totally different type of feature with an unusual nose is seen on the orthostat reliefs   *92–97*
of Alaca Hüyük. The figures of the vase from Bitik reproduce this type almost identically.   *XIV*

A gold statuette from Boghazköy with a hooked nose seems to represent the Hattian   *53 centre*
section of the population which appears to have still been numerous in the time of the
Empire. The Egyptian reliefs of various Hittite types, especially those of Hittite infantry,
show an ethnic type similar to the gold statuette of Boghazköy and may be regarded as
Hattian.

THE LION SCULPTURES AND THE IMPERIAL STYLE

As lions are a frequent motif in Hittite art, let us briefly examine the type of lion from the
time of the Empire.

In Hittite art lions occur chiefly as guardians of portals or supporting statue bases.
Sometimes, however, they are an attribute of the gods or part of a hunting scene.

In the art of the Empire we meet with perfectly formed lions whose type does not   *41*
change during this entire period. Already in a vessel shaped like a lion's head of the old
Hittite period we find the basic features of the Hittite type of lion. The most important
characteristics of these beasts may be summed up as follows: the ears, if cocked, are   *XVII, 83*
rounded, but when laid back, are heart shaped. The knob-shaped lumps appearing on the
upper ear, near the mane, are Hittite characteristics. The fold of the neck round the lower   *90, 91*
jaw is usually thick; when missing it is replaced by a collar mane distinct from the head.
The nose, sometimes wrinkled at the lower ridge, runs in a straight line. The cheekbones
are always high and sometimes encircled by thick folds of flesh. There are no wrinkles

under the eyes; the jaws are open or tightly closed. The tongue resting on the lower open

91 jaw is characteristic. It even shows in the lions with closed jaws. The mane is seldom
76, Fig. 19 stylized. The chest is usually curved. On the reliefs the paws show stylized claws. The tail
52 above, is either raised or pointing downwards, ending in a wide spiral like the *Kalmush*, the
83, 90 symbol of sovereignty of Hittite kings.

As regards themes too the sculpture of the Empire shows a unified style. Subjects are generally religious. Ceremonies of the cult, libations and prayer are frequent. Animals
47, 52, 79 like the lion, bull and stag are often seen. Hybrid beings, lion, bull or bird-demons are
XXI, 87 among the most popular motifs.

In his revealing study published some years ago, Anton Moortgat classified an important group of sculptures from the Great Empire as Hurrian. It may be that a considerable number of Hittite motifs are derived from a Hurrian source, but it must be said that Hittite sculptors entirely re-created whatever they adopted from Hurrian art.

It is difficult to assert at the present stage of our knowledge that the Hurrians had important monumental sculpture. Thanks to the research of Edith Porada we are very well informed on the subject of Hurrian glyptic. A seal impression from Mitanni with fine motifs in relief was found in Boghazköy. But a comparison of Hurrian glyptic with Hittite sculpture shows that a strong influence from Mitanni is out of the question. The Hittites, who held sway over a large part of the then civilized Near East, needed a national sculpture which proclaimed their power everywhere. The political situation therefore favoured the deployment of a specifically Hittite style over the whole realm. The finds from Ras Shamra show us that in Carchemish, where subsidiary kings ruled
53, above at times, the glyptic was purely Hittite. The gold leaf statuettes found there by Sir Leonard Woolley are indistinguishable from those found in Boghazköy.

The beautiful ivory relief from Megiddo with characteristically Hittite motifs shows that Hittite influence had penetrated to Syria. As Gordon Loud has pointed out, this work of art is a local product in which Hittite motifs are used, but devoid of their significance.

The interesting gold disk now at the Oriental Institute of Chicago is a similar work with Hittite motifs, correctly localized by Helene Kantor as coming from Syria. A bronze
50, 51 statuette from Latakia in Syria is almost identical with the bronze statuette from Boghaz-köy. That both are Hittite products is evident from the square features, the large ear-rings, the skirt, and the typically Hittite way of treating the muscles, met with in the god of the King's Gate. The perfectly preserved statuette of Latakia shows how the long plait was worn by the men. Had it not been known that the relief was found by Sir Leonard Woolley in Tell Atchana near Antakya, one would have classed them without hesitation
45 above with the sculptures of Alaca Hüyük and Yagri. In Tarsus seal impressions with hieroglyphs

XX King Muwatalli (1315–1282 BC). Rock relief at Sirkeli near Adana

were found which correspond to those of Boghazköy, although the figurine of rock crystal
discovered there differs in style and ethnic type from the specifically Hittite carving. The
posture of the arms recurs in the sculptures depicting gods which Bahadir Alkim found in
Yesemek. Hetty Goldman compares the triangular shape of the eyes with those of the
god at the King's Gate, and declares them, probably correctly, to be Hittite. But this
may be a local style influenced by the Hittites.

53 below

We may mention in conclusion that a small Hittite bronze figurine now at the Ashmolean Museum at Oxford was found in Greece. It proves that Hittite art was not unknown in the western world. Moreover, the figurine at the Ashmolean Museum will not
have been the only Hittite work of art exported to Greece.

In coming back to the artistic remains in Anatolia we may say that the basic features
of Hittite sculpture given above are common to all reliefs of the Empire. Existing minor
deviations may be interpreted as the differences between various workshops. The oldest
relief of Muwatalli, dating from about 1285 BC, represents the type of Great King described earlier. The figures depicting an embrace on the seal impression of Muwatalli
recur two generations later in the side chamber of Yazilikaya on the relief of the god
Sarruma and king Tudhaliya IV. The figures of the next oldest relief of Fraktin
belong to the same style. The flame-like ornament on the tunics of male figures from
Fraktin occurs on similar garments of a relief at Chagdin near Adana. The short peaked
cap worn here by female figures appears, as we saw, on many other Hittite sculptures.

98
45

85

100

The style of the Empire was dominant in the whole realm. Thus iconographic details
of the kings of Karabel near Izmir, the Mother of the Gods on Mount Sipylos near
Manisa, and the divine reliefs of Gâvurkale near Ankara are identical with those of
Yazilikaya, Fraktin and Sirkeli.

XXII, 102
XXIII, 99
98

The relief of Karabel represents a king holding a bow and spear, and girt with a
sword ending in a crescent-shaped pommel. The partly damaged hieroglyphic inscription
between the two royal signs seems to repeat the ideogram of Tudhaliya found on the
cartouche scene of Yazilikaya. The tall elegant peaked cap testifies to the evolved style
of the time of Tudhaliya IV.

We have already pointed out that the Mother of the Gods of Sipylos wore a walled
city crown, like the goddesses at Yazilikaya. The style and iconography of the rock
reliefs of Immankulu, Tasci and Hanyeri not reproduced in this book, all three of them
from the ante-Taurus, belong to the same tradition. The images of Eflatun Pinar, with
their figures in deep relief, show a different mode, but the iconographic details are typically Hittite. The wings of the sun disks are upturned at the ends as was the custom in
Hittite Empire art. The peaked cap of the seated god and the Hathor head-dress of the
goddess are found on other Hittite sculptures. The gold statuette of a deity from Yozgat
mentioned earlier, with its protruding eyes, full cheeks and high cheekbones, perfectly
corresponds to the type of sculpture found in the heart of the Hittite region.

XXI

53 above
76–79, 85

*53, below
left*

116

A gold statuette of unknown provenance in the British Museum is almost identical with   *53, below*
that in the Louvre and must come from the same goldsmith's workshop.

A finely chiselled ivory figurine from Boghazköy is a mountain-god. His horned cap
has already been discussed. The lower body has the shape of a mountain. The semi-
anthropomorphic representation of mountain-gods was evolved in Mesopotamia. The
ivory statuette of Boghazköy is a Hittite adaptation from Akkadian models. But the
specifically Hittite type of a mountain-god is one we meet with in the reliefs of Yazilikaya,   *78, Fig. 19*
Immankulu, Hanyeri, and on royal seals of the Empire.

In this characteristic Hittite representation the mountain-god is entirely humanized,
and his mountain character is indicated merely by rounded humps attached to his tunic
and jagged thorns on either side. The god of Boghazköy has two pairs of horns on his
peaked cap, which show him to be a high-ranking mountain-god. To these were added
five superimposed horns on the front of the peaked cap, protuberant because it is a sculpture in the round. If one regards the statuette in profile one can see that these protuberances have a point, like horns on reliefs generally. The way in which they are dimini-
shing in size towards the top reminds one of the horns seen at Yazilikaya and Alaca
Hüyük.

The god on the monument at Fasiller, south-west of Konya, near lake Beyshehir, wears
a cap whose front appears to be adorned with similar horns. The ivory figurine of
Boghazköy exhibits the same kind of horns as those seen on reliefs, which speaks against
an earlier provenance of this piece, and in fact the statuette has been dated by the
excavators to the thirteenth century BC. The mountain-god wears a long, faultlessly
preserved plait with detailed strands of hair. It is slightly curled at the end in a way
otherwise found only on reliefs.

The small steatite relief of Alaca Hüyük represents the protective deity standing on a   *47 below*
stag and clutching a bird in his outstretched right hand. The cap with one horn only
labels him as a lesser deity. The iconographic details are the same as those met with on
other Hittite reliefs.

The bronze plaque from Alaca Hüyük with two bull-demons mounted on bulls   *47 above*
standing each side of a tree may be a local version of a Hurrian concept, but style and
techniques are purely Hittite.

The gold statuette of a seated goddess from Boghazköy adorned with round ear-rings   *53 centre*
and wearing up-turned shoes is a Hittite product of Central Anatolian workships. The
large nose with broad, fleshy nostrils proves that the Hattian population continued into
the time of the Empire.

The sculptures of Alaca Hüyük form a group in themselves. The iconographic details   *90–97*
are the same as on other Hittite figures; only the stylistic details differ slightly. They
are low reliefs with faintly modelled outlines. The body and the muscles are stylized.
The technique recalls that applied to metal works. A similar stylization occurs on a gold
disk in the Oriental Institute of Chicago. Helene Kantor has drawn our attention to the

likeness between the gold disk and the reliefs of Alaca Hüyük. The plant motifs of the hunting scenes also recur on this gold object. It is to be assumed that the plant motifs on reliefs owe much to Hurrian art, but they, nonetheless, achieve an absolutely original note. As H. G. Güterbock has shown, the stylized muscles at least are found on animals in Hittite glyptic. We might assume the existence of similar works by Hittite goldsmiths.

96 *95* It is true that the charging bull, the turning stag, and the crouching lion are motifs which did not originate in Hittite art, but came by various routes from Syria, where Mesopotamian ideoplastics were found with Cretan and Mycenaean ones.

The style and method of the sculptures from Alaca Hüyük are genuinely Hittite. The extreme flatness of the reliefs occurs in the carvings of Tell Atchana near Antakya, and *100, 101* on the stele from Yagri on the Sakarya river. The similarly shallow reliefs of Fraktin give the impression of being unfinished, since the outlines of the figures are barely indicated on the rockface.

As for their technique, it is the same as that applied by stone masons of Alaca Hüyük. *92, 93* Here too certain figures, like the marching priest and the worshipper, are rendered in full profile, like the women of the main scene of Yazilikaya.

76 above Only the juggler and the acrobats are shown in full face from the belt to the knees, probably in order to display the centre pleat of the skirt. With the figure of the seated *93* god the stone mason has indulged in an amusing rendering. The god does not clutch the sceptre leaning against his right shoulder in his right, but in his left, hand. The representation of the legs in profile is primitive. The artist obviously intended to include as much as possible of the carpet underneath the throne.

The sculptures of Alaca Hüyük are typical of the style of the Empire in the thirteenth century BC. They represent religious scenes and libations. The scene in which the king, accompanied by the queen, offers a libation, forms a whole with the reliefs of priests and sacrificial beasts, while the other scenes have no bearing on each other and should be envisaged as independent compositions.

In spite of their flat reliefs and several flaws in the execution, the sculptures of Alaca *88, 90* Hüyük are especially beautiful. Most attractive are the decorative animal motifs with *94–96* their clear calligraphic outlines.

The peak of the evolved Hittite style appears without doubt in the unique reliefs of the *74–87* rock shrine of Yazilikaya. The outcrop of rocks lying at two kilometres distance to the *Fig. 17* north-east of Hattusas contains two natural caves; the later one to the west, and the smaller one adjoining it on the east side. The west wall in the larger chamber is adorned with a long procession of gods and the east side with goddesses, all of whom converge on the north wall, but the division into male and female deities is not absolute. Three *79 below* *right* female divinities take part in the procession of the gods, and one male god is noticeable *76, Fig. 19* among the goddesses. The central scene represents a meeting of the chief divinities. To the left we notice the Great God bestriding the backs of two mountain-gods. Facing him is the Great Goddess mounted on her sacred animal, the lion. The two divinities are flanked by bulls with peaked caps, of whom only the forepart is seen.

Behind the Weather-God a second deity stands on rounded cones which typify mountain peaks. The Great Goddess is followed by a young god mounted, like herself, on a lion, and by two goddesses whose sacred emblem is the double-headed eagle. The names of the gods have been identified with the help of the hieroglyphs placed above their out-stretched hands. The god to the left is the Weather-God of Hattusas, the chief god in the centre is the Weather-God of the heaven. The Hurrian name of the chief goddess is Hepat. She is the Sun-Goddess of Arinna. The youthful divine son standing behind her is Sarruma. The three divinities, taken as one, form a trinity. The divine pair with their child is a concept found in the lead idols of the Early Hittite period.

The male cortège consisting of forty-two figures starts on the left of the entrance to the chamber, with a relief of twelve gods. Several religious functions are depicted between this and the main scene. The two antithetic bull demons mentioned earlier take part *79, 3rd row* in the procession. They stand on the hieroglyphic sign for earth and carry the crescent moon which signifies the sky. At the head of the procession, on the west wall, we can see the most important gods. Counting from the front to the rear we distinguish the goddess *79 below right* of war Shaushga accompanied by Ninatta and Kulitta. They are followed by the Moon-God with a pair of wings whose peaked cap is topped by a crescent moon. Further on we recognize the Sun-God represented by the divine king. His kingship is indicated by the *79 below left* *kalmush*, the symbol of his sovereignty, and by his skull-cap. The king's name is not given in hieroglyphics, but in the picture writing on the right, level with his face, he is called the Sun-God of the heaven, so we presume the figure to be the personification of the Sun-God in the Great King, perhaps with the object of stressing the idea of divine kingship.

On the north wall to the extreme left stands a god on two blunt peaks. The ear of *76 below* wheat above his left hand defines him as a god of vegetation.

Unfortunately the goddesses on the west wall of the main chamber depicted as a row of identical figures have yet to be identified.

The place of honour in the main chamber is taken up by the relief of the king on the *XIX, 78* east wall. It is the largest relief in this gallery and measures 2.95 metres, that is, one third more than the main scene which stands 2.18 metres high. The king faces this main scene at an angle. We assume that Tudhaliya had his portrait placed in the large chamber while it was being completed. He is represented armed, in conformity with the usual conception of a Hittite Great King. He wears a skull cap. The *kalmush*, the sign of sovereignty, is at his side. At the same time the blunt peaks on which he stands characterize him as a god. He seems to have allowed himself to be venerated as the representative of the divinity during his lifetime.

The large relief of Tudhaliya IV is one of the most superb Hittite sculptures. The details are carried out with the greatest care. The composition is graceful and harmonious. The Great King had handsome features and a straight nose. The raised position of the relief on the rock wall, with the figure poised on mountain ranges, the fluid draperies and the royal staff combine to create an impression of his floating in the atmosphere and dominating the earth.

The whole arrangement of the reliefs in the main chamber, where the two processions converge towards the north wall, not unlike the Parthenon frieze, is informed by the artistic vigour of the Hittites.

When discussing Hittite religion and architecture we have pointed out that the main
74 chamber of Yazilikaya was the holy of holies of the temple whose foundations can be seen near the entrance to the shrine. Religious rites performed in the temples of the capital in a closed room, before the statue of the god, took place here under the open sky, in front of the reliefs which can be regarded as a simplified version of the Hittite pantheon.

As we have tried to show, the side chamber was destined for the royal worship. Formerly
80–87 the statue of Great King Tudhaliya, whose pedestal can still be seen, stood on the north side of the side chamber. The cartouche of the king with the mountain-god facing north is turned towards the statue. The other reliefs of the chamber also face north, in the direction of the statue.

The side chamber, as the place of royal worship, will have been completed under
Fig. 17 Great King Tudhaliya IV, when he erected and completed buildings C and D within a short time of each other. Whoever stepped into the side chamber through the southern entrance which is no longer accessible, saw the statue of the ruler placed in a dominant position in front of the north wall.

86–87 The relief of the twelve gods in the side chamber is the best preserved. It is covered in a yellowish patina, like the two attendants Ninatta and Kulitta of the outer chamber. The twelve gods are an important find for the history of art. The Hittite sculptor has made a bold and successful attempt to portray a row of human figures with overlapping limbs marching in succession.

83 The significance of the sword-god who, on account of his horns and peaked cap must be considered a high ranking deity, is ambiguous. It is true that the relief is a transposition of a motif occurring in minor sculpture into monumental proportions, but in the concept of this sword-god we must look for some profound religious significance.

85 The scene in which the god Sarruma holds king Tudhaliya in his embrace is one of the most important reliefs of the side chamber. As transpires from the testament of Hattusili I, the embrace is a gesture indicating honour and protection.

The relief of the god Sarruma and Tudhaliya is another great work of Hittite art. Here too we may admire the accomplished mastery of calligraphic lines which was the strong point of Hittite sculpture. But the scene in which the god embraces the king

XXI Shrine at a spring by Eflatun Pinar near Beyshehir

afforded the artist greater scope to prove his skill than could a single figure. The pyramidal composition is most successful. The sculpture rests on a rhythmic horizontal line achieved by the alignment of up-turned shoes. The steeply rising sweep of the garments and the ruler's staff merge in the rounded forms of the bodies of the king and god. The vertical pointed cap of the god with its superimposed horns and divine ideograms opposes the horizontal rhythm of the up-turned shoes, and with its fine proportions provides a graceful finish to the entire composition.

87   The apotropaic lion-demons who guard the entrance to the side chamber on the west wall are derived from Hurrian symbolism. The way in which their wings are represented is not Hittite, although iconographic and stylistic details are the same as on the other lion sculptures of Yazilikaya, Boghazköy and Alaca Hüyük.

In conclusion a few words are necessary concerning the period of the reliefs. E. Laroche has made it clear that the two divine processions of Yazilikaya correspond to male and female deities enumerated in Hurrian sacrificial lists from Boghazköy. He was able to prove his thesis by considering the Hurrian reading of phonetically written hieroglyphic names. He is of the opinion that Hittite religion submitted to Hurrian influence during the reign of Hattusili III and his spouse, queen Puduhepa.

In connexion with his investigations we might say that the relief in the main chamber, with the exception of that of Great King Tudhaliya, may have been completed under the reign of Hattusili and Puduhepa. It must have been during that period that the two chambers of the sanctuary were isolated from the outside world. As was shown earlier, Great Queen Puduhepa, allied to the Hurrian Hepat through her name, may have played a considerable part in this religious reform.

Tudhaliya IV, who shared the first years of his reign with his illustrious mother, might have built temples in front of the shrine of Yazilikaya, and planned the reliefs in the side chamber and his own portrait in the main chamber. As we have said earlier, he should
Fig. 17   have completed the projecting structure D at the same period.

GLYPTIC ART

During the Hittite Empire stamp seals only were in use. The subordinate kings of Carchemish and the Princes ruling over the south-eastern vassal states of the Hittite Empire were the only ones to use cylinder seals in their commercial dealings with Syrian vassals. Some handsome examples with original Hittite designs are preserved in private collections. One seal forms part of the Pierpont Morgan Library. The finest cylinder seals of the kings Ini-Teshup and Talmi-Teshup of Carchemish originate from Ras Shamra. These, as we have said, are in pure Hittite style.

45
Fig. 1   We have already discussed the Muwatalli seal and have compared the embrace of the king depicted there with that on the Tudhaliya seal from Ras Shamra and the Tudhaliya
52 above   relief in the side chamber of Yazilikaya. A gold signet ring from Konya shows scenes

122

closely related to those of Yazilikaya. The figure standing on a double-headed hybrid *79 below*
mythical beast is the goddess Shaushga at Yazilikaya. The lions with raised tails and
jaws agape recall the lions there. Sedat Alp translates the antithetically spelt name, lion
plus volute, GAL: UR.MAH.

The fine seal from Tarsus with five stamping surfaces is incised with ritual scenes *52*
whose figures are of the same style as the carvings from Central Anatolia. The altar here
closely resembles that on a relief from Alaca. The hieroglyphs are the same as on the
sculptures of the Anatolian high plateau. The bird-demon offering a libation before an
altar may be one of the motifs which we find only in the art of the Empire. The elegant
gold signet ring from Alaca Hüyük adorned with a plaited band belonged to a rich *45 below*
Hittite of the Empire. Sedat Alp has deciphered his name as La-La-Lu.

POTTERY

Monochrome pottery of the early and the old Hittite period continued to be used during
the Empire, but compared with other branches of art of this period it played a subordinate
role. The perfection of a polychrome style is noticeable in a few examples. A very handsome vessel in relief from Bitik is a specimen of this category of courtly artifact. On the *XIV*
existing large fragment we see men bearing offerings, musicians, and an interesting
scene: two figures face each other on low stools. The male figure on the left unveils his
partner, and with his other hand offers her a drinking cup which she receives with her
left hand. It may be a wedding scene and the oldest example of a 'sacred marriage'.
Although the iconographic and stylistic details are entirely Hittite, oriental influence is
undeniable in the frieze of men offering gifts. This precious object is dated from about
1400 BC.

A vessel shaped like a double-headed duck from Boghazköy can be dated according *48, 49*
to its layer as belonging to the fifteenth century BC.

V

THE LATE HITTITE PERIOD

1200–700 BC

After the collapse of the Empire, Hittite civilization did not survive in Asia Minor. In almost every Hittite site of the second millennium BC so far excavated, the Hittite cultural strata cease with a layer of conflagrations. It is, however, significant that the succeeding Phrygian culture showed no signs that might connect it in any way with the foregoing Hittite civilization. None of the present day city names of Central Anatolia, like Gordion, Ankara, Yozgat, Corum, Tokat, Boghazköy, Kirshehir and so on can be traced back to a Hittite source, as is the case with the centres south of the bend of the Halys river and the cities of South Anatolia, Nigde, Adana, Malatya, Marash, Carchemish, and so on. It is hardly accidental that precisely those cities which were focal points of Hittite culture bear no Hittite names, and is perhaps due to the fact that Hittite tradition could not survive there for various reasons. Especially the almost total ignorance of the Greeks concerning the Hittites shows the cessation of Hittite tradition. It is significant that Herodotus believed the armour of the typically Hittite figures of Karabel to be Egyptian and Ethiopian, and mistook the Hittite hieroglyphs there for sacred Egyptian writing.

It is true that in the Odyssey a race called Ketaioi are mentioned once, but this is generally connected with a people associated with the river Keteios or Kaiteios in Mysia. Whether this name is, as some scholars now believe, to be identified with the Hittites we cannot decide. But should these people be the Hittites it would not mean much, as their casual mention in the Odyssey tells us nothing.

Furthermore it is striking that up to date not only no Phrygian, but no cultural remains of any sort have been found which might belong to the period between 1200 and 800 BC. This could indicate that Central Anatolia at that period was either very thinly populated or occupied by nomad tribes who left no material remains in the dwelling mounds. The results of Thracian invasion must have been altogether catastrophic if no urban settlements could be formed until the emergence of the Phrygian state about 750 BC. Only

102

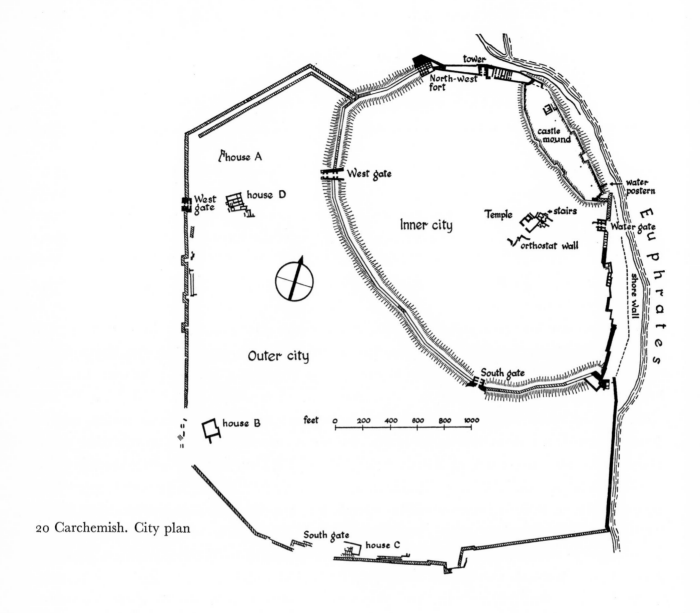

20 Carchemish. City plan

the southern centres of Hittite civilization, which had flourished as Hittite vassal states since the second millennium BC, could carry on their existence. Although Henri Frankfort has asserted that in Syria too a dark period followed between 1200 and 850 BC, W. F. Albright convincingly explained soon afterwards that historical tradition suffered no break in Syria. It is undeniable that in north Syrian and south Anatolian cities brief dark periods can be noted, but Albright is right in saying that the southern states on the whole show an uninterrupted historical tradition. A stratum absent in one town will be found in another, so that one cannot really speak of a break of tradition in these parts. Malatya and Carchemish are the sites best able to show us that the various phases of the period between 1200 and 800 BC existed in uninterrupted succession in this region. The

Fig. 20 site of Carchemish, which played a paramount role in the first millennium, appears to be most promising in this respect. The main historical events are recorded in the strata of this site. It should be noted that Carchemish is mentioned in the inscription of Rameses III as a city destroyed by 'Peoples from the Sea', and that the layer of conflagration left by this catastrophe gives us a precious starting point for determining the cultural strata. We are convinced that the new Italian excavations in Malatya will yield valuable contributions to this question.

Our study of the works of art from the Empire has shown us that the style of the realm prevailed in all parts of the Hittite Kingdom and was unrivalled in Hittite vassal states. The culture of Carchemish was almost a dependency of Anatolian Hittite art. The works of art from north Syrian and south Anatolian centres of civilization show that in the second millennium BC the style of Mitanni and the Syro-Hittites prevailed. We shall see presently that late Hittite art of the first millennium absorbed Assyrian and Aramean influences as well.

The term 'late Hittite art' therefore needs some explaining and justification, the more so as we now know that the inhabitants of the north Syrian and south Anatolian small states were proved by their idioms to have been Luvians. We have pointed out the influences of Mitanni, Syro-Hittite, Assyrian and Aramaean elements in late Hittite sculpture, but have none the less classified this art as a continuation of Anatolian Hittite tradition because its basic elements are Hittite. If one considers moreover that these small states continued to use the picture writing of the Empire and derived their religious cult and symbols and the names of their gods and kings (Lubarna-Labarna, Qataziliu Hattusili, Mutalli-Muwatalli) from the tradition of Hattusas, and that from the time of Tiglathpilesar I, they were called the Hatti (Hittites) by their Assyrian enemies, one must admit that the designation of 'late Hittite' is entirely justified. Recently H. G. Güterbock has devoted himself to this question, and, we believe, has given it an excellent definition. He says: 'The term "Hittite" applies to south Anatolian and Syro-Hittite small states of the late period, but this name does not merely define a new period; it also describes something altogether different from the Hittite Empire.' We believe that in the following stylistic analysis of late Hittite works of art we have confirmed this formulation.

The south Anatolian and north Syrian principalities existed in part even before the collapse of the Empire. Thus Carchemish, as we have seen, was an important kingdom in the second millennium BC. But the majority of northern Syro-Hittite small states seem to have come into existence after the downfall of the Empire. The art of these principalities is not unified. It varies from place to place and shows three distinct styles: the traditional style, the style with Assyrian influence, and that with Aramaean influence.

THE TRADITIONAL STYLE
1050–850 BC

This style perpetuates the Hittite art which flowered during the second millennium in Anatolia and north Syria. Examples of the traditional style are found mainly among the sculptures of Malatya and Carchemish.

104, 105
above

The iconographic elements of the traditional style go back chiefly to models of the Empire. Here too, as in the sculptures of Hattusas, male figures wear the wedge-shaped beard and smooth upper lip, the long plait reaching to the elbow and curled at the tip, the short tunic with a centre pleat and the curved seam above the knees, and up-tilted boots. On the monuments of the late Hittite period the god is still known by his peaked cap. The gods on the reliefs of Malatya wear the same headgear as the gods of Yazilikaya. Their caps are adorned with the divine symbols which do not occur elsewhere, save at Yazilikaya. The sword worn by the gods of the traditional style has a crescent pommel and a slightly curved blade. The sceptre and the mace are held against the shoulder. At Carchemish and Malatya, as in Yazilikaya and Alaca Hüyük, the sceptre and the mace are shouldered. Some goddesses of Malatya wear the dress with flowing pleats of the goddesses of Yazilikaya and Alaca Hüyük. The royal image with the winged sun and the *kalmush* is identical with models from the Empire. The type of lion of that epoch persists in the traditional style.

108–116

104

This style, however, contains a great number of iconographic details that are alien to Anatolian Hittite art. The tassel at the upper tip of the horned cap, fewer horns, the absence of ear pendants and the uplifted position of the arms are details which distinguish the traditional style from that of the previous epoch. The way in which the god grasps an object is non-Hittite. On the reliefs of the Empire the gods never carry an object in their outstretched hand but they close their fist. It is therefore entirely non-Hittite for the Weather-God to clutch a sheaf of thunderbolts, although it occurs in his ideogram. All these details, which are missing from the carvings of the Empire, go back to models of Mitannian and Syro-Hittite art of the second millennium. The hybrid beings of the traditional style are, as we have said in an earlier work with reference to Anton Moortgat, figurative concepts taken from the same Mitannian and Syro-Hittite cultural sphere. These heterogeneous elements of the traditional style show that most sculptures of the late Hittite period are a mixture based on three different traditions, the strongest being the Anatolian Hittite.

111–113

Lion sculptures are the link between Hittite and late Hittite art. Thus the lions of Sam'al (Zincirli), where there is least of the Hittite character, are, to begin with, purely Hittite. The older gate lions and those on the orthostat reliefs of Sam'al are Anatolian Hittite, like the lion sculptures of Carchemish; with their round, massive ears, gaping

109
XVII jaws, hanging tongues, and noses wrinkled at their lower edges they are faithful copies of the gate lions of Hattusas.

110 The small pillar lions and the lion's head of a double-headed sphinx, both from Carchemish, on the other hand, resemble the type of lion with heart-shaped, stylized, flat ears and thick folds round the neck, from Alaca Hüyük.

90, 91, 103 At first sight the gate lions of Malatya give the impression of being less like their Anatolian models than the lions of Carchemish. The wrinkled nose, the hanging tongue, the fold of the neck, however, are Hittite, and so are the position of the legs, the paws and the tail. Only the incised brows form an exception.

104, 105
above The handsome reliefs on the orthostats from Malatya which formerly adorned the face of the city walls close to the main gate, represent the king performing a religious rite, a motif found in the art of the great period. On two reliefs the king named Sulumeli appears twice as a prince, and once, on the third relief, as a king. On the former, where he is represented merely as a prince, only his name is given, without titles. The two lower signs 'li' and 'mi' or 'ma' we know from the names of Mursili and Suppiluliuma. The upper sign can be deduced from the name Sulumeli found in cuneiform texts. In these scenes the king offers a libation to the Moon-God, the Sun-God, and a protective deity. On the other reliefs the same name is rendered by antithetic royal signs. The most beautiful relief is the one on which Sulumeli offers a libation to four gods. The first is the Weather-God followed by his spouse and their divine child. To the far left is a sacrificial animal, a bull led by an acolyte.

105 On the large relief two scenes are represented in succession. The Weather-God is seen to the left riding in his chariot drawn by a pair of bulls. To the right he has descended from his chariot and receives a libation from the hands of king Sulumeli. In his right hand he holds a boomerang and in his left a thunderbolt. Two hieroglyphs placed behind him, level with the divine ideogram above the Weather-God, confirm his nature. The horns and divine ideograms on his cap are rendered schematically. These are most distinctly seen on the relief of figures with the dragon Illuyanka, where the monster is slain by the Weather-God in the presence of his son. The ball-shaped protuberances on this relief may be the hail sent by the Weather-God on to his adversary.

110, 114 The best preserved reliefs in the traditional style came from Carchemish. The faces of the double-headed male sphinx and the women in the procession are almost intact. Their hooked noses indicate a Luvian or Hittite ethnic type. The goddess identified as
115 Kubaba by her horn and the pomegranate shows the same physiognomy.

108 Other examples of the traditional style from Carchemish are the pedestal with twin
111–113 bulls and the relief with bird daemons, bull daemons, and the 'Gilgamesh'. They show the same iconographic and stylistic details as the other carvings.

XXII Rock relief of Kemal Pasha (Karabel) east of Izmir. Great King Tudhaliya
and his hieroglyph

Unfortunately we cannot fix dates for determining the time of the traditional style with any certainty. According to the date of destruction of the Hittite Empire the upper time margin of late Hittite art must be placed about 1200 BC. But since the art of the small states does not seem to have undergone a change in style, we are not in a position to determine the characteristics which distinguish the two periods. Add to this the fact that none of the sculptures that have come down to us belong to the beginning of the late Hittite period. Not even the oldest late Hittite sculptures from Malatya can be dated as early as one might assume at first glance. We may say that in Arslantepe, where the sculptures of Malatya were found, no layers of the second millennium with Hittite ceramics have been observed, while a dwelling mound close by contains characteristic Hittite monochrome pottery. These circumstances make it clear that the reliefs of Malatya do not originate from the Empire, but it is hard to say how soon after 1200 BC they were made. The close stylistic affinity of the gate sculptures suggests an early date. In a special study we have placed the upper time margin of these works of art in the middle of the eleventh century BC. The lower time margin of the traditional art is indicated by the emergence of a style with Assyrian influence beginning about 850 BC. We shall speak of this in the following section.

104, 105 above

THE ASSYRIAN STYLE

Assyrian influence in late Hittite art did not infiltrate uniformly everywhere. We can observe this process earlier in some localities than in others. One might speak of strong and slight Assyrian tendencies in various places. The degree of Assyrian influence, however, offers a safe starting point for chronology only within the same place, but not within workshops of different principalities with disparate political orientation. More important still is the fact that during this period Assyrian influence penetrated in some cases indirectly, through the intervention of the Aramean peoples.

On the whole a slight and a strong Assyrian phase can be noted. The first may date from about 850–745 BC, and the second from about 745–700 BC.

THE FIRST PHASE 850–745 BC

In the first Assyrian phase isolated Assyrian motifs only appear, while most elements of the traditional style persist and several late Hittite characteristics are added.

117, 118
124, 126

The chief characteristic of this phase is the emergence of a new specifically late Hittite hair fashion. The hair is arranged in concentric curls caught in a tuft at the nape of the neck. Each curl consists of a strand of hair whose ends are rolled to form a ringlet. It was widely diffused and worn, and occurs for instance on the gold helmet of Mes-kalam-dug of Ur, but also on the head of the Apollo on the west pediment of the temple of Zeus at

Olympia. Now since in the first half of the first millennium BC this curl is nowhere to be found in the Near East outside the Syro-Hittite domains, it could be used to classify the styles of late Hittite art. This lock of hair occurs on all male heads of the late Hittite style with Assyrian influence. It remains the dominant fashion until the middle of the eighth century BC, and in the second half of this century is replaced by the Assyrian-Aramaean ringlet. The tuft of hair worn by the men which we have mentioned may be derived from Assyrian art of the ninth and eighth centuries. The concentric arrangement of curls is a fashion of late Hittite workshops. Since it was invariably used in Hittite sculptures characterized by many other Assyrian motifs it is of particular importance for the chronological dating of late Hittite art. *125, 134*
138–140

The new hair fashion can be observed chiefly in Sam'al where it might have been introduced in the first place. It is found also in Carchemish, on reliefs of the traditional style, and is absent only from the gate sculptures of Malatya. The wounded lion of Malatya, on the other hand, represented in a characteristically Assyrian motif of an attacking lion, has a fashionably stylized mane. *126, 127*

104, 105 below

As for the rest, this phase is distinguished by Assyrian fashion. War chariots are the chief motif borrowed by late Hittite workshops from Assyrian art. Assyrian stags and lions also appear. More important still are Assyrian fashions in dress. The long tunic tied with a sash that ends in a tassel is an Assyrian fashion. The replacement of the Hittite sword with a crescent shaped pommel and curved scabbard by the new long sword, sometimes with a long tassel, is a further sign of Assyrian influence. As another result of this influence up-turned shoes went out of fashion. Hybrid beings still wear them, but the gods are shod with sandals. *105, below*

127, 128

The ninth century was the high period of Assyrian dominance and civilization. King Assurnasirpal III (883–859 BC) consolidated his realm from within. To Shalmanesar III (854–824 BC), the 'King of the Four Cardinal Points', Assyria owes its greatest development. Only during that period did Assyria exercise a far reaching influence on its neighbours; it must have affected late Hittite art in the middle of the ninth century BC. During the waning period of Assyrian power, lasting from 824 to 745 BC, late Hittite art did not feel Assyrian influence, but a new and stronger impetus, as we shall presently see, is to be observed under the reign of Tiglathpilesar III (745–727 BC). *126*

In this connexion let us examine the best example of the first Assyrian phase in late Hittite art. From Malatya we know the above-mentioned relief of a lion hunt, and those with genii and other demons. The lion and chariot carvings of the first derive from Assyrian models. The genius wears a New-Babylonian feather crown and has Assyrian wings. The attributes he carries are taken from Assyrian art. *105 below*

The style of the first Assyrian phase occurs in a series of sculptures from Carchemish, side by side with late Hittite characteristics. The plaques with reliefs of war chariots and with the inscriptions of victory are, as transpires from the lock of hair, executed in the new *124*
117, Fig. 21

21 Orthostat relief with seal inscription from Carchemish (*v*. detail of plate 117)

109   style. The fact that the seated figure of Carchemish does not wear a horned cap or other Hittite attributes and is shod with sandals, characterizes him as an Assyrian god. That he is shown bare-headed and in a seated position are traits that go back to foreign models. The lions, on the other hand, are, as we saw, traditional.

Figs. 22–25   On the orthostats of Sam'al the lions only are rendered in the traditional style, while the human figures betray the influence of the new style. The hair is either stylized in the shape of bundle curls, or, in rare cases, is treated in the Assyrian mode. Assyrian belts and sandals appear. The loops of hair on various orthostats are Assyrian. The god

126–127   with the Hittite lock of hair standing on two lions is a typical example of this stage. He has a long sword attached to his side which is adorned with a trailing tassel. In his right hand he once held a staff, like king Katuwas. Only the lower section is preserved. The god follows the new fashion in wearing sandals and no headgear, but his lions, in spite of their Assyrian manes, are in the traditional Hittite style, like those of Carchemish and Malatya.

116   The relief with the Moon- and the Sun-God also shows a mixture of styles. The curled strands of hair and beard and the stylization of the lions' manes are marks of the new style, while all the other details of the figure are traditional.

117, Fig. 21   An inscription with severed heads and hands, apart from the curled beards and hair, indicates Assyrian influence by the very inhumanity of the subject.

181   The relief of king Katuwas from Carchemish, with its concentrically arranged curls, the small tuft of hair at the nape of the neck and the long sword, is a copy of the type of

132

seated god from Carchemish. The figure of the king who raises one hand to his mouth is the first letter of the hieroglyphic inscription and signifies 'I am'.

The orthostat with war chariots from Carchemish, with the exception of the hair   *124*
fashion of the figures, is a faithful copy of Assyrian models.

A basalt relief from Sam'al shows a god in the traditional style with the peaked cap, long plait, thunderbolt, up-tilted boots and short tunic, while the curls of the head,   *128*
long sword and anklet on his right leg are characteristic of the early Assyrian style.

THE SECOND PHASE 745–700 BC

When the Assyrians achieved new eminence under Tiglathpilesar III (745–727 BC), his   *106, 107,*
successor Sargon (721–705 BC) and Sennacherib (704–681 BC), late Hittite workshops   *119–123,*
once more submitted to the influence of Assyrian art, which this time had a stronger   *125, 132,*
and more intensive impact. The most essential change of style was marked by the dis-   *135–137*
appearance of the bundle curl in favour of the spiral ringlet of Assyria. The concentric arrangement of curls of the early style with Assyrian influence was maintained, so that from this peculiarity we are able to determine the time and provenance of late Hittite works of art. Further Assyrian elements are to be observed in dress; the new cloak, the   *107*
handsome belt, and the fine long sword. Remarkable is the new Sargonid stylization   *109, 121*
of the arm muscles on the reliefs of Araras and Kamanas which offers a safe point of reference for dating the works. Loose curls on the nape of the neck and the tufts of hair on both figures are Sargonid elements which date them from the end of the eighth century BC. The vertical folds which adorn the back of the cloaks on the Araras reliefs are of the same date, since such folds are seen on Babylonian carvings of the late eighth century.

In spite of these Assyrian stylistic elements the reliefs of Araras retain a certain Hittite character. The concentric arrangement of curls and the postures of the arms are still Hittite. King Araras embraces his eldest son Kamanas precisely as the god Sarruma   *121*
enfolds king Tudhaliya at Yazilikaya. It is a Hittite custom for the king to introduce   *85*
his successor to the dignitaries and nobles of his realm, as happens on this relief. The   *119*
remaining reliefs portray the members of the royal family, the young Princes and the   *122, 123*
Queen. The youngest child is in the mother's arms. The children are playing with dice and a top. In the time of king Araras plaques bearing old-fashioned reliefs were re-used; the sculptors smoothed the surfaces and carved reliefs of the new royal family. On the lower ledge of the plaque with the children, for instance, remains of a bearded figure can be seen, and the lower ledges of the other plaques also bear remains of older reliefs.   *121–123*

The royal colossus from Malatya is nothing but a local imitation of Assyrian models.   *106–107*
The arrangement of the wavy hair, the treatment of the beard and the tuft of hair in the nape of the neck are Assyrian. The king is bareheaded. His cloak with diagonal folds and the elegant, dainty sandals are faithful copies of Assyrian fashions.

A pair of sphinxes from Sam'al, used as a base for pillars, are fine sculptures in the   *125*
late style with Assyrian influence. The locks and the tuft of hair in the nape of the neck

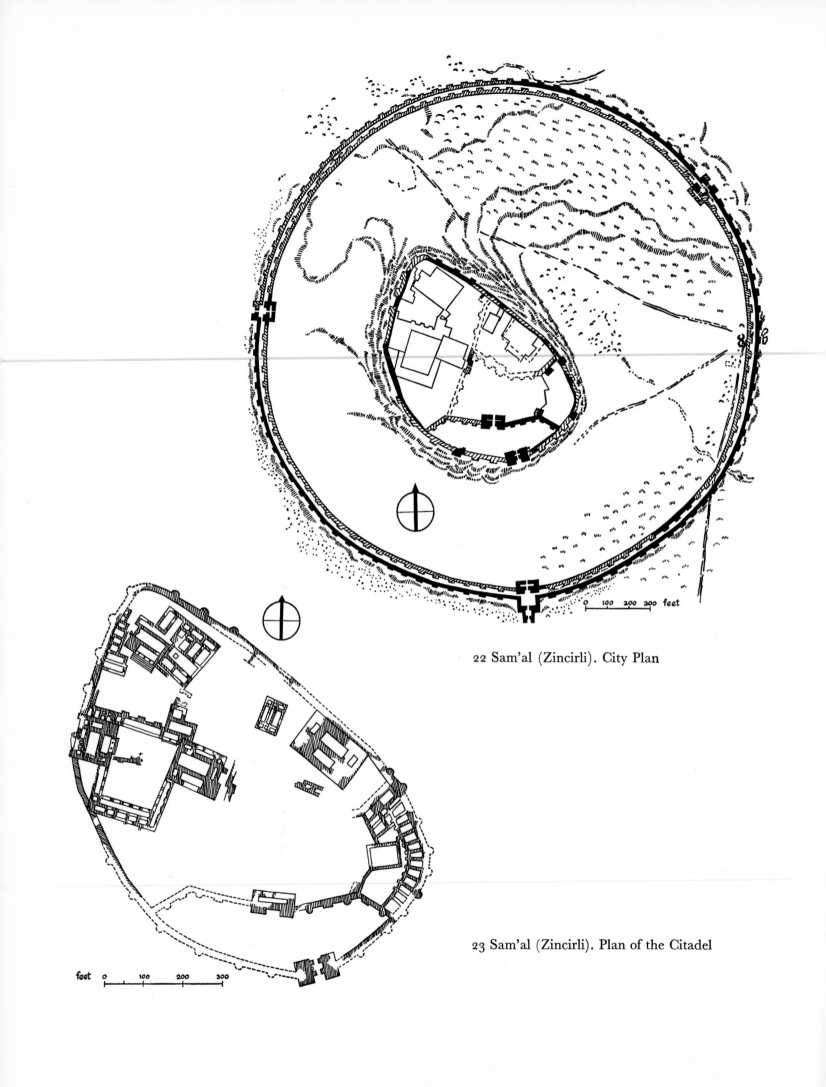

22 Sam'al (Zincirli). City Plan

23 Sam'al (Zincirli). Plan of the Citadel

feet 0   100   200   300

24 Sam'al (Zincirli).
City Gate from the north-east

25 Sam'al (Zincirli). Southern Gate
(reconstruction)

are treated in the Sargonid style. The gate lions of Sam'al and Sakçagözü reproduced *132*
here are handsome examples of the Assyro-Hittite type of lion. They lack the most im- *135*
portant characteristic of Hittite lions, i.e. the hanging tongue, the wrinkles on the lower
ridge of the nose and the heart-shaped, stylized ears. Typical of this kind of lion with a
strong Assyrian influence are the double and triple lobes of the ear, the wrinkled centre
part of the nose, and the folds beneath the eyes in palmette form. Typically Assyrian is the
naturalistic rendering of the bodies which in the Hittite lions are also square. The triple
knobs on the lower joints of the legs are characteristic of the workshops of Sam'al and
Sakçagözü.

The twin lions of Göllüdag with bold profiles are further examples of markedly Assyrian *136*
lion sculptures. It is significant that they have no cheekbones, as is the case with Assyrian
lions. The shape of the body and slender proportions are unmistakably Assyrian. But two
characteristics of these sculptures from South Anatolia, the spiral paws and the tail
hidden between the legs, betray a certain affinity with late Hittite art.

A lion relief from the outskirts of Ankara represents the last stage of Assyrian infiltration. *137 above*

Here even the popular rendering of the lion's tail in Hittite art has been ousted by that seen on Assyrian reliefs. The remaining reliefs from Ankara, especially that of a griffin, indicate that these sculptures belong to late Hittite art with strong Assyrian influence.

137 below The lion and bull reliefs from Ankara and others found on this site must have been made for a Phrygian prince about 700 BC.

ARAMAEAN ART

If we examine the works of art at Sam'al and their various inscriptions, we can see that all develop stylistic marks which exist neither in Assyrian nor in Hittite art. Thus

129–131 the figures of Sam'al wear a sort of turban headgear which at first sight looks Assyrian, but which in shape and arrangement is an unique modification of the Assyrian tiara. Characteristic of this art is the ringlet adopted from Assyria, but developed in such a way that the Assyrians of the time of Sargon took it for their new style. The curl by the ear seems to be another Aramaean invention. Folds too are never absent from Aramaean reliefs. It may be that these were inspired by Hittite, Babylonian and Assyrian models, but it is important that these folds existed on Aramaean sculptures, or on late Hittite ones that have been strongly influenced by them.

We should not ignore the secular outlook of the Aramaeans as reflected in their art, as we believe that it had repercussions on late Hittite art.

The erection of stelae with reliefs depicting a funerary meal are a specifically Aramaean feature of late Hittite art.

130, 138, 139 From the study of the sculptures from Sam'al it transpires that since the middle of the ninth century at least, a decidedly Aramaean courtly art existed side by side with that traditional folk art of the small states. We know that in Sam'al two different ethnic elements lived side by side. Kilamuwa boasts of having stopped 'the feuds between the Mushkabim and the Ba'ririm'. We think that these two ethnic groups can be distinguished by their art. The Aramaeans were the ruling class; their courtly art is elegant and graceful. The Luvians, who followed Hittite tradition and represented the autochthonous population, were their subjects, but were allowed to preserve their own rugged, archaic art. In order to show the people that the indigenous customs were being respected, the Semitic ruler adorned the gateways and orthostats by the entrance of the citadel with Hittite sculptures. But in the palaces this old-fashioned art finds no place. Aramaean sculptures were given preference there. The peaceful coexistence of the Mushkabim and Ba'ririm seems to have lasted for some time, for only in the second half of the eighth

132, 134, 135 century BC were the Hittite lions dismantled and replaced by new ones of Assyrian design.

XXIII Rock monument of the Mother of the Gods on Mount Sipylos by Akpunar near Manisa

Having become the uncontested masters of the country, Aramaeans no longer needed to consider the Luvian-Hittite tradition. Hittite culture, which here was never as vigorous as in Carchemish and Malatya, disappeared after the middle of the eighth century BC. The carvings of the Barrekup period are almost wholly free from Hittite tradition, as we saw from the lions in the second Assyrian style. In human figures no Hittite characteristics survive.

129   The oldest Aramaean work of art is the relief of a king from Sam'al. As we can ascertain from Assyrian models, the tuft of hair gathered in the nape of the neck dates the relief from the ninth century BC. The headgear and the spiral curls are, as mentioned, Aramaean. The dress too, in spite of a strong affinity with Assyrian fashion, strikes an Aramaean note. The foremost figure may be king Kilamuwa whose name we know from inscriptions. The figure behind him is dressed in the same way. In its left hand it holds a pouch the size of a fist, and in its right, blossom, evidently a royal emblem. It may be the king's son. Both figures have strongly Semitic features with hooked noses. The shaven upper lip of the king could be taken as an indication of Hittite fashion to which, in the beginning, Aramaean kings adhered.

   The colossus of Sam'al, now in Berlin, displays the god Hadad as part of an archaic inscription of king Panammu, son of Karal, on the front of his robe. The statue dates from about 790 BC and has a beard of stylized Aramaean ringlets.

131   A remarkable relief from Sam'al represents the Aramaean king Barrekup and his scribe. The brief inscription to the right and left of a lunar symbol names the founder and his deity: 'I, Barrekup, son of Panammu. My God Baal Harran.' Both figures have Semitic noses. The king wears an Aramaean tiara: the hair and beard are arranged in stylized Aramaean ringlets, with the curl beside the ear. The shoulder folds of the cloak, which are a peculiarity of Aramaean sculptors, appear for the first time. The king is seated on a richly carved throne. He raises his right hand to emphasize his words addressed to the scribe: in his left he holds a palmette, perhaps in token of his royal dignity. The scribe, dressed in a simple garment without ornaments, carries what appears to be a roll of papyri tucked under his left arm and his left hand holds a box with ink and brushes. He raises his right fist to salute his king.

130   Another Aramaean work from Sam'al is the funerary stele of a princess with her lady-in-waiting. It has a point at the base which fitted into the pedestal. The custom of placing a stele upon a grave was unknown in Mesopotamia and is specifically Aramaean. If we add up the funerary reliefs of late Hittite Asia Minor known to date, we can see that they are either Aramaean or at least influenced by Aramaean art. On top of the tombstone we see the winged disk with palmette leaves, here, as in Assyria and Egypt, the emblem of royal sovereignty. The princess is seated on a simple throne with knotted cushions, before a table with a funereal meal. A ribbon with trailing ends, sewn with flowers, adorns the brim of her cap. Her skirt is folded, like the cloak of king Barrekup.

Among her jewels let us mention the Phrygian clasp on her breast, which was the great fashion in the third half of the eighth century and about 700 BC. The flowers in her left hand may be another princely emblem. On the richly laid table is a dish with flat loaves and meatballs which are still the favourite food in South-eastern Anatolia. Next to it stands a small dish with a roast fowl and two smaller vessels, perhaps with salt and spice. The female attendant holds a knife in her left hand, and in her right a fly-whisk. Both figures are the same as those on the Aramaean reliefs. The stylistic relationship of the figures with the relief of king Barrekup dates the funerary stele as from the beginning of the eighth century BC. The Phrygian clasp of the princess confirms the date.

The orthostats of Sakçagözü are works of art with Assyrian influence. The hair and *133, 134* beard of the huntsman is dressed in Aramaean ringlets. The relief of the king with genii, a winged disk and a stylized palm tree are Aramaean. The lion sculptures are in the *135* second Assyrian style, while the bird demons continue to be partly Hittite. It is true that *111* the Hittite bird head is combined with that of an Assyrian lion, so that in Sakçagözü during the last part of the eighth century we meet with the first examples of griffin, found after 700 BC in Etruria and Greece.

The funerary stele of a rich lady from Marash combines Aramaean Hittite elements. *138* The seated woman is clothed in the traditional costume of Carchemish. But her son, who *114* carries a clay tablet and a stiletto to show that he could read and write, has Aramaean curls while the loop of hair gathered in the nape of his neck is Hittite, like that of the *138* huntsman from Sakçagözü. We have seen similar long hair on the gate reliefs of Malatya. *133* In the centre, between the figures, stands a table with a funerary meal. *104, 105*

From this period dates a masterpiece of great value; a funerary stele of a wedded pair *139* from Marash. They appear full face, seated side by side. Both have footstools, like the princess from Sam'al. Each lovingly lays his arm round the shoulder of the other. The *130* mournful expression of their faces indicates they are the Dead. The husband's hair and beard are dressed in Aramaean curls. The wife wears the richly adorned, low polos in the traditional style of the Kubaba from Carchemish. The way in which, facing the *115* beholder, the woman is shown on the right and the man on the left, is an ancient Hittite motif occurring in the early historical period, which became a fixed rule under the Empire. The bunch of grapes held by the husband perhaps indicates his profession. He may have been a rich wine merchant. His wife holds a mirror in her left hand, like the high-born Hittite ladies. Her dress is fastened with a Phrygian clasp—the fashion of the day. The cloak, with ends tucked into her belt, reminds us of the costume seen on Ionian sculptures of the sixth century. This work of art, and other reliefs from Marash dating from the beginning of the seventh century BC, may be connected with Ionian civilization through some links of which we are as yet ignorant. Greek funeral art of the archaic period shows a similarity in form and content to the funereal reliefs of Marash.

The large rock relief of Ivriz, unlike Hittite-Aramaean sculpture, is an example of the *XXIV, 140*

Aramaean Hittite style. The cap of the god and the ringlets on both figures are Aramaean. The way in which the horns are attached to the divine cap is non-Hittite. The king is *107* fashionably dressed in a rich garment and an Assyrian cloak familiar from the royal statue of Malatya with Assyrian influence. His headgear is original and occurs again on an ivory figurine of a priest from Ephesus. The profiles of both figures too, with their strongly hooked Semitic noses, indicate the Aramaean character of the reliefs.

A large number of iconographic and stylistic indications, on the other hand, are *93 below* the marks of Hittite influence. The god's gesture of salute is familiar from the art of the Empire. Above all his dress and gesture are almost purely Hittite. The short tunic has the curved seam above the knees found on Hittite reliefs. The position of the hands and arms, apart from the fact that the hand in the background holds an object, are rendered in the manner of the Hittite reliefs. The stylization of the muscles reminds us of the technique of Hittite sculpture under the Empire. It should be noted that both figures, in spite of their Aramaean fashions, continue to wear up-turned shoes. They are no longer as plain as those seen on the original Hittite reliefs, but fashionable and more elaborate. The general character of the sculpture makes it clear that its Aramaean donor erected it for his Luvian-Hittite subjects. The picture writing too, not generally in use among the Aramaeans, who had their own script, is employed here for the benefit of the indigenous population. This script gives the king's name as Warpalawas, known from Assyrian annals as a contemporary of Tiglathpilesar III. The rock relief must therefore date from about 730 BC.

141–150 The interesting sculptures from Karatepe discovered by H. T. Bossert and his colleagues are among the latest examples of the Hittite-Aramaean style, unthinkable without the influence of Aramaean sculpture from Sam'al of the Barrekup period. They are Aramaean works of art which by their choice of subjects, including jugglers, monkeys and palm trees, betray a Phoenician influence not otherwise found in Anatolian sculpture. Phoenician inscriptions used side by side with hieroglyphs indicate the close link between the rulers of Karatepe and the Semitic centres of the south.

The basic character of sculptural representation, however, remains Assyro-Aramaean. The hair of the musicians is stylized in the Assyrian mode, the lock of hair is rendered in Sargonid fashion. The pointed helmets of the warriors resemble Assyrian ones of the eighth and seventh centuries BC. The 'Phrygian cap' with forward tilted peak worn by warriors from Karatepe, has its parallel in Assyrian art of the late eighth or early seventh centuries, though the plume, which reminds us of Greek art, is not found in the Mesopotamian world.

143, 147, 148 The majority of figures, like the above-mentioned carvings, wear Aramaean caps above a Semitic profile. But it is interesting to note that the left half of the banquet

XXIV Rock relief. King Warpalawas paying homage to the god of plenty. Aramaean influence. Second half of the 8th century BC—at Ivriz near Konya

140

142   scene with servants and musicians is in a totally different style from the main scene,
143   where we find the king attending a sumptuous dinner. The musicians, unlike the figures
of the main scene, have straight profiles and rather regular features. Their hair style is,
as we have said, Assyrian. Their dress too is that of the reliefs of Sam'al while that found
in the main scene and other reliefs is quite different. Other variations in style show that
the sculptures of Karatepe must be attributed, as Halet Cambel has pointed out, to
artists of different provenance.

Hittite tradition is almost totally absent in these works of art with a marked foreign
148   influence. Only the way in which a calf is carried over the shoulder is a Hittite motif
found in Sam'al and Carchemish. The sword worn by the man who carries the calf is
similar to those of the first style with Assyrian influence in late Hittite art. Since the
autochthonous population was Luvian-Hittite, the Semitic ruler was obliged to add hieroglyphic inscriptions to Phoenician ones.

The Aramaean characteristics of the sculptures from Karatepe are decisive in con-
142   firming their date to the last part of the eighth century BC. Two vessels with tall handles
carried by servants recall Phrygian vases of the early seventh century. Earlier comparisons
with Assyrian art also point to the seventh century. This date, fixed by us after the
publication of the finds from Karatepe on the grounds of stylistic comparisons, was
confirmed after the descriptions had been deciphered.

141   The fortress of Karatepe, the 'Black Mountain', handsomely situated above the
Ceyhan valley, was the summer seat of king Asitawanda whose name is given on the
inscriptions of the orthostats. We see him in the main banqueting scene, partaking of a
143   festive meal. With his right hand he reaches for a flat loaf in a large dish, while in his
left hand he holds a meatball. Three more meatballs lie on his plate. We saw them on
130   the table of the princess from Sam'al. Two servants with fans chase the flies away. The
cooks and servants on the left of the relief bring more dishes: roast hares, meat, fruit and
drink.

Below the main scene servants lead in an ox and a lamb for the banquet. The musicians
play monotonous but probably rhythmic and compelling tunes. The lyre they use is
very similar to its early Greek form. Terpander of Lesbos, who lived at the beginning
of the seventh century BC, may have fashioned his lyre of seven strings on such oriental
models.

146, 147   The sculptures of Karatepe on the whole are gay and even humoristic. The monkey
underneath the table, the scene of birds of prey and a hare, the performing bear and
the two jesters with monkeys on their shoulders are burlesque scenes which lend a special
interest to this primitive sculpture. Inspired by Mediterranean gaiety they are not ceremonial reliefs of the palace, but rather merry scenes from the king's summer residence.
The mother suckling her child is a different sort of masterpiece. It does not compel
150   admiration on account of an excellent technique or naturalistic rendering of form but it
displays the attractive and powerful expression inherent in a naïve and primitive style.

THE INFLUENCE OF LATE HITTITE ART

Late Hittite art did not produce outstanding creative works. The geographically favourable position of Luvian small principalities on the fringes of the Mediterranean caused late Hittite art with Assyrian and Aramaean influence to reach the countries of the Mediterranean and especially Greece. The fact that in the earliest phase of Greek archaic art not Assyrian, but late Hittite influences were at work, proves that in the eighth century BC the south Anatolian and north Syrian small states played their part in the peaceful encounter of Orient and Occident. Throughout the ninth century Assyria was the foremost great power in the Middle East. Shalmaneser III seems indeed to have been the 'King of the Four Coasts' and during that period late Hittite workshops came under the spell of Assyrian art. But with the close of Shalmaneser's reign the high period of the Assyrian Empire seems to come to an end. No more is heard of the Assyrians until Tiglathpilesar III, and even this great monarch was obviously powerless to prevent the Hittite-Luvian small states, who had acquired new eminence under the Aramaeans, from maintaining their political ascendancy between the Euphrates and the Mediterranean, and thereby keeping control over the shipping trade along the coast.

Into this period falls the initial contact of the Greeks with the East. Towards the end of the eighth century and the beginning of the seventh new motifs suddenly appear in Greek art: lions, griffins and sphinxes whose nearest prototypes are found in the Syro-Anatolian small states. Thus a number of oriental stylistic elements in Greek hair-styles, dress, and ornamentation may have been inspired by Hittite originals of the eighth and seventh centuries. The presence of the Greeks in the north Syrian port of Al Mina in the second half of the eighth century is convincing proof that the Greeks had immediate access to late Hittite art. Their real inspiration, however, lay in the late Hittite exports which found their way into all Greek cities of the period, as today's excavations show. Although by the end of the eighth century BC the small states were absorbed by the Assyrian Empire their artistic output remained unimpaired during the first half of the seventh century. The excavators of Carchemish report that the sculptures there remained untouched during the entire seventh century. G. M. A. Hanfmann has demonstrated that at the time Hittite statuary was still standing. The fact that Corinthian vase painters adopted Hittite motifs until the middle of the seventh century, that is to say, at a time when the North Syro-Anatolian states had ceased to be a political unit, can be explained only if we assume that Hittite workshops were still active at that date.

The geographical position of the small principalities, and the favourable historical conditions in the eighth century enabled the Hittites, Luvians and Aramaeans, who had created a common civilization in peaceful co-ordination, to confront the Greeks as worthy ambassadors of the oriental world.

	WESTERN ANATOLIA	CENTRAL AND EASTERN ANATOLIA	UPPER MESOPOTAMIA	EGYPT	
3500	Hacilar				3500
3000	Chalcolithic	Chalcolithic	Jemdet-Nasr-Period	Earlier Negâde Civilization	3000
				Archaic Period 1st–2nd Dynasty	
			Mesilim-Period		
2500	Troy I	Early Bronze Age	Ur I-Period	Old Kingdom 3rd–6th Dynasty	2500
	Troy II		Dynasty of Akkad		
2000	Troy III–V	Royal Graves of Alaca Hüyük, Horoztepe	3rd Dynasty of Ur	Middle Kingdom 11–12th Dynasty	2000
1900			Old Assyrian Empire		1900
1800		Old Assyrian Trade Settlements. First appearance of the Hittites	Mari-Period		1800
1700				Hyksos Period	1700
1600	Troy VI	Hittite Old Kingdom	Mitanni-Kingdom		1600
1500					1500
1400				New Kingdom 17th–20th Dynasty	1400
1300	Troy VIIa	Great Hittite Empire			1300
1200	Troy VIIb	—Decline—	Nairi–States		1200
1100					1100
1000		Late Hittite States			1000
900	Phrygian Civilization		Aramaeans New Assyrian Empire		900
800					800
700					700

The Ancient Near East. Comparative Table

LIST OF HITTITE KINGS

THE EARLY HITTITE PERIOD

Pithana of Kussara	18th century BC
Anitta of Kussara	18th century BC

THE OLD KINGDOM

Tabarna	c. 1680–1650 BC
Hattusili I	c. 1650–1620 BC
Mursili I	c. 1620–1590 BC
Telepinu	c. 1525–1500 BC

THE EMPIRE

Tudhaliya	1460–1440 BC
Arnuwanda I	1440–1420 BC
Hattusili II	1420–1400 BC
Tudhaliya III	1400–1380 BC
Suppululiuma I	1380–1346 BC
Mursili II	1345–1315 BC
Muwatalli	1315–1282 BC
Mursili III (Urhi-Teshup)	1282–1275 BC
Hattusili III	1275–1250 BC
Tudhaliya IV	1250–1220 BC
Arnuwanda III	1220–1190 BC
Suppululiuma II	c. 1190 BC

THE MONOCHROME PLATES

THE HATTIANS
Early Bronze Age. *c*. 2500–2000 BC

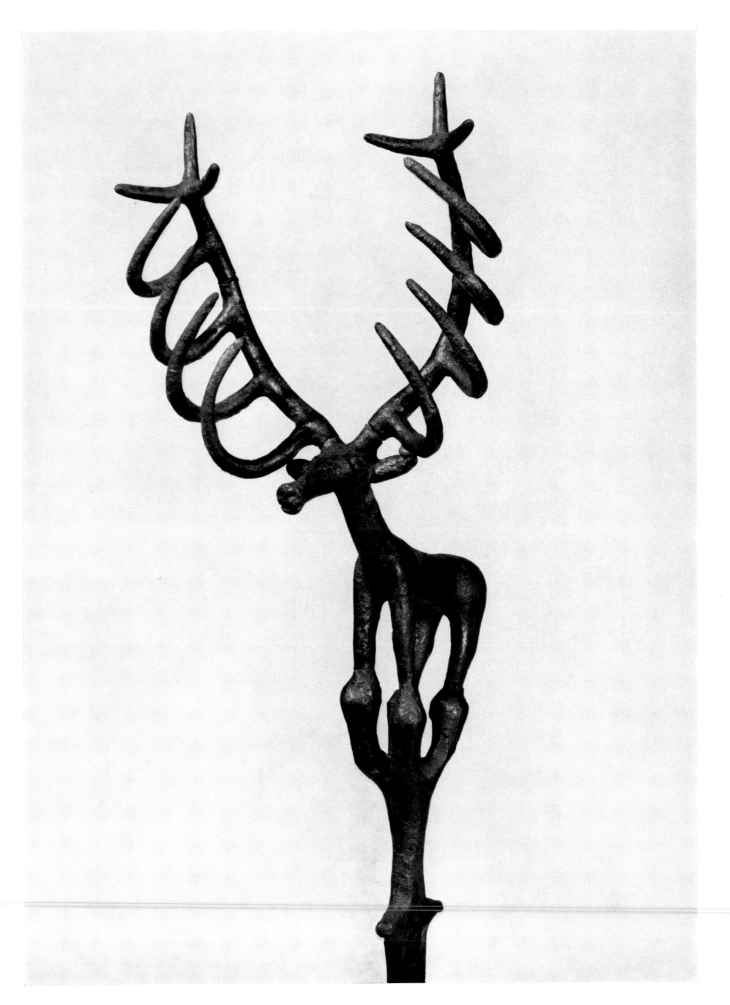

1 Ritual standard of a stag. Bronze. Height 45,5 cm. (18 in.), from Alaca Hüyük – Ankara

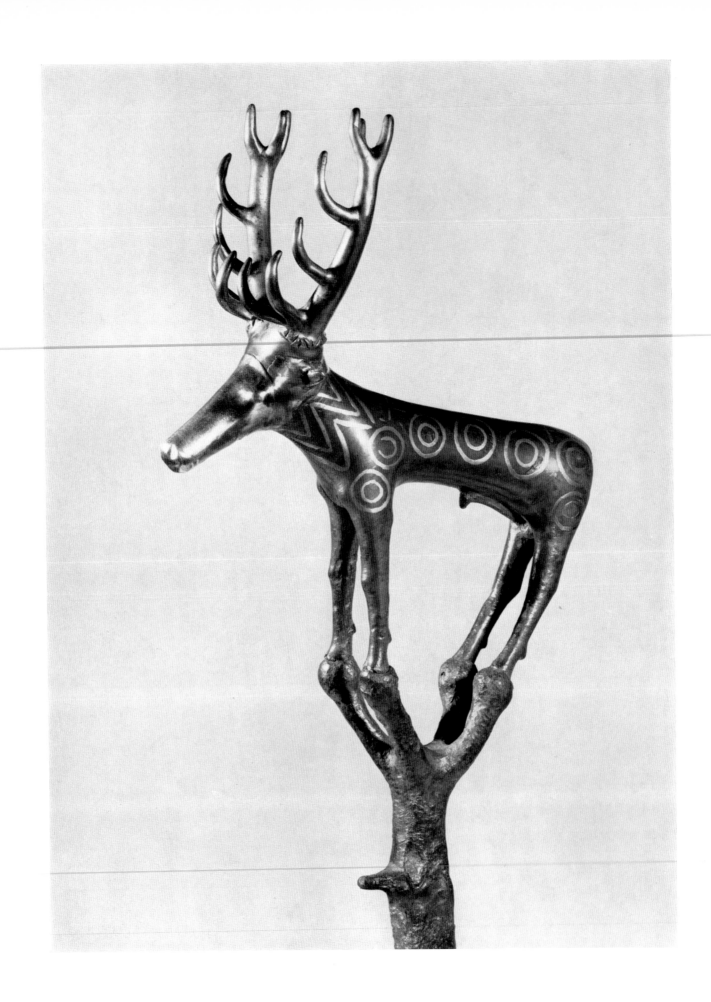

2 Ritual standard of a stag. Bronze inlaid with silver. Height 52 cm. (20½ in.), from Alaca Hüyük – Ankara

3 Ritual standard of a bull. Bronze. Height 41 cm. (16⅛ in.), from Alaca Hüyük – Ankara

4 Ritual standard of a bull. Bronze inlaid with silver. Height 36,5 cm. (14⅜ in.), from Alaca Hüyük – Ankara

5 Ritual standard of a bull. Bronze with dots in electrum. Height 57 cm. (22½ in.), from Alaca Hüyük – Ankara

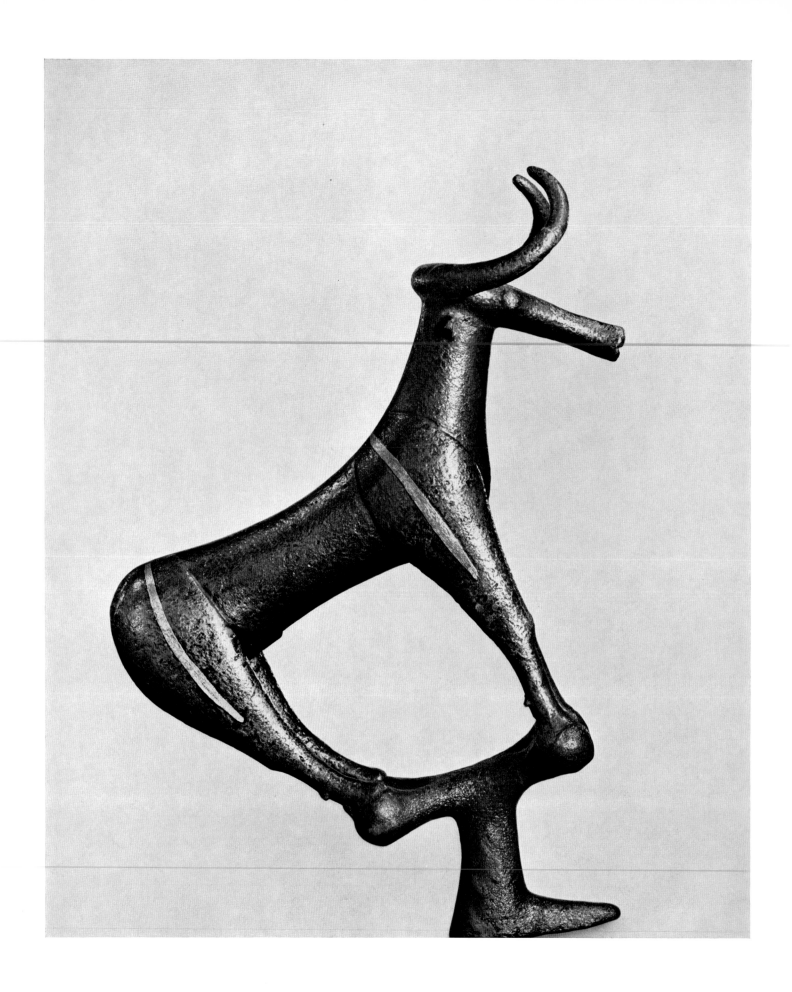

6 Ritual standard of a bull. Bronze with electrum stripes. Height 48 cm. (18⅞ in.), from Alaca Hüyük – Ankara

7 Above: Ritual standard with swastikas. Bronze. Height 34 cm. (13¾ in.). Below: Ritual standard in disk form. Bronze. Height 27,5 cm. (10¾ in.), both from Alaca Hüyuk – Ankara

8 Ritual standard in disk form with blossoms and birds. Bronze. Height 34 cm. (13¾ in.), from Alaca Hüyük –
Ankara

9 Detail of the standard in plate 8

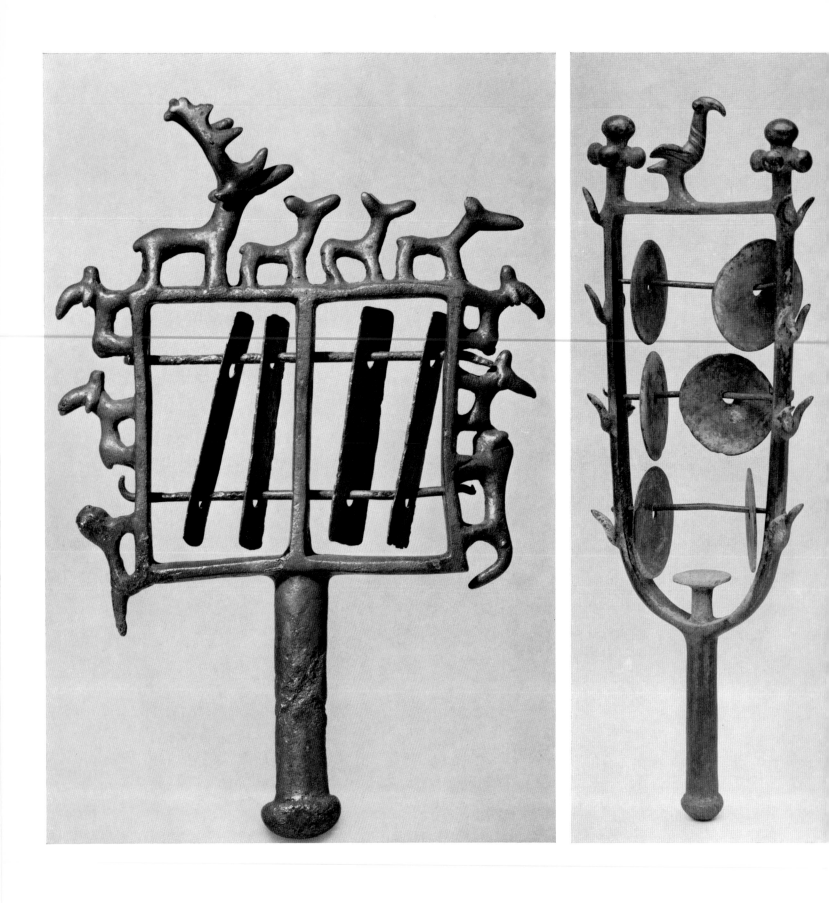

12 Left: Sistrum. Bronze. Height 25,4 cm. (10 in.), from Horoztepe – Ankara
Right: Sistrum. Bronze. From Central Anatolia – New York

13 Vessel. Clay with black slip. Height 23,2 cm. (9⅛ in.), from Alaca Hüyük – Ankara

14 Flagon. Gold. Height 15,3 cm. (6 in.), from Alaca Hüyük – Ankara. Cf. plate V

15 Above: Flagon. Gold. Height 15 cm. (6 in.). Below left: Base of the same gold flagon. Below right: Base of the gold vessel in VI below. Both from Alaca Hüyük – Ankara

16 Jug. Gold. Height 17,7 cm. (7 in.), from Central Anatolia – New York

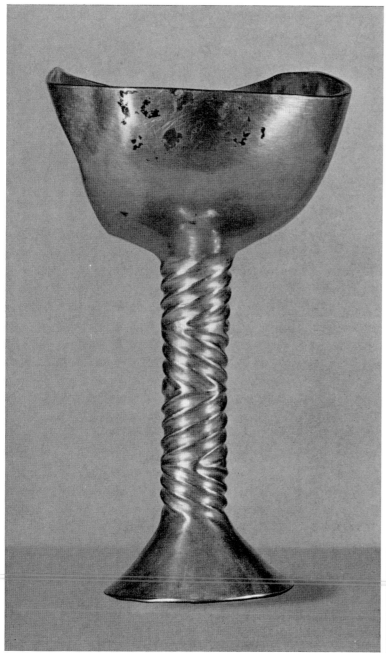

17 Above: Cup. Gold. Diameter 7,8 cm. (3 in.). Below left: Goblet. Gold. Height 12,5 cm. (5¼ in.).
Below right: Goblet. Gold. Height 12,5 cm. (4⅞ in.), all from Alaca Hüyük – Ankara

18 Headband. Gold. Diameter 16,2 cm. (6⅜ in.), from Alaca Hüyük – Ankara

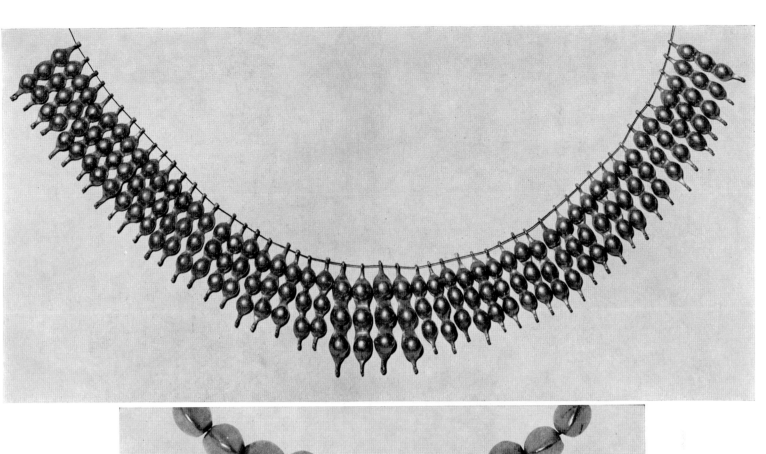

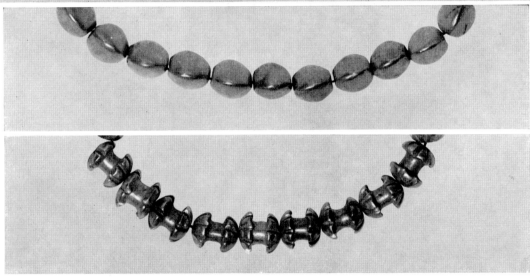

19 Above: Necklace. Gold. Longest link 2,7 cm. (1 in). Centre: Necklaces. Gold. Size of links 0,9 cm. and
0,8 cm. ($\frac{3}{8}$, $\frac{1}{4}$ in.). Below: Clasp with fitted pin. Gold. Length 13 cm. (5$\frac{1}{8}$ in.). All from Alaca Hüyük – Ankara

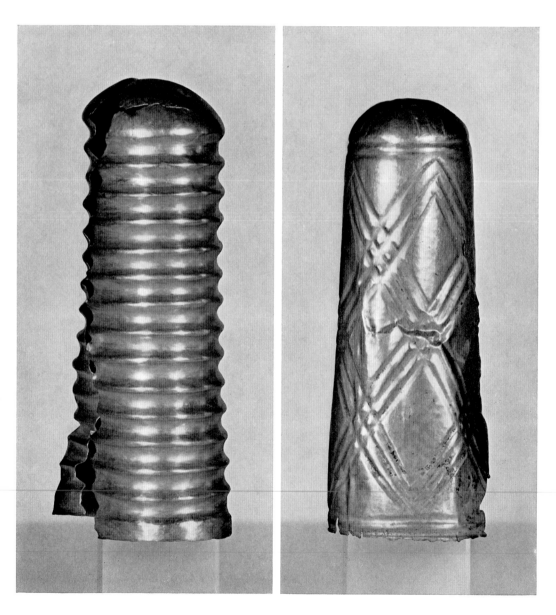

20 Above: Sceptre head with globular ornaments. Gold. Height 3,7 cm. 1½ in.).
Below: Two sceptre handles. Gold. Height 12,3 cm. (4¾ in.), (left) and 12 cm. (4¾ in.), (right). All from
Alaca Hüyük – Ankara

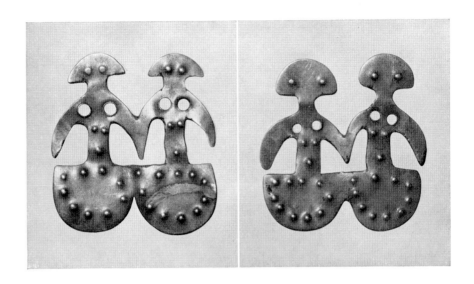

21 Above: Twin idols. Sheet gold. Height 3,1 cm. (1¼ in.). Below left: Female statuettes. Bronze. Height 16,3 cm. (6½ in.), 11,8 cm. (4⅝ in.), and 8,8 cm. (3½ in.). Below right. Female idol. Silver inlaid with gold. Height 10,8 cm. (4¼ in.). All from Alaca Hüyük – Ankara

22 Details of the statuette in plate VIII

23 Statuette of mother and child. Bronze. Height 20,4 cm. (8 in.), from Horoztepe – Ankara

24 Two clay letter-tablets in old Assyrian cuneiform script still in the original broken clay cases. On the case of the left-hand one the impression of three cylinder-seals. Left: Height 13 cm. (5⅛ in.), from Kültepe. Right: height 9,1 cm. (3½ in.), from Alishar – Ankara

25 Two idols. Alabaster. Height 16 cm. (6¼ in.) (left) and 20 cm. (7⅞ in.) (right),
from Kültepe. End of the 3rd millennium BC – Kayseri

26. Vessels. Polychrome clay. Old geometrical style.
Height of the vessel on the left: 22,6 cm. (8⅞ in.), from Kültepe. 19th/18th century BC – Ankara

27 Flagon. Polychrome clay. Evolved geometrical style. Height 52,6 cm. (20¾ in.), from Kültepe.
18th century BC – Kayseri

28 Tall cup with six handles. Clay with reddish-brown slip. Height 43,7 cm. (17¼ in.), from Kültepe.
18th century BC – Ankara

29 Above: Two jugs. Clay with reddish-brown slip. Height of the right hand beaker-jug 12,8 cm. (5 in.), from Kültepe. 19th/18th century BC. Below: Two vessels. Clay. Height of the right-hand vessel 34,2 cm. (13½ in.), from Kültepe. 18th century BC – Ankara

30 Jug. Clay with reddish-brown slip. Height 39,8 cm. (15¾ in.), from Kültepe.
18th century BC – Ankara

31 Above left: Male head. Fragment of a vessel. Height 5,6 cm. (2¼ in.). Above right: Rhyton in the shape of a wild boar's head. Height 6,5 cm. (2½ in.). Below: Vase with the heads of a male and female divinity. Height 15,5 cm. (6⅛ in.). All of dark grey clay, from Kültepe. 19th/18th century BC – Ankara

32 Above: Bull-rhyton. Brown clay. Length of head 12,2 cm. (4¾ in.). Centre: Boat-shaped rhyton with ram's head and oarsman. Clay with grey slip. Height 7,7 cm. (3 in.). Below: Ointment jar with ram's head. Clay with blackish brown slip. Length 18,9 cm. (7½ in.). All from Kültepe. 19th/18th century BC – Ankara

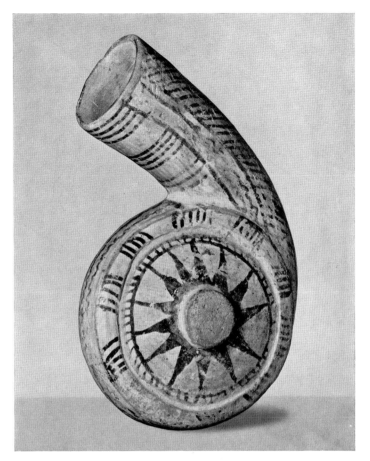

33 Above: Snail-rhyton. Height 15 cm. (6 in.). Below: Rhyton shaped like a boot. Height 8,9 cm (3½ in.). Both evolved geometrical style, from Kültepe. 19th century BC – Ankara

34 Lion-rhyton. Pale grey, dark painted clay. Height 17,8 cm. (7 in.), from Kültepe. 18th century BC – Paris

35 Above left: Two pairs of divinities. Lead. Height of the tallest figure 6,2 cm. (2½ in.), from Alishar. 18th century BC – Ankara. Above right: Figurine of a female deity. Ivory. Height 5 cm. (2 in.), from Kültepe. 18th century BC – Ankara. Below left: Steatite mould. Divine pair with two children. Height 5,7 cm. (2¼ in.), from Kültepe. 18th century BC – Ankara. Below right: Steatite mould. Divine pair with a child. Height 5,4 cm. (2⅛ in.), from Alishar. 18th century BC – Ankara

36 Flagon. Clay with reddish-brown slip. Height
29,8 cm. (11¾ in.), from Tokat. *c.* 1700 BC – Istanbul

37 Beaker-jug. Clay with reddish-brown slip.
Height 35,8 cm. (14⅛ in.), from Alaca Hüyük. 17th century BC – Ankara

38 Two beaker-jugs. Clay with reddish-brown slip. Height of the one on the left 51,8 cm. (20⅜ in.), from
Alaca Hüyük. 17th century BC – Ankara

39 Above: Small jug. Clay with reddish-brown slip. Height 16,5 cm. (6½ in.), from Amasya. *c*. 1700 BC – Istanbul
Below: Three vessels. Clay with reddish-brown (centre) and earth-coloured slip.
Height of the vessel on the left 21 cm. (8¼ in.), from Alishar. *c*. 1700 BC – Ankara.

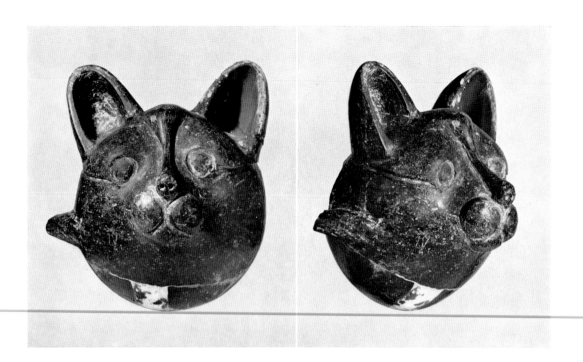

40 Above: Cat-rhyton. Clay with dark grey slip.
Width of the head 8,9 cm. (3½ in.), from Alishar. *c.* 1700 BC – Ankara
Below: Vessel shaped like a duck. Clay. Height 15,2 cm. (6 in.), from Beycesultan. *c.* 1700 BC – Ankara

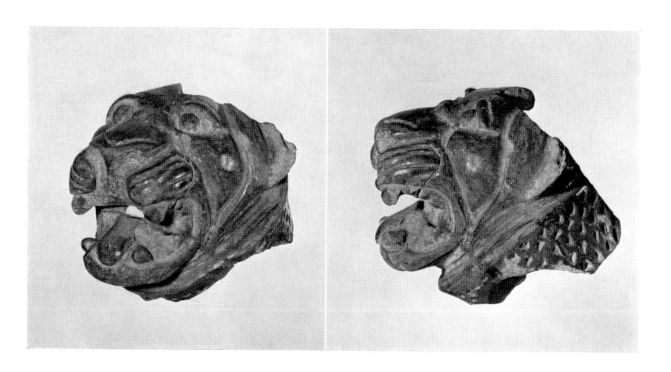

41 Above: Lion's head. Fragment of a rhyton. Clay with dark grey slip. Height 7,7 cm. (3 in.), from Alishar. *c.* 1700 BC – Ankara. Below: Vessel shaped like a duck. Cf. plate 40

42 Left: Figurine. Ivory. Height 3,9 cm. (1½ in.), from Alaca Hüyük. Imported from Syro-Phoenicia. 17th/16th century BC – Ankara. Right: Statuette of a goddess. Bronze. South Anatolian-Hittite. 16th century BC – St. Louis. Missouri

43 Statuette of a deity. Bronze. Height 23,7 cm. (9¼ in.), from Syria. Syro-Hittite. 15th century BC – Istanbul

44 Statuette of a god. Bronze. Height 11,4 cm. (4½ in.), from Tokat. 16th century BC – Ankara

45 Seals from the Old Kingdom and the Hittite Empire.
1st row: King Ishputashu. *c.* 1525–1500 BC. 2nd row, left: King Suppiluliuma. *c.* 1380–1340 BC; right: King
Muwatalli. *c.* 1306–1282 BC. 3rd row, left: King Urhi-Teshup (Mursili III). *c.* 1282–1275 BC; right: Queen
Puduhepa, the wife of Hattusili III. *c.* 1275–1250 BC. 4th row: Gold signet ring. *c.* 1400–1200 BC

48 Vessel shaped like a double-headed duck. Clay.
Height 20,2 cm. (8 in.), from Boghazköy. 15th century BC – Ankara

49 Vessel shaped like a double-headed duck. Clay.
Height 20,2 cm. (8 in.), from Boghazköy. 15th century BC – Ankara

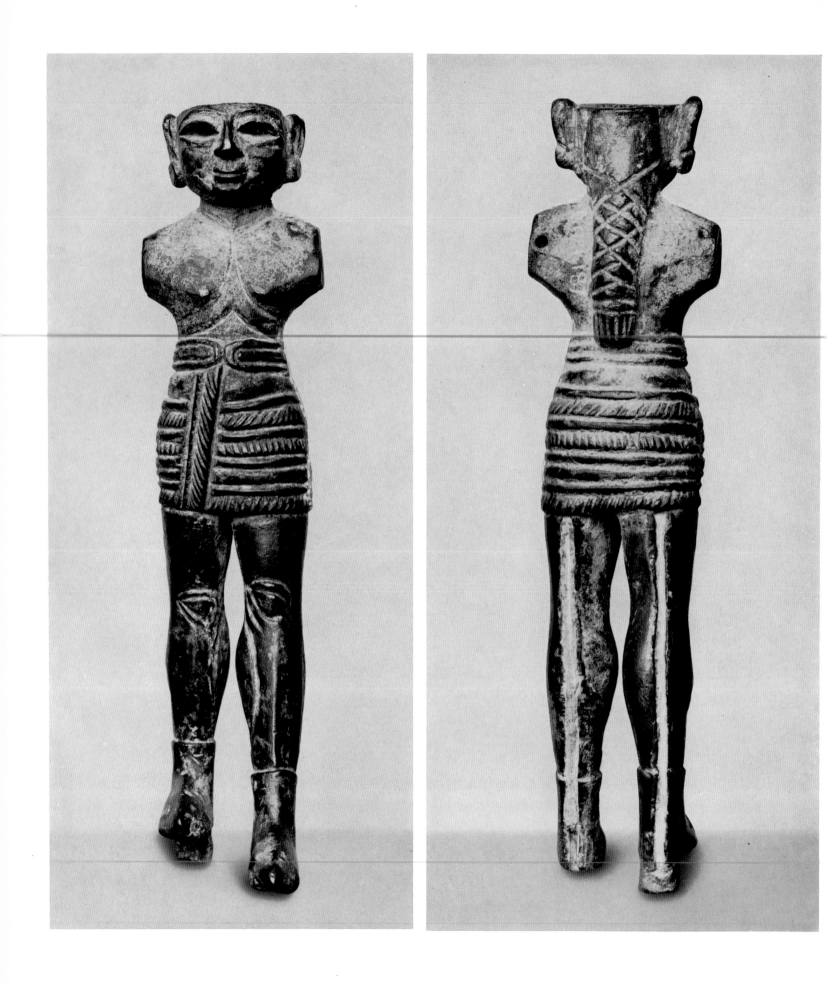

50 Male statuette. Bronze. From Latakiya. 15th/13th century BC – Paris

51 Male statuette. Bronze. From Boghazköy. 15th/13th century BC – Berlin

52 Above: Seal impression of a gold ring 15th/13th century BC – Oxford.
Below: Seal with five surfaces for sealing. Incised with gods and ritual scenes. 15th/13th century BC – Oxford

53 Above: Figurines of gods and demons. Gold inlaid with lapis lazuli and steatite. Maximum height 1,8 cm. (¾ in.), from a grave in Carchemish. 14th century BC – London. Centre: Seated goddess. Gold. Height 2 cm. (¾ in.). Below centre: Figurine of a mountain god. Ivory. Height 3,6 cm. (1½ in.). Both from Boghazköy – Ankara. Below left: Statuette of a deity. Gold. Height 4,2 cm. (1⅝ in.), from Yozgat, Boghazköy – Paris. Below right: Statuette of a deity. Rock-crystal. Height 6,1 cm. (2⅜ in.), from Tarsus – Adana. All 15th/13th century BC.

54 Above: The ruins of Hattusas. Below: Hattusas. The southern slope of Büyükkale

55 The great temple of the Weather-God (temple 1). *c.* 1400 BC. View from Büyükkale

56 Hattussas. The great temple of the Weather-God (temple 1). Above: South west front of the temple with the main portal. Below: Inner courtyard seen from the north east

57 Hattusas. The great temple of the Weather-God (temple 1). Above: Temple and south western storehouses.
Below: Main portal

58 Hattusas. The great temple of the Weather-God (temple 1). Above: South east side of the temple. Below: South west side of the temple—both seen from the north

59 Hattusas. The great temple of the Weather-God (temple 1).
Above: The Adyton (ritual chamber). In the background the rocks of Büyükkaya.
Below: The inner courtyard seen from north north west. In its east corner the room for lustrations

60 Hattusas. The great temple of the Weather-God (temple 1).
Above: The courtyard lying between the temple and the south western storehouses. On the left, three threshold stones belonging to the storehouses. In the centre, one of the big water basins. Below: A threshold of one of the temple rooms opening to the south

61 Hattusas. View from the south wall near Yerkapi of temple II (right) and III (left).
In the background, almost above temple II, the rock sanctuary of Yazilikaya

64 Relief of a god in martial dress.
Height 200 cm. (78¾ in.), from the King's Gate, Hattusas. 14th century BC – Ankara

65 Relief of a god in martial dress. Cf. plate 64

66 Hattusas. One of the two sphinxes from the inner side of the Sphinx Gate near Yerkapi – Berlin

67 Hattusas. The second of the two sphinxes from the inner side of the Sphinx Gate near Yerkapi – Istanbul

68 Head of the sphinx in plate 67

69 Head of the sphinx in plate 67

70 Hattusas. Büyükkale with the royal palace.
Above: The foundations of building A, the site of the archives of cuneiform tablets, seen from the east
Below: A complex of buildings and a paved road on the south west side of the royal palace

71 Base of a statue. Worshipper before an altar. Height 67,6 cm. (36⅝ in.), from Hattusas – Istanbul

72 Hattusas. Postern gate near Yerkapi at the southern extremity of the city walls.
Outer entrance with view into the tunnel

73 Hattusas. Postern gate near Yerkapi. View from the inner entrance of the corbel vault

74 Yazilikaya. Above: The rock sanctuary behind the temple ruins seen from the south east. *c.* 1350–1250 BC
Below: View of the rock sanctuary and the temple ruins from the opposite hill

75 Yazilikaya. Above: General view of the large rock chamber A from the south west.
Below: View of the north and west walls of chamber A seen from the south west

76 Yazilikaya. Above: The meeting of the gods. Relief on the north wall of rock chamber A.
Below: Further details to the left of the relief above

77 Yazilikaya. Above: A procession of female divinities. Relief on the east wall of rock chamber A.
Below: Detail of the relief depicting the meeting of the gods, cf. plate 76 above. From a plaster
cast made during the excavations – Berlin

78 Yazilikaya. King Tudhaliya IV. Detail of the relief in plate XIX

79 Yazilikaya. Details of the long procession of gods on the west wall of rock chamber A

80 Yazilikaya. Rock chamber B seen from the north

81 Yazilikaya. View of the east wall of rock chamber B, cf. plates 83 and 85

82 Yazilikaya. The Dagger-God. Relief on the east wall of rock chamber B.
From a plaster cast made during the excavations – Berlin

83 Yazilikaya. The Dagger-God. Relief on the east wall of rock chamber B

84 Yazilikaya. King Tudhaliya IV in the embrace of the god Sarumma. Relief on the east wall of rock chamber B. From a plaster cast made during the excavations – Berlin

85 Yazilikaya. King Tudhaliya IV in the embrace of the god Sarumma. Relief on the east wall of rock chamber B

86 Yazilikaya. Three gods. Detail from the relief of twelve gods, cf. plate 87 above

87 Yazilikaya. Above: Procession of twelve gods. Relief on the west wall of rock chamber B.
Below: One of the apotropaic demons at the entrance to rock chamber B

88 Alaca Hüyük. Above: Cartouche. Double-headed eagle gripping two hares. Below: The Sphinx Gate

89 Alaca Hüyük. Above: North east view of the entrance to the temple seen from within.
Below: Panoramic view of the temple ruins from the north west

90 Lion siezing a calf. Basalt. Height 98 cm. (38½ in.), from Alaca Hüyük – Ankara

91 Frontal view of the lion in plate 90

92 Orthostat reliefs from the city walls of Alaca Hüyük. Basalt – Ankara.
Above: A king and queen offering a libation before a bull. Height 126 cm. (49⅝ in.).
Below: Three priests in adoration. Height 133 cm (52¾ in.)

93 Orthostat reliefs from the city walls of Alaca Hüyük. Basalt – Ankara.
Above: Jugglers and acrobats. Height 116 cm. (45¾ in.). Below: Seated god and worshipper. Height 112 cm. (44 in.).

94 Orthostat relief from the city walls of Alaca Hüyük.
Stag and wild boar hunt. Basalt. Height 131 cm. (51½ in.) – Ankara

95 Orthostat relief from the city walls of Alaca Hüyük.
Lion Hunt. Basalt. Height 130 cm. (51¼ in.) – Ankara

96 Orthostat reliefs from the city walls of Alaca Hüyük. Basalt – Ankara
Above: Stag hunt. Fragment. Height 81 cm. (31⅞ in.). Below: Charging bull. Height 93 cm. (36⅝ in.).

97 Archer from the orthostat relief in plate 94

98 King Muwattali (1315–1282 BC). Rock relief at Sirkeli near Adana

99 Gâvurkalesi near Ankara. Above: Two gods confronting a seated goddess. Rock relief. In the background to the right, part of the adjoining grave monument. Below: Entrance to the above grave of the Isopata type

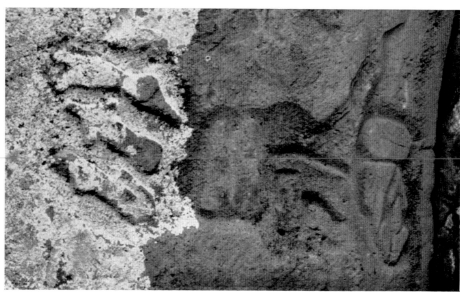

100 Rock relief of Fraktin near Kayseri. Above: General view of the relief. Great King Hattusili III offering a libation to the Weather-God, and Great Queen Puduhepa offering a libation to the goddess Hepat. Below: Hieroglyphic inscription from the right of the relief

101 Rock relief at Fraktin near Kayseri. Above: On the left-hand side of the relief Great King Hattusili III offering a libation to the Weather-God. Below: To the right Great Queen Puduhepa offering a libation to the goddess Hepat

102 Rock relief near Kemal Pasha (Karabel) east of Izmir.
Great King Tudhaliya and his hieroglyph, cf. plate XXII

103 Gate lion. Basalt. Height 131 cm. (51½ in.), from Malatya. Traditional style. 1050–850 BC – Ankara

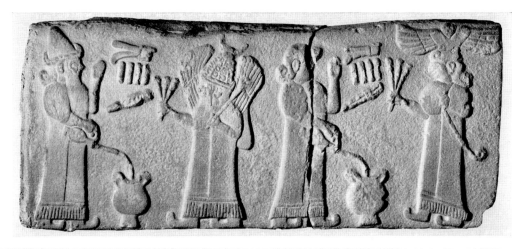

104 Orthostat reliefs from Malatya. Basalt. Traditional style. 1050–850 BC – Ankara.
From top to bottom: King Shulumeli offering libations. Height 44,5 cm (17½ in.). King Shulumeli offering libations to four divinities. Height 44,5 cm. (17½ in.). King Shulumeli offering libations to a tutelary god. Height 44,5 cm. (17½ in.). The Weather-God slaying the Dragon Illujanka. Height 47 cm. (18½ in.)

105 Orthostat reliefs from Malatya. Basalt – Ankara.
Above: King Shulumeli offering a libation to the Weather-God. Height 86,2 cm. (34 in.). Traditional style.
1050–850 BC. Below: Lion hunt. Height 53,4 cm. (21 in.). Assyrian influence. 850–700 BC

106 Statue of a king. Limestone. Assyrian style.
End of the 8th century BC, from Malatya – Ankara. Cf. plate 107

107 Statue of a king. Limestone. Height 3 m. 18. (125¼ in.), from Malatya.
Assyrian style. End of the 8th century BC – Ankara

108 Pair of bulls. Pedestal of a statue from Carchemish.
Basalt. Height 102 cm. (40⅛ in.). Traditional style. *c*. 1050–850 BC – Ankara

109 Statue of a seated god on a lion pedestal. Basalt. Height about 160 cm. (63 in.), from Carchemish.
Traditional style 1050–850 BC – Lion pedestal in Ankara; statue of the god destroyed

112 Orthostat relief from Carchemish.
Lion and bull demons. Basalt. Traditional style. Height 129,6 cm. (51 in.), *c.* 1050–850 – Ankara

113 Orthostat relief from Carchemish. 'Gilgamesh'.
Basalt. Height 128,5 cm. (50½ in.). Traditional style. 1050–850 BC – Ankara

114 Orthostat relief from Carchemish. Procession of women. Basalt. Height 112 cm. (44 in.).
Traditional style. 1050–850 BC – Ankara

115 The Goddess Kupaba. Fragment of a relief. Basalt.
Height 82 cm. (32¼ in.), from Carchemish. Traditional style. 1050–850 BC – Ankara

116 Orthostat relief from Carchemish. Sun-God and Moon-God mounted on a lion.
Tufa. Height 250 cm. (137¾ in.). Traditional style. 850–700 BC – Ankara

117 Detail of an orthostat relief from Carchemish. Inscription recording a victory. Tufa.
Height 151,3 cm. (59½ in.). Assyrian influence. 850–700 BC – Ankara

118 Orthostat relief from Carchemish. King Katuwas.
Basalt. Height 128,5 cm. (50½ in.). Assyrian style. 850–700 BC – Ankara

119 Orthostat relief from Carchemish. Officers. Basalt. Height 111 cm. (43⅝ in.). Assyrian style. Second half of the 8th century BC – Ankara

120. Orthostat relief from Carchemish. Hieroglyphic inscription. Continuation of plate 119. Basalt. Height 111 cm. (43⅝ in.). Second half of the 8th century BC – Ankara

121 Orthostat relief from Carchemish. King Araras and his son Kamanas. Basalt. Height 114,6 cm. (45⅛ in.).
Second half of the 8th century BC – Ankara

122. Orthostat relief from Carchemish. The children of King Araras. Basalt. Height 119 cm. (46⅞ in.).
Second half of the 8th century BC – Ankara

123 Orthostat relief from Carchemish. Queen Tuwarisas, wife of King Arasas, with her youngest child and a goat. Basalt. Height 115,2 cm. (45¾ in.). Assyrian style. Second half of the 8th century BC – Ankara

124 Orthostat relief from Carchemish. Battle chariot.
Basalt. Average height 175 cm. (69 in.). Assyrian influence. 850–700 BC – Ankara

125 Pair of sphinxes. Pedestal of a statue from Sam'al (Zincirli). Basalt. Height 97 cm. (39⅛ in.). Assyrian influence, 8th century BC – Istanbul

126 Statue of a king on a pedestal of lions. Basalt.
Height about 320 cm. (126 in.), from Sam'al (Zincirli). 850–700 BC – Istanbul. Cf. plate 127

127 Statue of a king on a pedestal of lions. Basalt. Height *c.* 320 cm. (127 in.), from Sam'al (Zincirli).
850–700 BC – Istanbul. Cf. plate 126.

128 Relief. Basalt. Height 127,5 cm. (50¼ in.), from Sam'al (Zincirli). *c.* 850 BC – Istanbul

129 Relief from the outer palace gate of Sam'al (Zincirli). Prince Kilamuwa with his son or attendant. Basalt. Height 58,5 cm. (23 in.), *c.* 850 BC – Berlin

130 Tomb stele. Princess with her attendant, between them a table with a funeral meal. Basalt. Height 134 cm.
(52¾ in.), from Sam'al (Zincirli). Aramaean style. 8th century BC – Berlin

131 Orthostat relief from Sam'al (Zincirli). King Barrekup and his scribe. Basalt. Height 112 cm. (44 in.). Aramaean style. 8th century BC – Berlin

132 Lion. Part of a portal. Basalt. Height 148 cm. (58¼ in.), from Sam'al (Zincirli).
Aramaean influence. 8th century BC Ankara

133 Detail of a relief. Hunter attacking a lion. Basalt. Height of the detail 72 cm. (28⅜ in.),
from Sakçagözü. Aramaean style. Second half of the 8th century BC – Ankara

134 Orthostat relief and lion from a portal. Basalt. Height of the relief 86,3 cm. (34 in.), from Sakçagözü. Aramaean influence. Second half of the 8th century BC – Ankara

135 Lion. Part of a portal. Basalt. Height 84 cm. (33 in.), from Sakçagözü.
Assyrian style. Second half of the 8th century BC – Ankara

136 Pair of lions. Limestone. Height 147 cm. (57⅞ in.), from Göllüdag.
Assyrian influence. *c.* 700 BC – Kayseri

137 Reliefs from the vicinity of Ankara. Basalt. Assyrian influence. *c.* 700 BC
Above: Lion. Height 93,4 cm. (36¾ in.). Below: Bull. Height 104 cm. (41 in.).

138 Tomb stele. Dead woman and scribe. Basalt. Height 105 cm. (41¼ in.), from Marash. Aramaean influence.
End of the 8th/beginning of the 7th century BC – Adana

139 Tomb stele Husband and wife. Basalt. Total height 100 cm. (39¾ in.), from Marash. Aramaean influence. End of the 8th/beginning of the 7th century BC – Adana

140 Rock relief. Detail of plate XXIV. King Warpalawas paying homage to the god of plenty
Aramean influence. Second half of the 8th century BC – near Ivriz

141 Karatepe. View of the Ceyhan valley from the north portal

142 Orthostat relief from the south portal.
Scene with musicians. Basalt. Aramaean influence. *c*. 700 BC – Karatepe

143 Orthostat relief from the south portal.
A king attending a feast. Basalt. Aramaean influence. *c.* 700 BC – Karatepe

144 Sphinx from the south end of the western orthostat frieze of the north portal Basalt. Aramaean influence.
c. 700 BC – Karatepe

145 Sphinx and orthostat relief with man carrying a calf, from the south end of the western orthostat frieze of the north portal. Basalt. Aramaean influence. *c*. 700 BC – Karatepe

146 Bear hunt and dancing bears, from the western orthostat frieze of the north portal.
Basalt. Aramaean influence. *c.* 700 BC – Karatepe

147 Bear hunt and demon, from the western orthostat frieze of the north portal.
Basalt. Aramaean influence. *c.* 700 BC – Karatepe

148 Man carrying a calf, from the western orthostat frieze of the north portal – Karatepe. Cf. plate 145

149 Bird demon, from the western orthostat frieze of the north portal, adjoining the orthostat of plate 148

150 Mother suckling her child, from the western orthostat frieze of the north portal, adjoining the orthostat of plate 149

NOTES ON THE PLATES

COLOUR

I *Ritual standard of a stag with twelve tines*. Bronze. Ornaments on the body inlaid with silver, head and twelve tines plated with silver. Height 52 cm., length of the body 26 cm. From Alaca Hüyük, grave B. 2300–2100 BC—Ankara, Museum of Archaeology, Cat. No. 11878.

II *Ritual standard of a bull*. Bronze. The neck covered in silver. Concentric rings on the body inlaid with silver. Height 37 cm. From Alaca Hüyük, grave L. 2300–2100 BC—Ankara, Museum of Archaeology, Cat. No. ALDL 27.

III *Ritual standard of a stag with twelve tines and two small panthers*. Bronze. Attached to the rim eight pairs of bull's horns and seven blossoms. The central blossom is somewhat larger than the rest. The muzzle of the panther is covered in silver, that of the stag with silver gilt. The arch and the animals are mounted on bull's horns. The support with a crossbar served to raise the standard. Height 22 cm. From Alaca Hüyük, grave B. 2300–2100 BC—Ankara, Museum of Archaeology, Cat. No. 11849.

IV *Ritual standard of a stag with fourteen tines* under an arch. Bronze. Height 22 cm. From Alaca Hüyük, grave D. 2300–2100 BC—Ankara, Museum of Archaeology, Cat. No. 7020.

V *Flagon*. Gold. Height 15·3 cm. From Alaca Hüyük, grave B. 2300–2100 BC—Ankara, Museum of Archaeology, Cat. No. 11722.

VI Above: *Vessel*. Gold. Decorated with six carnelians fitted on with gold pins. Height 5·8 cm. From Alaca Hüyük, grave H. 2300–2100 BC—Ankara, Museum of Archaeology, Cat. No. 6052.

VI Below: *Vessel*. Gold. Height 8·2 cm. From Alaca Hüyük, grave K. 2300–2100 BC—Ankara, Museum of Archaeology, Cat. No. 8774.

VII *Headband with open-work pattern*. Gold. Diameter 19·4 cm. From Alaca Hüyük, grave A. 2300–2100 BC—Ankara, Museum of Archaeology, Cat. No. 11857.

VIII. *Female statuette*. Silver. The head is plated with sheet gold. Cruciform bands across the breast and back. Gilt navel and gold anklets. Height 24·4 cm. From a grave in Hasanoglan near Ankara, *c.* 2000 BC—Ankara, Museum of Archaeology.

IX. *Pitcher*. Polychrome clay. Height 71·3 cm. Old geometrical style. From Kültepe, layer II. 19th–18th century BC—Ankara, Museum of Archaeology, Cat. No. g/k 99.

X *Vessel*. Polychrome clay. Height 52·6 cm. Evolved geometrical style. From Kültepe. 18th century BC—Ankara, Museum of Archaeology, Cat. No. d/k 21.

XI *Jug*. Clay with reddish-brown slip. Height 39·8 cm. From Kültepe. 18th century BC—Ankara, Museum of Archaeology, Cat. No. 12469.

XII *Lion-rhyton*. Clay with reddish-brown slip. Height 21·1 cm. From Kültepe, 18th century BC—Ankara, Museum of Archaeology, Cat. No. 15017.

XIII *Three vessels*. Clay with different coloured slips. Height of the vessel on the left including the spout 32·8 cm. From Alishar, *c.* 1700 BC—Ankara, Museum of Archaeology, Cat. Nos. 12394, 12398, 12402.

XIV *Vessel in relief with polychrome slip*. Fragment. Height of the fragment 36·5 cm. From Bitik near Ankara. *c.* 1400 BC—Ankara, Museum of Archaeology, Cat. No. 567.

XV *Hattusas*. View from Büyükkale towards the 'Narrow Defile', the rocks of Büyükkaya and the country to the north-west.

XVI, XVII *Hattusas. The Lion Gate* in the city walls on the south-west side.

XVI The Lion Gate seen from without.
XVII The right-hand lion of the Gate.

XVIII *Hattusas, Büyükkale.* South-west view of the building E and the terraced walls of the royal palace.

XIX. *The rock sanctuary of Yazilikaya.* 2 km. to the north-east of Hattusas. Limestone. *c.* 1350–1250 BC. Great King Tudhaliya IV (1250–1220 BC), the founder of the rock sanctuary, striding across the mountain peaks. In his right hand he carries his lituus; in front of him the cartouche with his name. The figure in the centre of the cartouche depicts a mountain-god. Relief on the east wall of rock chamber A (No. 64). Height of the figure without mountains 220 cm.

XX *Great King Muwatalli* (1315–1282 BC). Rock relief at Sirkeli near Adana.

XXI *Shrine at a spring by Eflatun Pinar* near Beyshehir. On the front, sculptural panels represent beings supporting winged suns.

XXII *Rock relief near Kemal Pasha* (Karabel) east of Izmir. Great King Tudhaliya and his hieroglyph. Mentioned by Herodotus (II, 106).

XXIII *Rock monument of the Mother of the Gods* on Mount Sipylos by Akpunar near Manisa. Pausanias calls it 'the oldest image of the Mother of the Gods in the country of Magnesia, on the north side of Mount Sipylos'. The goddess is seated on a throne. Her hands seem to support her breasts. On her head she wears the cylindrical polos.

XXIV *Rock relief at Ivriz near Konya.* King Warpalawas paying homage to the god of plenty.

MONOCHROME

1 *Ritual standard of a stag with fourteen tines.* Bronze. Height 45·5 cm., from Alaca Hüyük, grave A. 2300–2100 BC—Ankara, Museum of Archaeology, Cat. No. 11826.

2 See note for colour plate I.

3 *Ritual standard of a bull.* Bronze. Height 41 cm., from Alaca Hüyük, grave D. 2300–2100 BC—Ankara, Museum of Archaeology, Cat. No. 5973.

4 *Ritual standard of a bull.* Bronze with silver inlay on the forehead, the eyes and the neck. Height 36·5 cm. From Alaca Hüyük, grave K. 2300–2100 BC—Ankara, Museum of Archaeology, Cat. No. ALDK 24.

5 *Ritual standard of a bull.* Bronze with dots soldered in electrum. Height 57 cm. From Alaca Hüyük, grave E. 2300–2100 BC—Ankara, Museum of Archaeology, Cat. No. 7126.

6 *Ritual standard of a bull.* Bronze, with electrum stripes inlaid on the body. Height 48 cm. From Alaca Hüyük, grave C. 2300–2100 BC—Ankara, Museum of Archaeology, Cat. No. 11850.

7 Above: *Lozenge-shaped ritual standard* with swastika ornaments on three corners. Bronze. Height 34 cm. From Alaca Hüyük, grave B. 2300–2100 BC—Ankara, Museum of Archaeology, Cat. No. 11851.

7 Below: *Ritual standard in disk form* with seven spherical 'satellites'. Bronze. Height 27·5 cm. From Alaca Hüyük, grave E. 2300–2100 BC—Ankara, Museum of Archaeology.

8, 9 *Ritual standard in disk form* with open work pattern originally with twelve blossoms attached to the rim. Bronze. Above the three central blossoms birds in flight, above the others undefined animals. Suspended from the upper border are three hammered spherical ornaments. Below a pair of bull's horns. Height 34 cm. From Alaca Hüyük, grave B. 2300–2100 BC—Ankara, Museum of Archaeology, Cat. No. 11849.

10 *Ritual Standard of a stag and two does.* Bronze. From Alaca Hüyük 2300–2100 BC—Ankara, Museum of Archaeology, Cat. No. 18728.

11 Above: *Ritual standard in disk-form of a deer emerging from a radiant circle.* Bronze. Height 23 cm. From Alaca Hüyük, grave D. 2300–2100 BC—Ankara, Museum of Archaeology, Cat. No. 7019.

11 Below: *Arc-shaped ritual standard with flower buds.* Bronze. Height 19 cm. From Alaca Hüyük, grave D. 2300–2100 BC—Ankara, Museum of Archaeology, Cat. No. 7022.

12 Left: *Sistrum.* Bronze. Height 25·4 cm. From Horoztepe. 2100–2000 BC—Ankara, Museum of Archaeology.

12 Right: *Sistrum*. Bronze. From Central Anatolia. 2100–2000 BC—New York, The Metropolitan Museum of Art.

13 *Vessel*. Clay with black slip. Hand-made without the potter's wheel. Height 23·2 cm. From Alaca Hüyük, grave A. 2300–2100 BC—Ankara, Museum of Archaeology, Cat. No. 11748.

14 See note for colour plate V.

15 Above and below left: *Flagon*. Gold. Height 15 cm. From Alaca Hüyük, grave K. 2300–2100 BC—Ankara, Museum of Archaeology, Cat. No. 8773.

15 Below right: Base of vessel, plate VI Below.

16 *Jug*. Gold. Height 17·7 cm. From Central Anatolia. 2300–2100 BC—New York, The Metropolitan Museum of Art, Cat. No. 57–67.

17 Above: *Cup*. Gold. Diameter 7·8 cm. From Alaca Hüyük, grave L. 2300–2100 BC—Ankara, Museum of Archaeology, Cat. No. 8804.

17 Below left. *Goblet*. Gold. Height 13·5 cm. From Alaca Hüyük, grave B. 2300–2100 BC—Ankara, Museum of Archaeology, Cat. No. 11727.

17 Below right: *Goblet*. Gold. Height 12·5 cm. From Alaca Hüyük, grave K. 2300–2100 BC—Ankara, Museum of Archaeology, Cat. No. 8776.

18 *Headband*. Gold. Diameter 16·2 cm. From Alaca Hüyük, grave K. 2300–2100 BC—Ankara, Museum of Archaeology, Cat. No. 8779.

19 Above: *Necklace*. Gold. Modern reconstruction. Longest link 2·7 cm. From Alaca Hüyük, grave B. 2300–2100 BC—Ankara, Museum of Archaeology, Cat. No. 11648.

19 Centre: *Necklaces*. Gold. Modern reconstruction. Size of the links 0·9 cm., and 0·8 cm. (each having 19 pieces in all). From Alaca Hüyük, grave A. 2300–2100 BC—Ankara, Museum of Archaeology, Cat. Nos. 11654, 11708.

19 Below: *Clasp* with fitted pin. Gold. Length 13 cm. From Alaca Hüyük, grave A. 2300–2100 BC—Ankara, Museum of Archaeology. Cat. No. 11854.

20 Above: *Sceptre head* with twelve globular ornaments. Gold. Height 3·7 cm. From Alaca Hüyük, grave B. 2300–2100 BC—Ankara, Museum of Archaeology, Cat. No. 11725.

20 Below: *Two sceptre handles*. Gold. Height 12·3 cm. (left) and 12 cm. (right). From Alaca Hüyük. 2300–2100 BC—Ankara, Museum of Archaeology, Cat. Nos. 11724, 6070.

21 Above: *Twin idols*. Sheet gold. Height 3·1 cm. From Alaca Hüyük, grave H. 2300–2100 BC—Ankara, Museum of Archaeology, Cat. Nos. 6042, 6041.

21 Below left: *Female statuettes*. Bronze. Height 16·3, 11·8, and 8·8 cm. From Alaca Hüyük, grave H. 2300–2100 BC—Ankara, Museum of Archaeology, Cat. Nos. 7025, 7026, 7027.

21 Below right: *Female idol*. Silver. The breasts, ears and shoes inlaid with gold. Two blue dots instead of eyes. Height 10·8 cm. From Alaca Hüyük, grave L. 2300–2100 BC—Ankara, Museum of Archaeology, Cat. No. 8801.

22 See note for colour plate VIII.

23 *Statuette of mother and child*. Bronze. Height 20·4 cm. From Horoztepe. 2100–2000 BC—Ankara, Museum of Archaeology, Cat. No. 18529.

24 Left: *Clay letter-tablet* in old Assyrian cuneiform script, still in its clay case. On the case three separate seal impressions. They depict the presentation of deities, in the centre to a seated god, above to a Bull-God. Between the seal impressions on one side a cuneiform text. Height 13 cm. From Kültepe. 19th century BC—Ankara, Museum of Archaeology, Cat. No. 19394.

24 Right: *Clay letter-tablet* in old Assyrian cuneiform script, still in its original broken clay case. Height 9·1 cm. From Alishar, in Central Anatolia. 18th century BC—Ankara, Museum of Archaeology, Cat. No. g/l 132.

25 *Two idols*. Alabaster. Height 16 cm. (Left) and 20 cm. (Right). A small twin idol attached to the breast of the right-hand idol. From Kültepe. End of the 3rd millennium BC—Kayseri, Museum.

26 *Vessels*. Polychrome clay. Height of vessel on the left 22·6 cm. Old geometrical style. From Kültepe, layer Ib and Ia. 19th–18th century BC—Ankara, Museum of Archaeology, Cat. No. a/k 777, H/K85, b/k 78.

27 *Flagon*. Polychrome clay. Height 52·6 cm. Evolved geometrical style. From Kültepe. 18th century BC—Kayseri, Museum.

28 *Tall cup with six handles.* Clay with reddish-brown slip. Height 43·7 cm. From Kültepe, level II 19th–18th century BC—Ankara, Museum of Archaeology, Cat. No. d/k 27.

29 Above: *Two jugs.* Clay with reddish-brown slip. Height of the right-hand beaker-jug 12·8 cm. From Kültepe. 19th–18th century BC—Ankara, Museum of Archaeology, Cat. No. g/k 217.

29 Below: *Two vessels.* Clay. Height of the right-hand vessel 34·2 cm. From Kültepe. 18th century BC—Ankara, Museum of Archaeology, Cat. No. g/k 82, 15001.

30 See note for colour plate XI.

31 Above left: *Male head.* Fragment of a vessel with dark grey slip. Height 5·6 cm. From Kültepe. Level Ib. 18th century BC—Ankara, Museum of Archaeology, Cat. No. 11289.

31 Above right: *Rhyton in the shape of a wild boar's head.* Clay. Height 6·5 cm. From Kültepe. 18th century BC—Ankara, Museum of Archaeology, Cat. No. I/k 173.

31 Below: *Vase with the heads of a male and female divinity.* Dark grey clay. Height 15·5 cm. From Kültepe, level II. 19th–18th century BC—Ankara, Museum of Archaeology, Cat. No. j/k 267.

32 Above: *Bull-rhyton.* Brown clay. Length of the head 12·2 cm. From Kültepe. 19th–18th century BC —Ankara, Museum of Archaeology, Cat. No. f/k 299.

32 Centre: *Boat-shaped rhyton with ram's head and oarsman.* Clay with grey slip. Height 7·7 cm. From Kültepe, level II. 19th.18th century BC—Ankara, Museum of Archaeology, Cat. No. e/k 98.

32 Below: *Ointment jar with ram's head.* Clay with dark grey slip. Length 18.9 cm. From Kültepe. 18th century BC—Ankara, Museum of Archaeology, Cat. No. c/k 195.

33 Above: *Snail-rhyton.* Evolved geometrical style. Height 15 cm. From Kültepe. 19th century BC—Ankara, Museum of Archaeology, Cat. No. 3267.

33 Below: *Rhyton shaped like a boot.* Evolved geometrical style. Height 8·9 cm. From Kültepe. 19th century BC—Ankara, Museum of Archaeology, Cat No. 11364a.

34 *Lion-rhyton.* Clay. Pale grey with dark paint. Height 17·8 cm. From Kültepe. 18th century BC—Paris, Musée du Louvre.

35 Above left: *Two pairs of divinities.* Lead. Height of the tallest figure 6·2 cm. From Alishar. 18th century BC—Ankara, Museum of Archaeology, Cat. Nos. 12357–59.

35 Above right: *Figurine of a female deity.* Ivory. Height 5 cm. From Kültepe, level Ib. 18th century BC—Ankara, Museum of Archaeology.

35 Below left: *Steatite mould.* Divine pair with two children. Height 5·7 cm. From Kültepe, level Ib. 18th century BC—Ankara, Museum of Archaeology.

35 Below right: *Steatite mould.* Divine pair with a child. Height 5·4 cm. From Alishar. 18th century BC —Ankara, Museum of Archaeology.

36 *Flagon.* Clay with reddish-brown slip. Surface symmetrically decorated with incised rings. Probably a ritual vessel. From Tokat. c. 1700 BC—Istanbul, Museum of Archaeology, Cat. No. 12890.

37 *Beaker-jug.* Clay with reddish-brown slip. Height 35·8 cm. From Alaca Hüyük. 18th–17th century BC —Ankara, Museum of Archaeology, Cat. No. 12432.

38 *Two beaker-jugs.* Clay with reddish-brown slip. Height of the one on the left 51·8 cm. From Alaca Hüyük. 17th century BC—Ankara, Museum of Archaeology, Cat. Nos. 12431, 5704.

39 Above: *Small jug.* Clay with reddish-brown slip. Height 16·5 cm. From Amasya, c. 1700 BC—Istanbul, Museum of Archaeology, Cat. No. 5289.

39 Below: *Three vessels.* Clay with reddish-brown (centre) and earth-coloured slip. Height of the vessel on the left 21 cm. From Alishar. c. 1700 BC—Ankara, Museum of Archaeology, Cat. Nos. 12392, 12397, BS 55/535.

40 Above: *Cat-rhyton.* Clay with dark grey slip. Width of the head 8·9 cm. From Alishar. c. 1700 BC—Ankara, Museum of Archaeology, Cat. No. 12391.

40 Below; 41 Below: *Vessel shaped like a duck.* Clay. Height 15·2 cm. From Beycesultan. c. 1700 BC—Ankara, Museum of Archaeology, Cat. No. BS 56/624.

41 Above: *Lion's head*. Fragment of a *rhyton*. Clay with dark grey slip. Height 7·7 cm. From Alishar. *c.* 1700 BC—Ankara, Museum of Archaeology, Cat. No. c 964.

42 Left: *Figurine*. Ivory. Height 3·9 cm. From Alaca Hüyük. Imported from Syro-Phoenicia. 17th–16th century BC—Ankara, Museum of Archaeology.

42 Right: *Statuette of a goddess*. Bronze. South Anatolian-Hittite. 16th century BC—St. Louis, Missouri. Vladimir Golschmann Collection.

43 *Statuette of a deity*. Bronze. Height 23·7 cm. From Syria. Syro-Hittite. 15th century BC—Istanbul, Museum of Archaeology, Cat. No. 4513.

44 *Statuette of a god*. Bronze. Height 11·4 cm. From Tokat. 16th century BC—Ankara, Museum of Archaeology, Cat. No. 8825.

45 *Seals from the Old Kingdom and the Hittite Empire.* 1st row: *Clay edict of the Great King Ishputashu* (*c.* 1525–1500 BC) the son of Pariyawatri, King of Kizzuwatna, and contemporary of Telepinu. Diameter 2·2 cm.—Adana, Museum.

2nd row, Left: *Clay edict of the Great King Suppiluliuma.* *c.* 1380–1346 BC. Diameter 3·4 cm. From Boghazköy—Ankara, Museum of Archaeology, Cat. No. 3614.

2nd row, Right: *Clay edict of the Great King Muwatalli.* In the embrace of his god. *c.* 1315–1282 BC. Diameter 5·4 cm. From Boghazköy—Ankara, Museum of Archaeology, Cat. No. 815–1.

3rd row, Left: *Clay edict of the Great King Urhi-Teshup* (Mursili III), *c.* 1282–1275 BC. Diameter 4·5 cm., from Boghazköy—Ankara, Museum of Archaeology, Cat. No. 15169.

3rd row, Right: *Clay edict of the queen Puduhepa*, the wife of Hattusili III. *c.* 1275–1250 BC. Diameter 2·7 cm.—Adana, Museum.

4th row: *Gold signet ring*. From Alaca Hüyük. *c.* 1400–1200 BC—Ankara, Museum of Archaeology.

46 *Border of a vase with Hittite city walls.* Fragment. Clay. Height 12·3 cm. From Boghazköy. 15th century BC—Ankara, Museum of Archaeology, Cat. No. 342/P.

47 Above: *Plaque with relief*. Bronze. Two male figures with bulls' heads raise a winged sun. Height 13·9 cm. 15th–13th century BC—Ankara, Museum of Archaeology, Cat. No. 6292.

47 Below: *Steatite relief*. Male divinity standing on a stag. Height 6·3 cm. From Alaca Hüyük. 15th–13th century BC—Ankara, Museum of Archaeology, Cat. No. 12467.

48, 49 *Vessel shaped like a double-headed duck.* Clay. Height 20·2 cm. From Boghazköy. 15th century BC—Ankara, Museum of Archaeology, Cat. No. 364P.

50 *Male statuette*. Bronze. The headgear is lost. From Latakiya. 15th–13th century BC—Paris, Musée du Louvre.

51 *Male statuette*. Bronze. The headgear is lost. From Boghazköy. 15th–13th century BC—Berlin, Staatliche Museen.

52 Above: *Seal impression of a gold ring*. 15th–13th century BC—Oxford, Ashmolean Museum.

52 Below: *Seal with five surfaces for sealing*. Incised with gods and ritual scenes. From Tarsus. 15th–13th century BC—Oxford, Ashmolean Museum.

53 Above: *Figurines of gods and demons*. Gold inlaid with lapis lazuli and steatite. Maximum height 1·8 cm. From a grave in Carchemish. 14th century BC—London, British Museum.

53 Centre: *Seated goddess*. Gold. Height 2 cm. From Boghazköy. 15th–13th century BC—Ankara, Museum of Archaeology, Cat. No. 13164.

53 Below centre: *Figurine of a mountain god*. Ivory. Height 3·6 cm. From Boghazköy. 14th–13th century BC—Ankara, Archaeological Museum, Cat. No. 387/N.

53 Below left: *Statuette of a deity*. Gold. Height 4·2 cm. From Yozgat, Boghazköy, 15th–13th century BC—Paris, Musée du Louvre.

53 Below right: *Statuette of a deity*. Rock-crystal, Height 6·1 cm. From Tarsus. 15th–13th century BC—Adana Museum.

54 Above: *The ruins of Hattusas.*

54 Below: *Hattusas*. The southern slope of Büyükkale.

55–60 *Hattusas. The great temple of the Weather-God (temple I). c.* 1400 BC.

55 View of the temple from Büyükkale.

56 Above: South-west front of the temple with the main portal.

56 Below: Inner courtyard seen from the north-east.

57 Above: Temple and south-western storehouses.

57 Below: Main portal.

58 Above: South-east side of the temple seen from the north.

58 Below: South-west side of the temple seen from the north.

59 Above: The Adyton (ritual chamber). In the background the rocks of Büyükkaya.

59 Below: The inner courtyard seen from north-north-west. In its corner to the east the room for lustrations.

60 Above: The courtyard lying between the temple and the south-western storehouses. On the left, three threshold stones belonging to the storehouses. In the centre, one of the big water basins.

60 Below: A threshold of one of the temple rooms opening to the south with the original gimlet holes.

61 *Hattusas.* View from the south wall near Yerkapi of temple II (right) and III (left). In the background, almost above temple II, the rock sanctuary of Yazilikaya.

62 *Hieroglyphic inscription of Great King Suppiluliuma.* 1380–1346 BC, on the Nishantepe, south-west from Büyükkale.

63 *Hattusas. The King's Gate* seen from without. 14th century BC.

64, 65 *Relief of a god* in martial dress, with a pointed helmet, carrying an axe and a sword. From the inner side of the King's Gate of Hattusas. Height 200 cm. 14th century BC—Ankara, Museum of Archaeology.

66 *Sphinx.* Limestone. From the inner side of the Sphinx Gate at Hattusas near Yerkapi. 14th century BC—Berlin, Staatliche Museen. Cat. No. VA 1098.

67–69 *Sphinx.* Limestone. From the inner side of the Sphinx Gate at Hattusas. 14th century BC—Istanbul, Museum of Archaeology, Cat. No. 7868.

70 *Hattusas, Büyükkale, with the royal palace.*

Above: The foundations of building A, the site of the archives of cuneiform tablets seen from the east.
Below: A complex of buildings and a paved road on the south-west side of the royal palace.

71 *Base of a statue.* Worshipper before an altar. Height 67·6 cm. From Hattusas. *c.* 1300 BC—Istanbul, Museum of Archaeology, Cat. No. 7776.

72, 73 *Hattusas. Postern gate near Yerkapi* at the southern extremity of the city walls.

72 Outer entrance with view into the 70 m. tunnel.

73 View from the inner entrance of the corbel vault.

74–87 *The rock sanctuary of Yazilikaya,* 2 km. to the north-east of Hattusas. Limestone. *c.* 1350–1250 BC.

74 Above: The rock sanctuary behind the temple ruins seen from the south-east.

74 Below: View of the rock sanctuary and the temple ruins from the opposite hill.

75 Above: General view of the large rock chamber A to the west (main chamber) seen from the south-west.

75 Below: View of the west and north walls of chamber A approached from the south-west.

76 Above: The meeting of the gods. Relief on the north wall of rock chamber A.

76 Below: Further details to the left of the relief above.

77 Above: A procession of female divinities (Nos. 49–55), the best preserved among the sixteen figures of goddesses (Nos. 46a–63). Relief on the east wall of rock chamber A.

77 Below: Detail of the relief depicting the meeting of the gods, cf. plate 76 above. From a plaster cast made during the excavations—Berlin, Staatliche Museen.

78. See note for colour plate XIX.

79 Details of the long procession of gods on the west wall of rock chamber A. Upper row: male gods (Nos. 1–13). Height of the figures varies between 77 and 88 cm. Second row: Mountain-God (No. 17) and unidentified gods (Nos. 18–24). Third row (Nos. 25–33): unidentified gods (Nos. 26 and 27); two bull-demons (Nos. 28 and 29). standing on the hieroglyph for earth and carrying the crescent moon, symbol for the firmament.
Bottom row, from the left: a deceased divinized Great King topped by the winged sun (No. 34): and the Moon-God (No. 35); Ninatta and Kulitta (Nos. 36 and 37), the attendants of the War-Goddess Shaushga; Shaushga with unfolded wings (No. 38). Height of the figures 75–88 cm.

80 Rock chamber B (Inner chamber) seen from the north.

81 View of the east wall of rock chamber B. Cf. plates 83 and 85.

82, 83 The Dagger-God of the east wall of rock chamber B (No. 82). Plate 82 is from a plaster cast made during the excavations. Height of the figure 323 cm.—Berlin, Staatliche Museen.

84, 85 King Tudhaliya IV in the embrace of the god Sarumma (No. 81). Relief on the east wall of rock chamber B. Plate 84 is from a plaster cast made during the excavations. Height of the figure: 170 cm.—Berlin, Staatliche Museen.

86, 87 Above: A procession of twelve gods dressed as warriors and armed with sickle-shaped swords. Relief on the west wall of rock chamber B (Nos. 69–80). Height of the figures: 80 cm.

87 Below: A human figure with a lion head and claws: one of the apotropaic demons who guard the entrance to rock chamber B. Height of the figure: 100 cm.

88 Above: *Alaca Hüyük. Double-headed eagle gripping two hares.* Cartouche on the inner side of the southern portal-sphinx.

88 Below: *Alaca Hüyük.* South view of the Sphinx Gate.

89 *Alaca Hüyük. The Temple.*

89 Above: North-east view of the entrance to the temple seen from within.

89 Below: Panoramic view of the temple ruins from the north-west.

90, 91 *Lion seizing a calf.* Basalt. Height 98 cm. From Alaca Hüyük—Ankara, Museum of Archaeology.

92–97 *Orthostat reliefs from the city walls of Alaca Hüyük.* Basalt—Ankara, Museum of Archaeology.

92 Above: *A king and queen offering a libation before a bull.* Height 126 cm.

92 Below: *Three priests in adoration.* Height 133 cm.

93 Above: *Jugglers and acrobats.* Height 116 cm.

93 Below: *Seated god and worshipper.* Height 112 cm. Relief near the entrance of the building.

94 *Stag and wild boar hunt.* Height 131 cm.

95 *Lion hunt.* Height 130 cm.

96 Above: *Stag hunt.* Fragment. Height 81 cm.

96 Below: *Charging bull.* Height 93 cm.

97 *Archer.* From the orthostat relief in plate 94.

98 See note for colour plate XX.

99 *Gâvurkalesi* (Gâvurkale) near Ankara.

Above: Two gods confronting a seated goddess. Rock relief. In the background to the right, part of the adjoining grave monument.

Below: Entrance to a grave of the Isopata type.

100, 101 *Rock relief at Fraktin near Kayseri.* Great King Hattusili III (1275–1250) offering a libation to the Weather-God (left) and Great Queen Puduhepa offering a libation to the goddess Hepat (right).

102 See note for colour plate XXII.

103 *Gate lion from Malatya.* Basalt. Height 131 cm. Traditional style. 1050–850 BC—Ankara, Museum of Archaeology.

104, 105 Above: *Orthostat reliefs from Malatya*. Basalt. Traditional style—Ankara, Museum of Archaeology.

104 (Top to bottom): King Shulumeli offering libations. Height 44·5 cm. Cat. No. 12254. King Shulumeli offering libations to four divinities. Height 44·5 cm. Cat. No. 12253. King Shulumeli offering libations to a tutelary god. Height 44·5 cm. Cat. No. 12249. The Weather-God slaying the dragon Illujanka. Height 47 cm. Cat. No. 12250. All 1050–850 BC.

105 Above: King Shulumeli offering a libation to the Weather-God. Height 86·2 cm. 1050–850 BC. Cat. No. 55.

105 Below: Lion hunt. Height 53·4 cm. Assyrian influence. 850–700 BC. Cat. No. 12245.

106, 107 *Statue of a king*. Limestone. Height 3·18 m. From Malatya. Assyrian influence. End of the 8th century BC—Ankara, Museum of Archaeology.

108 *Pair of bulls*. Pedestal of a statue from Carchemish. Basalt. 102 cm. Traditional style. 1050–850 BC—Ankara, Museum of Archaeology, Cat. No. 10103.

109 *Statue of a seated god on a lion pedestal*. Basalt. Height about 160 cm. From Carchemish. Traditional style. Statue of the god destroyed; one lion's head in the British Museum, London; rest of the pedestal in Ankara, Museum of Archaeology, Cat. No. 69.

110–114, 116–124 *Orthostat reliefs from Carchemish*—Ankara, Museum of Archaeology.

110 Sphinx with a human and a lion's head. Basalt. Height 133·6 cm. Traditional style. 1050–850 BC. Cat. No. 95.

111 Two bird-men. Basalt. Height 123·5 cm. Traditional style. 1050–850 BC. Cat. No. 96.

112 Lion and bull demons. Basalt. Height 129·6 cm. Traditional style. 1050–850 BC. Cat. No. 9669.

113 'Gilgamesh'. Basalt. Height 128·5 cm. Traditional style. 1050–850 BC. Cat. No. 9665.

114 Procession of women. Basalt. Height 112 cm. Traditional style. 1050–850 BC. Cat. No. 9665.

116 Sun-God and Moon-God mounted on a lion. Tufa. Height 250 cm. Traditional style. 850–700 BC. Cat. No. 10079.

117 Inscription recording a victory. Tufa. Detail of an orthostat relief. Height 151·3 cm. Assyrian influence. 850–700 BC. Cat. No. 10067.

118 King Katuwas. Basalt. Height 128·5 cm. Assyrian influence. 850–700 BC. Cat. No. 89.

119 Officers. Basalt. Height 111 cm. Assyrian style. Second half of the 8th century BC. Cat. No. 9663.

120 Hieroglyphic inscription. Continuation of the inscription in plate 119. Basalt. Height 111 cm. Assyrian style. Second half of the 8th century BC. Cat. No. 90.

121 King Araras and his son Kamanas. Basalt. Height 114·6 cm. Assyrian style. Second half of the 8th century BC. Cat. No. 91.

122 The children of king Araras. Basalt. Height 119 cm. Assyrian style. Second half of the 8th century BC. Cat. No. 93.

123 Queen Tuwarisas, wife of king Araras, with her youngest child and a goat. Basalt. Height 115·2 cm. Assyrian style. Second half of the 8th century BC. Cat. No. 92.

124 Battle chariot. Basalt. Average height 175 cm. Assyrian influence. 850–700 BC. Cat. No. 94.

115 *The Goddess Kupaba*. Relief from Carchemish. Fragment. Basalt. Height 82 cm. Traditional style. 1050–850 BC—Ankara, Museum of Archaeology, Cat. No. 103.

125 *Pair of sphinxes*. Pedestal of a statue from Sam'al (Zincirli). Basalt. Height 97 cm. Assyrian influence. From the palace of king Barrekup. 8th century BC—Istanbul, Museum of Archaeology, Cat. No. 7731.

126, 127 *Statue of an Aramaean king* on a pedestal of two lions led by a genie. Basalt. Height about 320 cm. From Sam'al (Zincirli). Assyrian influence. 850–700 BC—Istanbul, Museum of Archaeology, Cat. No. 7768.

128 *Relief*. Weather-God. Basalt. Height 127·5 cm. From Sam'al (Zincirli). Assyrian influence. 850–700 BC. From the museum at Nebuchadnezzar II's palace in Babylon. Istanbul, Museum of Archaeology, Cat. No. 7516.

129 *Relief from the outer palace gate of Sam'al* (Zincirli). Prince Kilamuwa with his son or attendant. Basalt. Height 58·5 cm. Aramaean style. *c.* 850 BC—Berlin, Staatliche Museen, Cat. No. S 6580.

130 *Tomb stele.* Princess with her attendant, between them a table with a funeral meal. Basalt. Height 134 cm. From Sam'al (Zincirli). 8th century BC—Berlin, Staatliche Museen, Cat. No. VA 2995.

131 *Orthostat relief* (Zincirli). King Barrelays and his scribe. Basalt. Height 112 cm. Aramaean style. (Zincirli). 8th century BC—Berlin, Staatliche Museen.

132 *Lion.* Part of a portal. Basalt. Height 148 cm. From Sam'al (Zincirli). Assyrian influence. 8th century BC—Ankara, Museum of Archaeology.

133 *Detail of a relief, hunter attacking a lion.* Basalt. Height of the detail 72 cm. From Sakçagözü. Aramaean influence. 2nd half of the 8th century BC—Ankara, Museum of Archaeology, Cat. No. 1804.

134 *Orthostat relief and lion from a portal.* Basalt. Height of the relief 86·3 cm. From Sakçagözü. Lion with Aramaean influence. 2nd half of the 8th century BC—Ankara, Museum of Archaeology, Cat. Nos. 1011, 10113.

135 *Lion from a portal.* Basalt. Height 84 cm. From Sakçagözü. 2nd half of the 8th century BC—Ankara, Museum of Archaeology, Cat. No. 1811.

136 *Pair of lions.* Limestone. Height 147 cm. From Göllüdag. Assyrian influence. *c.* 700 BC—Kayseri, Museum.

137 Above: *Relief of a lion.* Basalt. Height 93·4 cm. From the vicinity of Ankara. Assyrian influence. *c.* 700 BC—Ankara, Museum of Archaeology, Cat. No. 49.

137 Below: *Relief of a bull.* Basalt. Height 104 cm. From the vicinity of Ankara. Assyrian influence. *c.* 700 BC—Ankara, Museum of Archaeology, Cat. No. 8906.

138 *Tomb stele, dead woman with distaff and scribe.* Basalt. Height 105 cm. From Marash. Aramaean influence. End of the 8th/beginning of the 7th century BC—Adana, Museum.

139 *Tomb stele of a husband and wife.* Basalt. Height 100 cm. From Marash. Aramaean influence. End of the 8th/beginning of the 7th century BC—Adana, Museum.

140 See note for colour plate XXIV.

141 *Karatepe.* View of the Ceyhan valley from the north portal.

142–50 *Orthostat reliefs.* Basalt. From Karatepe. Aramaean influence. *c.* 700 BC.

142 Scene with musicians. From the south portal.

143 A king attending a feast. From the south portal.

144 The sphinx from the south end of the western orthostat frieze of the north portal.

145 Sphinx and orthostat relief with man carrying a calf, from the south end of the western orthostat frieze of the north portal.

146 Bear hunt and dancing bears. From the western orthostat frieze of the north portal.

147 Bear hunt and demon. From the western orthostat frieze of the north portal.

148 Man carrying a calf. From the western orthostat frieze of the north portal.

149 Bird demon. From the western orthostat frieze of the north portal adjoining the orthostat of plate 148.

150 Mother suckling her child. From the western orthostat frieze of the north portal adjoining the orthostat of plate 149.

BIBLIOGRAPHY

ABBREVIATIONS USED IN THE BIBLIOGRAPHY

AA	Archäologischer Anzeiger, Supplement to Jahrbuch des Deutschen Archäologischen Instituts.
AASOR	Annual of the American Schools of Oriental Research. New Haven 1920ff.
AfO	Archiv für Orientforschung.
AJA	American Journal of Archaeology.
AiS	Ausgrabungen in Sendschirli I–V. Mitteilungen aus den orientalischen Sammlungen der Berliner Museen, Heft XI–XV, 1893–1943.
AO	Der Alte Orient.
AS	Paterson, Assyrian Sculpture.
BASOR	Bulletin of the American Schools of Oriental Research (South Hadley, later New Haven 1920ff.).
Belleten	Belleten, Türk Tarih Kurumu, Ankara.
Bittel, Grundzüge	Kurt Bittel, Grundzüge der Vor- und Frühgeschichte Kleinasiens, 2. Aufl. Tübingen 1950.
Bittel, Kleinfunde	Kurt Bittel, Boğazköy, Die Kleinfunde der Grabungen 1906–12. Deutsche Orientgesellschaft Nr. 60, Leipzig 1937.
Bittel, Ruinen	Kurt Bittel, Die Ruinen von Boğazköy, der Hauptstadt des Hethiterreiches. Berlin–Leipzig 1937.
Bittel/Naumann, Boghazköy II	Kurt Bittel and Rudolf Naumann, Boğazköy II. Neue Untersuchungen hethitischer Architektur, in: Abhandlungen der Preussischen Akademie der Wissenschaften. Berlin 1938.
Bittel/Naumann, Boghazköy–Hattusas	Kurt Bittel and Rudolf Naumann, Boğazköy-Hattuša, Ergebnisse der Ausgrabungen des Deutschen Archäologischen Instituts und der Deutschen Orient-Gesellschaft in den Jahren 1931–39 (I. Architektur, Topographie, Landeskunde und Siedlungsgeschichte), 63.
	Wissenschaftl. Published by the Deutsche Orient-Gesellschaft. Stuttgart 1952.
Bossert, Altanatolien	Helmuth Th. Bossert, Altanatolien. Kunst und Handwerk in Kleinasien von den Anfängen bis zum völligen Aufgehen in der griechischen Kultur. Berlin 1942.
Carchemish	Report on the Excavations at Djerablus (Jerablus) on behalf of the British Museum.
	Part I Introduction by D. G. Hogarth. London 1914.
	II The Town Defences by C. L. Woolley. London 1921.
	III The Excavations in the Inner Town by C. L. Woolley. The Hittite Inscriptions by R. D. Barnett. London 1952.
DTFD	Ankara Üniversitesi. Dil ve Tarih-Cografya Fakültesi Dergisi (Bulletin of the Philosophical Faculty of Ankara University).
ESA	Eurasia Septentrionalis Antiqua.
Goetze, Kleinasien	Albrecht Goetze, Kleinasien. Kulturgeschichte des Alten Orients, 3. Handbuch der Altertumswissenschaft III, 1. 2. Aufl. 1957.
I. J. Gelb, HHM	Ignace J. Gelb, Hittite Hieroglyphic Monuments. Chicago 1939.
Iraq	Iraq. Published by the British School of Archaeology in Iraq. London 1934ff.
JAOS	Journal of the American Oriental Society. New Haven 1951ff.
JCS	Journal of Cuneiform Studies.
JKF	Jahrbuch für Kleinasiatische Forschung. Istanbul.
ILN	Illustrated London News.
JNES	Journal of Near Eastern Studies. Chicago 1942ff.

LAAA   Annals of Archaeology and Anthropology. University of Liverpool 1908ff.

MDOG   Mitteilungen der Deutschen Orient-Gesellschaft. Berlin 1899ff.

MVAeG   Mitteilungen der Vorderasiatisch-Ägyptischen Gesellschaft.

Naumann, Architektur Kleinasiens   Rudolf Naumann, Architektur Kleinasiens von ihren Anfängen bis zum Ende der hethitischen Zeit. Tübingen 1955.

Özgüç, Kültepe 1948   Tahsin Özgüç, Ausgrabungen in Kültepe, 1948. Türk Tarih Kurumu Yayinlari, Serie V, Nr. 10 (1950).

Özgüç, Kültepe 1949   Tahsin and Nimet Özgüç, Ausgrabungen in Kültepe 1949. Türk Tarih Kurumu Yayinlari, Serie V, Nr. 12 (1953).

OIC   Oriental Institute Communications. The Oriental Institute of the University of Chicago.

OIP   Oriental Institute Publications. The Oriental Institute of the University of Chicago.

OLZ   Orientalische Literatur-Zeitung. Berlin 1898ff.

RA   Revue d'Assyriologie. Paris 1886ff.

RHA   Revue Hittite et Asianique. Paris 1930ff.

SBo   H. G. Güterbock, Siegel aus Boğazköy I–II. Berlin 1940, 1942. Archiv für Orientforschung Beihefte 5 und 7.

Syria   Syria, Revue d'art orientale et d'archéologie publiée par l'Institut français d'archéologie de Beyrouth. Paris 1920ff.

TTAED   Türk Tarih Arkeoloj ve Etnograpya Dergisi, Ankara.

WVDOG 19   O. Puchstein, Boghasköi. Die Bauwerke. Wissenschaftliche Veröffentlichungen der Deutschen Orient-Gesellschaft, Bd. 19, 1912.

ZA, NF   Zeitschrift für Assyriologie, Neue Folge.

I THE HATTIANS

THE PEOPLE AND THE LANGUAGE

S. Alp, Die soziale Klasse der Nam-Ra-Leute, *JKF* I.

E. Bilgiç, *AfO* XV.

Bossert, *Altanatolien*.

Goetze, *Kleinasien*.

O. R. Gurney, *The Hittites*. Penguin Books, Harmondsworth, 1952.

A. Kammenhuber, *Die protohattisch-hethitische Bilinguis vom Mond, der vom Himmel gefallen ist.*
ZA, NF 17, 1955.
Protohattisch-Hethitisches, Munchener Studien zur Sprachwissenschaft, 1959.

E. Laroche, Etudes 'Protohittites', *RA* 41, 1947.
Hattic deities and their epithets, *ICS*, 1947.
Une Conjuration Bilingue Hatti-Hittite, *PKF* I, 1950.

J. B. Pritchard, *Ancient Near Eastern Texts*.

ART

The Hattian Style

R. O. Arik, *Alaca Hüyük*, 1935.

K. Bittel, *AA*, 1930.
Grundzüge.
Hethiter und Proto-Hattier, *Historia* I, 1950.
Kleinasiatische Stud.
Prähistorische Forschung in Kleinasien. Istanbuler Forschungen Bd. 6, 1934.
Reinecke-Festschrift.

Bossert, *Altanatolien*.

H. Frankfort, *Art and Architecture of the Ancient Orient*.

Goetze, *Kleinasien*.

H. Goldman, *Excavations at Gözlükule, Tarsus* II.

S. A. Kansu, *Etiyokuşu*.

H. Koşay, *Alaca Hüyük*, 1936.
Alaca Hüyük, 1937–39.
Ahlatlibel, *TTAED* II, 1934.

H. Koşay and M. Akok, *AJA* 51.
Belleten 14, 1950.

M. E. L. Mallowan, *Iraq* 9, 1947.

Sp. Marinatos and M. Hirmer, *Crete and Mycenae*, London, 1961.

M. Mellink, *The Royal Tombs at Alacahöyük*, 19 Studies presented to Hetty Goldman.

Özgüç, *Horoztepe*, Ankara 1958.
Kültepe-Kaniš 1948 and 1949.

I. J. v. d. Osten, Alishar III, *OIP* 30.

D. B. Stronach, Metal Types in Early Bronze Age Anatolia, *Anatolian Studies* VII, 1957.

B. Tezcan, *Anatolia* V, 1960.
Bulletin, The Metropolitan Museum of Art, April 1960.

M. M. Vieyra, *The Hittite Art*, London 1955.

The History of the Finds

E. Akurgal, Atatürk, *Belleten* 20, 1956.

R. O. Arik, *Alaca Hüyük* 1935.

H. Koşay, *Alaca Hüyük* 1936; 1937–39; 1937–54.

The Significance of the Standards

E. Akurgal, *Phrygische Kunst*, Ankara 1955.

R. O. Arik, *Alaca Hüyük*, 1935.

K. Bittel, *Neue Deutsche Ausgrabungen.*
Reinecke-Festschrift.

Bossert, *Altanatolien.*

H. Demircioglu, *Der Gott auf dem Stier*, Berlin 1939.

F. Hančar, Der Kult der grossen Mutter, *AfO* 13, 1939–41.
Wiener Beiträge zur Kunst- und Kulturgeschichte Asiens XII, Vienna 1938.

G. Karo, *Die Schachtgräber von Mykenai*, 1930–33.

H. Koşay, Ahlatlibel, *TTAED* II, 1934.
Alaca Hüyük, 1936 and 1937–39.
La Turquie Kemalist.

F. Matz, *Kreta, Mykene, Troja*, Stuttgart 1957.

J. Mellaart, *Anatolian Studies* VII, 1947.

M. Mellink, *The Royal Tombs at Alacahöyük*, 19 Studies presented to Hetty Goldman.

T. Özgüç, *Die Bestattungsbräuche.*
Horoztepe, Ankara 1958.

M. I. Rostovtzeff, *Iranians and Greeks in South Russia.*

Schmidt, Die Kurgane, *ESA* IV.

D. B. Stronach, *Anatolian Studies* VII.

A. J. B. Wace, *Mycenae*, 1949.

R. O. Arik, The Small-scale Sculpture: *Alaca Hüyük*, 1935.

Bossert, *Altanatolien.*
Altkreta, 3. Aufl. 1937.

N. Dolunay, *IV. Türk Tarih Kongresi.*

Goetze, *Kleinasien.*

H. Koşay, *Alaca Hüyük*, 1937–39.

M. E. L. Mallowan, *Iraq 9*, 1947.

F. Matz, Kreta, *Mykene, Troja*, Stuttgart 1957.

J. Mellaart, *ILN.*

T. Özgüç, *Anatolia III.*
Horoztepe, Ankara 1958.

II THE EARLY HISTORICAL PERIOD

THE PEOPLES AND LANGUAGES IN EARLY HISTORY

K. Bittel, *Historia I* 1950.
Neue Deutsche Ausgrabungen.

Goetze, *Kleinasien.*

H. Koşay, *Alaca Hüyük*, 1936.

ASSYRIAN TRADE SETTLEMENTS IN ASIA MINOR

W. F. Albright, New Light on the History of Western Asia in second Millennium B.C., *BASOR* 77/78, 1940.
A third Revision in the Early Chronology of Western Asia, *BASOR* 88, 1942.
BASOR 126, 1952.

K. Balkan, *Chronology*, Ankara 1956.
Letter of King Anum-Hirbi, Ankara 1957.
Observations on the chronological problems of the Karum Kaniš.

F. Cornelius, Zur Chronologie von Alalakh VII, *RHA* 66, 1960.

G. Dossin, *RHA* V.

P. Garelli/D. Kennedy, Un nouveau Prince anatolien?, *RHA* 18, 1960.
Seize tablettes Cappadociennes de l'Ashmolean Museum d'Oxford, *ICS* 14, 1960.

B. Landsberger, Assyrische Handelskolonien in Kleinasien, *AO* 1925.

J. Mellaart, *Anatolian Studies VII.*

Özgüç, *Kültepe* 1949.

T. Özgüç, *Belleten* 17, 1953; 18, 1954.
Kültepe-Kaniš.

H. Otten, *MDOG* 89.
Zu den Anfängen det hethitischen Geschichte, *MDOG* 83.

THE IMMIGRATION OF THE INDO-EUROPEANS

W. F. Albright, *BASOR* 77.

S. Alp, Die soziale Klasse der Nam-Ra-Leute, *JKF* I, 1951.
On the Occasion of a new book concerning the Hittites, *DTCFD.*
Zur Lesung von manchen Personennamen auf den Hieroglyphen, hethitischen Siegeln und Inschriften, Ankara, 1950.

K. Balkan, *Chronology*, Ankara 1956.
Letter of King Anum-Hirbi.

T. Beran, *MDOG* 91, 1958.

K. Bittel, *ZA* 12, 1940.
Historia I, 1950.

J. Danmanville, Deux empreintes cappadociennes inédites du Musée d'Oxford, *RHA* 66.

G. Dossin, Une mention de Hattuša dans un text de Mari, *RHA* V.

A. Goetze, *AJA* 40, 1936.
Kleinasien.

H. G. Güterbock, Die Bedeutung der Bilinguis vom Karatepe für die Entzifferung der hethitischen Hieroglyphen, *Eranos* 47, 1949.
Siegel aus Boğazköy, I–II, Berlin 1940–42.

D. A. Kennedy, The Inscribed Hittite Seals in the Ashmolean Museum, *RHA* 16, 1958.
Sceaux hittites conservés à Paris, *RHA* 17, 1959.

B. Landsberger, *JCS* 8, 1954.

E. Laroche, *L'inscription Hittite d'Alep*, Syria 35, 1958.
Le Panthéon de Yazilikaya.

J. Mareau, *Die Welt der Kelten*, Stuttgart 1958.

T. Özgüç, *Belleten* 18, 1954; 20, 1956.
Kültepe-Kaniš.

H. Otten, *MDOG* 83, 1951.
Text des Königs Anitta, 89, 1957.

C. F. A. Schaeffer, *Ugaritica* III.

A. Scharff and A. Moortgat, *Ägypten und Vorderasien im Altertum*, München 1950.

F. Sommer, *Hethiter und Hethitisch, zu Zitat S. 20, Gebet des Königs Muwatalli.*

ART

R. O. Arik, *Alaca Hüyük*, 1935.

T. Beran, *Boğazköy*, III.
MDOG 89, 1957; 91, 1958.

K. Bittel, *Beiträge zu Eflâtun Pinar, Bibliotheca Orientalis* X, 1953.
Grundzüge.
Historia I, 1950.
MDOG 77, 1939; 89, 1957.
Neue Deutsche Ausgrabungen.
Reinecke-Festschrift.
Bossert, *Altanatolien.*
Altkreta, 3 Aufl, 1937.
F. Fischer, *MDOG* 91, 1958.
Goetze, *Kleinasien.*
H. G. Güterbock, *Kaniš and Neša, Two Forms of one Anatolian place.*
Israel Exploration Society, Jerusalem 5, 1958.
G. Karo, *Die Schachtgräber von Mykenai*, 1930–33.
H. Koşay, *Alaca Hüyük*, 1936.
Alaca Hüyük, 1937–39.
H. Koşay and M. Akok, *AJA* 51.
B. Landsberger, *Belleten* 3, 1939.
Sp. Marinatos and M. Hirmer, *Crete and Mycenae*, London, 1961.
J. Mellaart, *AS.*
M. Mellink, *A Hittite Cemetery at Gordion*, Philadelphia 1956.
N. Özgüç, *Anatolia* 4, 1959.
Belleten 17, 1953; 18, 1954; 21, 1957; 22, 1958.
Kültepe, 1949.
T. Özgüç, *Belleten* 18, 19, 20.
Kültepe, 1948–1949.
Kültepe-Kaniš.
D. Opitz, *Altorientalische Gussformen.*
I. J. v. d. Osten, Alishar II, *OIP* 29.
Alishar II, *OIP* 30.
Alishar III, *OIP* 30.
I. J. v. d. Osten and Krogmann, Alishar III, *OIP* 30.
Schmidt, Alishar I, *OIP* 19.

III THE HITTITE OLD KINGDOM

HISTORY AND CULTURE

K. Bittel, *Neue Deutsche Ausgrabungen.*
H. Bozkurt, M. Çiğ and H. G. Güterbock, *Istanbul arkeoloji müzelerinde bulunan Bogazköy tabletleri*, I and II, Istanbul 1947–48.
J. Friedrich, Aus dem hethitischen Schrifttum, *AO* 24, 3, 1925.
G. Furlani, *Saggi sulla Civiltà degli Hittiti*, Udine 1939.
Goetze, *Kleinasien.*
R. S. Hardy, The Old Hittite Kingdom, *American Journal of Semitic Languages and Literatures* 57, 1941.
A. Kammenhuber, Protohattisch-Hethitisches, *Münchener Studien zur Sprachwissenschaft*, 1959.
H. Otten, Die hethitischen Königslisten und die orientalische Chronologie, *MDOG* 83, 1951.
MDOG, 91, 1957.
F. Sommer and A. Falkenstein, *Die Hethitisch-Akkadische Bilingue des Hattušili* I. (Labarna II.), *Abhandlungen der Bayerischen Akademie d. Wissenschaften NF*, Heft 6, 1938 (Testament des Königs Hattušili I.).

ART

S. Alp, *Personennamen.*

T. Beran, *Boğazköy* III.
MDOG 91, 1958.
K. Bittel, *Boğazköy* III.
Kleinfunde.
MDOG 75, 1937; 91, 1958.
Neue Deutsche Ausgrabungen.
Bossert, *Altanatolien.*
F. Fischer, *MDOG* 89, 91.
I. J. Gelb, *AJA* 40, 1936.
Goetze, *AJA* 40, 1936.
Kleinasien.
H. Goldman, *Tarsus* I.
H. G. Güterbock, *SBo* I.
G. M. A. Hanfmann, *The Art Quarterly*, Spring, 1955.
H. Koşay, *Alaca Hüyük*, 1937–39.
H. Koşay and M. Akok, *AJA* 51, 1947.
MDOG 86, 88, 89.
M. Mellink, *A Hittite Cemetery at Gordion*, Philadelphia 1956.
H. H. v. d. Osten, Alishar II, *OIP* 29; III, *OIP* 30.
H. Seyrig, *Syria* 30, 1953.
O. Sümer, *Annual of the Archaeological Museum of Istanbul* VI, 1953.

IV THE PERIOD OF THE EMPIRE

HISTORY AND CULTURE

E. Akurgal, *Die Kunst Anatoliens von Homer bis Alexander*, Berlin 1961.
Phrygische Kunst.
W. F. Albright, *AJA* 54, 1950.
S. Alp, Military Instructions of the Hittite King Tuthalija IV, *Belleten* 11, 1947.
Symbolea Hrozny.
K. Balkan, *Ankara Boğazköy-Tafeln.*
T. Beran, *Boğazköy* III.
MDOG 91, 1958.
K. Bittel, *AfO* 13.
Yazilikaya.
Bittel and Naumann, *Boğazköy-Hattuša.*
Yazilikaya.
Bossert, *Altanatolien.*
Asia.
Ein Hethitisches Königssiegel.
E. Cavaignac, *RHA* II.
Subbiluliuma et son temps.
G. Contenau, *La civilisation des Hittites.*
F. Cornelius, Hattušilis III, geographisch erklärt, *RHA* 65, 1959.
F. Friedrich, *Artibus Asiae* 6.
I. J. Gelb, *HHM*, Nr. 34.
A. Goetze, *AO* 27.
Das Hethiter-Reich, *AO* 27, 1929.
Die Annalen des Muršili, *MVAeG* 38, 1933.
Die Pestgebete des Muršili, Kleinasiatische Forschungen 1930.
Kleinasien.
Hattušilis, der Bericht über seine Thronbesteigung nebst den Paralleltexten, *MVAeG* 29, 1924.
Madduwattas, *MVAeG* 32.

Muršilis Sprachlähmung, Kopenhagen 1934.
in: J. B. Pritchard, *Ancient Near Eastern Texts*.
The Predecessors of Šuppiluliumas of Hatti, *JAOS*.
H. G. Güterbock, Hittite Religion.
  MDOG 86, 1953.
Muršili's accounts of Šuppiluliuma's dealings with Egypt, *RHA* 67, 1960.
  SBo I.
The deeds of Šuppiluliuma as told by his son, Muršili II, *JCSX* 1956.
  Ugaritica III.
R. O. Gurney, Mita of Pakhuwa, *LAAA* 28.
V. Korošee, Les Hittites et leurs Vassaux syriens à la lumière des nouveaux textes d'Ugarite, *RHA* 66, 1960.
E. Laroche, *Les Hieroglyphes Hittites*, Paris 1961.
  RA 47.
  Ugaritica III.
P. Montet, De Tjarou à Qadech, *RHA* 67, 1960.
H. Otten, Die hethitischen 'Königslisten' und die altorientalische Chronologie, *MDOG* 83, 1951.
  MDOG 87, 91.
  Bibliotheca Orientalis 8, 1951.
J. B. Pritchard, *Ancient Near Eastern Texts*.
C. F. A. Schaeffer, *Ugaritica III*.
F. Sommer, Ahhijawa-Urkunden, *Abhandlungen der Bayer. Akademie* 1932.
J. Sturm, Der Hethiterkrieg Ramses II, Vienna 1939, *Beihefte zur Wiener Zeitschrift für die Kunde des Morgenlandes*, Heft 4.
E. F. Weidner, Die Staatsverträge in akkadischer Sprache aus dem Archiv von Boğazköy, *Boğazköy-Studien*, Heft 9, Leipzig 1923.

RELIGION AND MYTH

E. Akurgal, *Die Kunst Anatoliens von Homer bis Alexander*, Berlin 1961.
W. F. Albright, The Anatolian Goddess Kupaba, *AfO* V, 1929.
K. Bittel, *Yazilikaya*.
Bittel and Naumann, *Boğazköy-Hattuša*.
Bossert, Altanatolien.
  OLZ 36, 1933.
C. G. v. Brandenstein, *Hethitische Götter nach Bildbeschreibungen*, Text I, II.
J. Danmanville, Un roi hittite honore Ishtar de Šamuha, *RHA* 59, 1956.
La Libation en Mésopotamie, *RA* 49, 1955.
H. Demircioğlu, *Der Gott auf dem Stier*.
G. Furlani, *La Religione degli Hittiti*, Bologna 1936.
A. Goetze, in: J. B. Pritchard, *Ancient Near Eastern Texts*, 1950.
  Kleinasien.
R. Graves, *The Greek Myths* I (Penguin Books).
H. G. Güterbock, *Belleten* 7, 1943.
Gedanken über das Wesen des Gottes Telepinu, Festschrift J. Friedrich, Heidelberg 1959.
Hethitische Götterdar Stelungen und Götternamen, *Belleten* 7, 1943.
  Hittite Religion.

Kumarbi, Istanbuler Schriften 16, Europa-Verlag, Zürich–New York 1946.
  SBo II.
Hesiod, *Theogony*.
A. Kammenhuber, *Protohattisch-Hethitisches*.
E. Laroche, in C. F. A. Schaeffer, *Ugaritica III*.
Le Panthéon de Yazilikaya, *JCS* 6, 1952.
J. Mellaart, Excavations at Hacilar, *Anatolian Studies* 8, 1958; 9, 1959.
P. Meriggi, *Glossar*.
A. Moortgat, *Die bildende Kunst des alten Orients und die Bergvölker*, Berlin 1933.
  Vorderasien bis zum Hellenismus.
J. Nougayrol, Une fable hittite, *RHA* 67, 1960.
H. Otten, *Bibliotheca Orientalis* 8.
Die Überlieferung des Telepinu-Mythos, *MVAeG* 46, 1, 1942.
Mythen vom Gotte Kumarbi, Neue Fragmente, Deutsche Akademie der Wissenschaften, Berlin 1950.
Pindar, *Pyth. Od.* 1.
E. Porada, *Corpus of Ancient Near Eastern Seals*.
  Seal Impressions of Nuzi.
W. Porzig, *Kleinasiatische Forschungen I*, 1930.
C. F. A. Schaeffer, *Ugaritica III*.
Schmidt, *Typhoeus, Typhon in Roscher Lexikon Bd.* V, 1916–24.
C. L. Woolley, *Carchemish III*.

FOREIGN COMPONENTS AND ELEMENTS IN HITTITE CULTURE

E. Bilgiç, Die Ortsnamen der Kappadokischen Urkunden, *AfO* 15, 1952.
J. Friedrich, Kleine Beiträge zur churritischen Grammatik, *MVAeG* 42, 2, 1939.
  Orientalia NS 12, 1943.
Goetze, *Kleinasien*.
H. G. Güterbock, *The Hurrian Element*.
Furuzan Kinal, *Géographie et l'Histoire des Pays d'Arzawa*, Ankara 1953.
B. Landsberger, *JCS* 8, 1954.
E. Laroche, in: C. F. A. Schaeffer, *Ugaritica III* (List of Queens).
  Onomastique.
A. Moortgat, *Vorderasien bis zum Hellenismus*.
R. T. O'Callaghan, *Aram Nahraim*, 1948.
H. A. Potratz, *Das Pferd in der Frühzeit*, 1938.
F. Sommer, *Boğazköy-Studien* 4, 1920.
E. A. Speiser, Introduction to Hurrian, *AASOR* 20, 1940–41.
E. F. Weidner, Die Staatsverträge in akkadischer Sprache aus dem Archiv von Boğazköy, *Boğazköy-Studien*, Heft 8, Leipzig 1923.

THE SPECIFIC CHARACTER OF HITTITE CULTURE

Bittel and Naumann, *Boğazköy II*.
J. Friedrich, *MVAeG* 34, 1930, Staatsverträge.
Goetze, *Kleinasien*.
H. G. Güterbock, *Boğazköy I*.
A. Kammenhuber, *Protohattisch-Hethitisches*.
C. F. A. Schaeffer, *Ugaritica III*.

ARCHITECTURE

Buildings on the Citadel

K. Bittel, *MDOG* 89, 1957.
Bittel and Naumann, *Boğazköy II*.
  Boğazköy-Hattuša.
H. Frankfort, *Iraq* 16, 1952.
  The Art and Architecture of the Ancient Orient.
Goetze, *Kleinasien*.
E. Laroche, La Bibliothèque de Hattuša, *Archiv Orientalni*, XVII 1949.
Lloyd and Gökçe, *Anatolian Studies* 3, 1953.
Sp. Marinatos and M. Hirmer, *Crete and Mycenae*, London, 1961.
MDOG 35, 1907.
Naumann, *Architektur Kleinasiens*.
  Boğazköy III.
N. Özgüç, *Belleten* 17, 1953.
H. Otten, Bibliotheken im Alten Orient, *Das Altertum I*, 1955. *Bibliotheca Orientalis* 8.
Troy III, 2.
E. F. Weidner, Die Bibliothek Tiglatpilesers I., *AfO* 16, 1953.
WVDOG 1912.

The City

K. Bittel, *Neue Deutsche Ausgrabungen*.

The Fortifications

K. Bittel, Beitrag zu Eflâtun Pinar, *Bibliotheca Orientalis X* 1953.
  Kleinfunde.
  Ruinen.
Bittel and Naumann, *Boğazköy-Hattuša*.
H. G. Güterbock, *Boğazköy I*.
E. Laroche, *Les Hieroglyphes Hittites*.
Naumann, *Architektur Kleinasiens*.

The Temples

Bittel, *Ruinen*.
K. Bittel and R. Naumann, *Yazilikaya*, Leipzig 1941.
Goetze, *Kleinasien*.
H. Koşay, *Les Fouilles d'Alaca Höyük*.
K. Krause, *Boğazköy, Tempel V, Istanbuler Forschungen Bd.* 11, Berlin 1940.
Sp. Marinatos and M. Hirmer, *Crete and Mycenae*, London, 1961.
Naumann, *Architektur Kleinasiens*.

The Tombs

E. Akurgal, Smyrne à l'Epoque Archaique, *Belletin IX* 1945. *Spähethitische Bildkunst*, Ankara 1949.
K. Bittel, Beitrag zu Eflâtun Pinar, *Bibliotheca Orientalis X*, 1953.
  Die hethitischen Grabfunde von Osmankayasi, Berlin 1958.
K. Bittel and R. Naumann, *Yazilikaya*, Leipzig 1941.
H. G. Güterbock, *Gedächtnisschrift für Halil Edhem, Türk Tarih Kurumu*, Ankara 1947.
  MDOG 86, 1953.

E. Laroche, Eflâtun Pinar, *Anatolia III*, 1958.
M. Mellink, *A Hittite Cemetery at Gordion*, Philadelphia 1956.
H. H. v. d. Osten, *OIC* 14, 1930.
H. Otten, *Hethitische Totenrituale*.
G. Rodenwaldt, *Kunst um Augustus*, Berlin 1942.

The Basic Characteristics of Hittite Architecture

K. Bittel, *Neue Deutsche Ausgrabungen*.
Sp. Marinatos and M. Hirmer, *Crete and Mycenae*, London, 1961.
Naumann, *Architektur Kleinasiens*.

SCULPTURE

AfO 14.
E. Akurgal, *Spähethitische Bildkunst*, Ankara 1949.
S. Alp, *Personennamen*.
R. O. Arik, *Les Fouilles d'Alaca Höyük* 1937.
Belleten 12 1938.
T. Beran, *Hethitische Rollsiegel der Grossreichszeit, Istanbuler Mitteilungen* 8, 1956; 9–10, 1959–60.
K. Bittel, *Boğazköy III*.
  Kleinfunde.
  Nur hethitische oder auch hurritische Kunst?, *ZA, NF* 15, 1950.
  Yazilikaya.
Bittel and Naumann, *Yazilikaya*, Leipzig 1941.
Bossert, *Altanatolien*.
H. Th. Bossert and R. Naumann, *Altsyrien*.
H. Frankfort, *Cylinder Seals*.
Goetze, *Kleinasien*.
H. G. Güterbock, *Siegel aus Boğazköy II*, Berlin 1942.
O. R. Gurney, *The Hittites*.
D. A. Hogarth, *Hittite Seals VII*.
H. Kantor, A 'Syro-Hittite' Treasure, *JNES* 16, 1957.
D. A. Kennedy, *RHA* 16, 1958.
E. Laroche, Importations Mycenniennes à Boghaz-Köy? *Minos III* 1954.
  Le Panthéon de Yazilikaya, *JCS* 6, 1952.
G. Loud, The Megiddo Ivories, Chicago 1939, *OIP* 52.
F. Matz, Zu den Sphingen vom Yerkapi in Boğazköy, *Marburger Winckelmanns-Programm* 1957.
A. Moortgat, *Die Bildende Kunst des Alten Orients und die Bergvölker*, Berlin 1933.
  Nur hethitische oder auch churrische Kunst?, *ZA, NF* 14, 1949.
Özgüç, *Kültepe* 1949.
T. Özgüç, *Anatolia II*, 1957.
H. Otten, *Anatolia IV*, 1959.
E. Porada, *Corpus of Ancient Near Eastern Seals in North American Collections*, Washington 1948.
  Mesopotamian Art in Cylinder Seals, New York 1947.
  Seal Impressions of Nuzi, *BASOR* 24, 1944–45.
M. Riemschneider, *Die Welt der Hethiter*, Stuttgart 1954.
C. F. A. Schaeffer, *Ugaritica I und III*.
Schaeffer and Andrae, Die Kunst des Alten Orients, *Propyläen-Kunstgeschichte*, Bd. II, 2 Aufl., Berlin 1925.
M. Tosun, *Mezopotamya Silindir Mühürlerinde Hurri-Mitanni Üslubu*, Ankara 1956.
C. L. Woolley, *Carchemish III*.

V THE LATE HITTITE PERIOD

HISTORY

W. F. Albright, *Northeast-Mediterranean Dark Ages, The Aegean and the Near East*, Studies presented to Hetty Goldman.
Some Oriental Glosses on the Homeric problem, *AJA* 54, 1950.
B. Landsberger, *Sam'al, Studien zur Entdeckung der Ruinenstädte, Karatepe I*, Ankara 1948.
E. Forrer, *Die Provinzeinteilung des Assyrischen Reiches*, Leipzig 1920.
P. Naster, *L'Asie Mineure et l'Assyrie au VIIIe et VIIe siècle*, Louvain 1938.

ART

E. Akurgal, *Späthethitische Bildkunst*, Ankara, 1949.
Remarques stylistiques sur les Reliefs de Malatya, Istanbul 1946.
Die Kunst Anatoliens, Berlin 1961.
A. Moortgat, *Die bildende Kunst des Alten Orients und die Bergvölker*, Berlin 1933.
Bildwerk und Volkstum Vorderasiens zur Hethiterzeit, 1934.
Tell Halaf III, Die Bildwerke, Berlin 1955.
R. Naumann, *Die Hethiter*, Berlin 1948.
Architektur Kleinasiens.
Bossert, *Altanatolien*.

Malatya

E. Akurgal, *Remarques stylistiques sur les Reliefs de Malatya*, Istanbul 1946.
H. Th. Bossert, *Felsefe Arkivi*, Istanbul 1947.
L. Delaporte, *Malatya, La Porte des lions*, Paris 1940.
R. Dussaud, *Datation des Bas-Reliefs Hittites de Malatya*, Comptes Rendus de l'Académie des Inscriptions et Belles-Lettres, 1945.

Carchemish

E. Akurgal, *Späthethitische Bildkunst*, Ankara 1949.
H. Th. Bossert, Zur Geschichte von Kargamis, *Studi Classici et Orientali*, Pisa 1951.
H. G. Güterbock, Carchemish, *JNES* 13, 1954.
F. Kinal, *Kargamis sehri tarihi hakkinda, DTC Fakültesi Dergisi XVI* 1958.
P. Meriggi, La Ricostruzione di Kargamis, *Rivista degli Studi Orientali XXIX*.
C. L. Woolley, *Carchemish I–III* (D. G. Hogarth, *Carchemish I*, 1914; C. L. Woolley, *Carchemish II*, 1921; Woolley and Barnett, *Carchemish III*, 1952).

Sam'al

E. Akurgal, *Späthethitische Bildkunst*, Ankara 1949.
B. Landsberger, *Sam'al*, Ankara 1948.
F. v. Luschan, *Ausgrabungen in Sendschirli I–V (1893–1943)*.

Sakçagözü

E. Akurgal, *Späthethitische Bildkunst*, Ankara 1949.
J. Garstang, *Liverpool Annals I*, 1908.
G. M. A. Hanfmann, On the date of the late Hittite palace of Sakçagözü, *BASOR* 160, 1960.

Karatepe

E. Akurgal, *Späthethitische Bildkunst*, Ankara 1949.
H. Th. Bossert, Die Phoenizisch-hethitischen Bilinguen vom Karatepe. *Oriens I* (1948), *Oriens II* (1949), *Archiv Orientalni* 18 (1950). *Jahrbuch für Kleinasiatische Forschung* I (1950–51), II (1952–53). H. Th. Bossert and H. Çambel, *Karatepe*. A preliminary report on a new Hittite site, Istanbul 1946.
H. Th. Bossert and U. B. Alkim, Karatepe, *Die Ausgrabungen auf dem Karatepe*, Ankara 1950.
H. Çambel, Some Observation on the Karatepe Sculptures, *Belleten XII*, 1949 (Oriens I).
M. Mellink, *Bibliotheca Orientalis* 7, 1950.

INDEX

Figures set in italic type indicate plate numbers

314